AQA Critical Thinking

AS

John Butterworth

Joe Chislett

with contributions from

Geoff Thwaites

ɔrnes

Published in 2009 by:
Nelson Thornes Ltd
Delta Place
27 Bath Road
CHELTENHAM
GL53 7TH
United Kingdom

09 10 11 12 13 / 10 9 8 7 6 5 4 3 2 1

A catalogue record for this book is available from the British Library

ISBN 1 978 4085 1387 3

Cover photograph/illustration: Photolibrary/ BrandX Pictures
Page make-up by Hart McLeod

Printed and bound in Spain by GraphyCems

Acknowledgements

The publishers would like to thank the authors where appropriate for use of images and drawings. We have attempted to contact all copyright holders and controllers. If any items are not fully credited this will be corrected in future editions. The author and publishers wish to thank the following for permission to use copyright material:

Text

P3 extracts from *Lord of the Flies* by William Golding reprinted with permission from Faber & Faber; p13 'Badgers must die' by Valerie Elliott, *Times Online* 9 April 2008 http://www.timesonline.co.uk/tol/news/environment/article3708956.ece reprinted with permission from © NI Syndication, London (2008); p29 'Prince flies multi-million helicopter' by Mathew Hickley *Daily Mail* 16 April 2008 http://www.dailymail.co.uk/news/article-559770/Prince-William-flies-multi-million-pound-RAF-Chinook-helicopter-cousins-Isle-Wight-stag--picks-Harry-way.html reprinted with permission from Solo Syndication; p35 'End of Line for Graffiti Pests' by Andy Russell, www.manchestereveningnews.co.uk/news/s/1014/1014831_end_of_line_for_graffiti_pests.html reprinted with permission from Manchester Evening News; p45 Unicellular life' from *Little Book of Science* pp80–1 by John Cribbin, Penguin Books 2000, reprinted with permission from David Higham Associates; p60 'Benefit cheats face telephone lie detector tests' by George Jones 6 April 2007 www.telegraph.co.uk/news/uknews/1547682/Benefit-cheats-face-telephone-lie-detector-tests.html reprinted with permission from Telegraph Media Group Ltd; p97 Car insurance intermediary the A&A Group extract; adapted from www.expressinsurance.co.uk/web/press_releases/car_insurance/young_drivers_17120353.html © Adfero Ltd.

Photos

P3 still from *Lord of the Flies*, p29 Chinook helicopter, p32 Clarence House and p35 graffiti train, all Alamy; p13 badger photo and p45 bacteria under microscope, istockPhoto; p60 man having lie detector test, Science Photo Library.

Joe Chislett would like to thank Laura, and also his father, Andrew Chislett, who was integral in his appreciating the importance of critical thinking – and its deep significance in the modern world.

Geoff Thwaites contributed the original material for Chapters 24 to 29.

Contents

Introduction

Nelson Thornes and AQA

Nelson Thornes has worked in collaboration with AQA to ensure that this book offers you the best support for your AS level course and helps you to prepare for your exams. The partnership means that you can be confident that the range of learning, teaching and assessment practice materials has been checked by the senior examining team at AQA before formal approval, and is closely matched to the requirements of your specification.

These print and online resources together **unlock blended learning**; this means that the links between the activities in the book and the activities online blend together to maximise your understanding of a topic and help you achieve your potential.

These online resources are available on **kerboodle!** which can be accessed via the internet at **www.kerboodle.com/live**, anytime, anywhere. If your school or college subscribes to this service you will be provided with your own personal login details. Once logged in, access your course and locate the required activity.

For more information and help visit **www.kerboodle.com**

Icons in this book indicate where there is material online related to that topic. The following icons are used:

Learning activity

These resources include a variety of interactive and non-interactive activities to support your learning.

Progress tracking

These resources include a variety of tests that you can use to check your knowledge on particular topics (Test yourself) and a range of resources that enable you to analyse and understand examination questions (On your marks …).

Research support

These resources include WebQuests, in which you are assigned a task and provided with a range of web links to use as source material for research.

Study skills

These resources support you in developing a skill that is key for your course, for example planning essays.

How to use this book

This book supports the specification for your course and is arranged with a structure and sequence approved by AQA. There is no one way of working through the book, but we have presented the material in different but complementary ways depending on its purpose:

Part 1 introduces **the main elements of critical thinking**. You'll find it helpful to read the first six chapters it contains in sequence as they build on one another, gradually introducing the basic ideas and skills.

Part 2 provides further **opportunities to apply the ideas** introduced in Part 1, and again the ideas build as you work through the chapters.

In both Parts 1 and 2 each topic is explored through one or more texts. For example, the first topic centres around a debate between farmers and wildlife campaigners, Chapter 7 is based on a news article about the young royals, and Chapter 8 is about graffiti.

The skills and concepts you need to learn about arise naturally from the texts, and the main ideas are introduced and reintroduced repeatedly in different contexts. This will help you become familiar with them and confident in applying them.

Part 3 is a **critical thinking 'toolkit'** that provides short focused coverage of key critical thinking skills and terminology; you can use this in a different way from Parts 1 and 2 – dipping in and out of topics that catch your interest or that support work you are doing during your course. We hope you'll also find it very useful for ready reference when you want to refresh your mind about key skills and terminology used in thinking critically.

Part 4 helps you think about **how to present longer and more complex arguments** as you become more adept at thinking critically.

Key features of this book include:

Learning objectives

At the beginning of each section you will find a list of learning objectives that contain targets linked to the requirements of the specification.

Critical questions

Questions are posed at regular intervals. These are to get you thinking about the texts in a focused and critical way, and to give you a foretaste of the kinds of question you will be set in a critical thinking exam.

The tinted side-bar indicates discussion of and response to the critical question.

Margin feature

Extra features and examples, each individually named, highlighting and adding to the discussion in the main text.

Key terms

Terms you will need to be able to understand and define.

Over to you

Activities to help you understand and engage with the ideas in the book or better prepare for your exams.

AQA Examiner's tip

Hints from AQA examiners to help you with your study and to prepare for your exam.

AQA Examination-style questions

An exam-style question is provided and discussed in detail. Specimen answers are given.

Web links in the book

As Nelson Thornes is not responsible for third party content online, there may be some changes to this material that are beyond our control. In order for us to ensure that the links referred to in the book are as up-to-date and stable as possible, the websites are usually homepages with supporting instructions on how to reach the relevant pages if necessary.

Please let us know at **kerboodle@nelsonthornes.com** if you find a link that doesn't work and we will do our best to redirect the link, or to find an alternative site.

About the AQA AS Critical Thinking specification

Assessment objectives

The assessment objectives (AOs) are common to AS and A level. The assessment units will assess the following AOs in the context of the content and skills set out in section 3 of the specification which details the subject content:

- **AO1** Analyse critically the use of different kinds of reasoning in a wide range of contexts.
- **AO2** Evaluate critically the use of different kinds of reasoning in a wide range of contexts.
- **AO3** Develop and communicate relevant and coherent arguments clearly and accurately in a concise and logical manner.

This table shows approximately how the AOs relate to each unit of the specification.

	Unit 1	Unit 2
AO1	27%	27%
AO2	35%	35%
AO3	38%	38%
Total	100%	100%

Unit 1 assessment

Unit 1, or CRIT1, is the Critical Thinking Foundation Unit. Candidates will be assessed by means of a written paper lasting 1 hour 30 minutes. The question paper will be based on a source booklet containing several short documents which may be accompanied by images and/or graphics. These will relate to a single topic or issue, or two or more related topics, and consist of background information and argument. One or more of the documents will be a debate or discussion, or exchange of views. The question paper will have two sections, A and B.

Section A will require short written answers, assessing a range of skills and understanding summarised in the specification (3.1 to 3.14). Not all the points in the list will necessarily be addressed by a specific question in every examination.

There are two main categories of questions in this section. The first sets specific tasks or questions, such as:

- Identify an implicit assumption …
- Is there a flaw … ?

Questions in the other category are more open and require you to select for yourself the point (or points) which are most relevant. These typically ask you to comment critically or evaluate critically.

Section B will comprise one or two questions which give you the opportunity to present your own reasoning on a subject related to the stimulus materials. No specialist knowledge of the subject matter will be assumed, nor will such knowledge give any advantage to candidates.

Unit 2 assessment

Unit 2, or CRIT2, is Information, Inference and Explanation. Assessment is by means of a written paper lasting 1 hour 30 minutes. The exam will be based on a set of source documents presenting information either on a single topic or two closely related topics. Between them, the documents will present data in a range of forms: verbal, numerical and graphical.

The question paper will consist of two sections, A and B.

Section A will contain a number of questions requiring short written answers. Candidates will engage in extracting and interpreting information, assessing claims and conclusions, drawing inferences, and offering explanations.

Section B will present candidates with a short statement or proposal related to the examination topic(s), which they will be invited to argue for or against.

Both sections of the paper will require candidates to draw on skills from Unit 1 as well as Unit 2.

1 Thinking critically

1 Introducing critical thinking

If you were asked to say in a word what critical thinking is, probably the best answer would be *questioning*. Much of the time we accept the things we read and hear without questioning them. Or we reject them without question, because we have set our minds against them already. Either way we are being *uncritical*. As often as not this doesn't matter. It can even be the right response on some occasions: life is too short to stop and question every bit of information or opinion that comes along. But at other times it matters very much. As well as learning *how* to be critical, we also have to learn *when*.

Another word that is often used with the same sense as 'critical' is 'reflective'. Reflecting on something means focusing on it, thinking deeply or carefully about it. It is a nice word to use because it also gives the idea of throwing light on something. The reason for both questioning and reflecting critically is to see things more clearly, to deepen understanding and insight.

Another reason for thinking critically is to assess claims to *knowledge*. We can only count something as knowledge if we are sure of our reasons for believing it. It is not enough just to accept a claim or piece of information on the strength of having heard it somewhere, or because it seems quite likely. Or, as can often happen, because we *want* to believe it. Or because our friends believe it and we don't want to upset or contradict them. The critical response to a claim is to inquire into its grounds and origins, and to make our own minds up, independently and objectively. We will see an example of this shortly.

It is very important to add that being critical does not just mean finding fault. In everyday use, the words 'critical' and 'criticise' do often have this meaning, but in critical thinking it is just as important to give credit where it is due as it is to look for flaws and weaknesses.

Reasoning and argument

If you were asked instead what critical thinking was *about*, what it focuses on, the one-word answer would be *reasoning*. Critical thinking is a set of skills and techniques which, with practice, will enable you to understand and respond more effectively to texts associated with reasoning. It will also give you opportunities to improve your own reasoning and arguing ability, both spoken and written.

'Reasoning' and 'argument' are closely related words. However, they are not identical in meaning, and they are not freely interchangeable. We can say we are having an argument, or that we are presenting an argument, or that we are thinking critically about an argument. But we can't say we are presenting or having or thinking about 'a reasoning'. Grammatically 'reasoning' does not have a singular and plural form, as 'argument' does.

Another difference is that argument can also mean a dispute or disagreement, a quarrel even, in which case there may or may not be any reasoning at all.

The text we are going to look at first helps to clarify the relationship. It is a short extract from William Golding's novel *Lord of the Flies*, about a large party of schoolchildren whose plane crashes on a desert island, leaving them to fend for themselves, without any adults. At first they try to organise their lives in a civilised way. They elect one of the older boys, Ralph, as their chief. They hold assemblies to make rules and decisions. Ralph finds a large seashell, called a conch, which they pass round at meetings to indicate whose turn it is to speak, and to stop everyone talking at once. But despite all this, it is not long before tempers get the better of them, and they argue – in the second sense as well as the first.

The argument they are having here is about the fears of some of the children that there is a mysterious beast on the island, a ghost perhaps. We pick up the story with Ralph trying to keep order. One of the main characters, nicknamed Piggy, has just said that it is childish to believe in ghosts, following a vote in which the majority say that they do. Piggy is holding the conch and speaking to the assembly. A third boy, called Jack, who is Ralph's rival and who hates Piggy, tries to interrupt.

> [Piggy] 'I didn't vote for no ghosts!'
>
> He whirled round on the assembly.
>
> 'Remember that all of you!'
>
> They heard him stamp.
>
> 'What are we? Humans? Or animals? Or savages? What's grown-ups going to think? Going off – hunting pigs – letting fires out – and now!'
>
> A shadow fronted him tempestuously.
>
> 'You shut up, you fat slug!' …
>
> Ralph leapt to his feet.
>
> 'Jack! Jack! You haven't got the conch. Let him speak.'
>
> Jack's face swam near him.
>
> 'And you shut up! Who are you, anyway? Sitting there – telling people what to do.' …
>
> 'I'm chief. I was chosen.'
>
> 'Why should choosing make any difference? Just giving orders that don't make any sense –'
>
> 'Piggy's got the conch.'
>
> 'That's right – favour Piggy as you always do –'
>
> 'Jack!'
>
> Jack's voice sounded in bitter mimicry.
>
> 'Jack! Jack!'
>
> 'The rules!' shouted Ralph, 'you're breaking the rules.'
>
> 'Who cares?'
>
> Ralph summoned his wits.
>
> 'Because the rules are the only thing we've got!'
>
> But Jack was shouting against him.
>
> 'Bollocks to the rules!'

*Source: **Lord of the Flies**, William Golding, 1954, pp98–99*

This is primarily a dispute or quarrel. That would be the natural way to describe it. But it would be wrong to say that it was devoid of any kind of reasoning. Even when people argue with each other in an adversarial way,

One word, several meanings

The English language is unusual in having only one word for both dispute and reason-giving. In Latin these were *disputatio* and *argumentum* and other European languages have followed the example of distinguishing in this way. The shared use of 'argument' in English is rarely a problem, however, since it is usually quite clear from the context how the word is being used.

A still from the 1990 film version of Lord of the Flies, *directed by Harry Hook*

Lord of the Flies

Lord of the Flies was first published by Faber and Faber in 1954. The page numbers used here refer to the 2002 paperback edition.

like this, they are often reasoning with each other as well. In many ways, dispute is the natural home of reasoning, because in a dispute the aim of both sides is to make a point, and to persuade others that it is right. Think of parliamentary debate, or law courts, club committees or student unions, and the way argument is conducted there. The boys in the story are imitating this. The outcome is not always very successful, but they try.

Giving reasons

So we have two kinds of argument going on in the same extract. Ralph is arguing *with* Jack in the sense that they are quarrelling. But Ralph is also arguing *for* certain things, or *that* certain things should be so; and Jack is arguing *against* them, or at least against him, Ralph.

Look at the exchange that begins:

> 'Jack! Jack! You haven't got the conch.'

Here Ralph is arguing for the view that Piggy should be allowed to speak. He is giving Jack a reason to accept this and let him have his turn. The reason he gives is that Jack hasn't got the conch. Piggy has. In the original form it may not look much like a reasoned argument, but it is easy enough to rephrase it so that it does:

> **You haven't got the conch (Piggy has). So you must let Piggy speak.**

By inserting the word 'so' between the two sentences, we can see that one is being given as a reason (or grounds) for the other. And that makes it a simple argument.

Next look at Ralph's answer to Jack's question, 'Who are you anyway?' Of course, this is not a real question but a **rhetorical question**. Jack knows perfectly well who Ralph is. What he is really up to is challenging his authority, his personal entitlement to 'sit there telling people what to do'. It's a weak and childish challenge, and Ralph has a simple answer to it:

> 'I'm chief. I was chosen.'

Again he presents an argument: two connected reasons implying that he does have the right. And again Jack rejects his reasons. He responds with a second rhetorical question, effectively saying that being chief makes no difference if all Ralph can do is give orders that make no sense.

This time Ralph has no easy answer. Jack rejects the whole basis of Ralph's argument for preserving some kind of law and order on the island. If the rules and the authority of the elected chief make no difference, what reasons can Ralph give to persuade Jack?

None of this is to say that either Jack or Ralph is reasoning well. Jack especially can hardly be described as reasoning at all. He may appear to get the better of Ralph, if we consider the argument simply as a contest of wills. But if you examine what he says, it is clear that he has no argument of his own. He just attacks Ralph personally, challenges his authority. All his replies are personal:

> 'Who are you?'
>
> '… giving orders that make no sense.'
>
> '… favour Piggy as you always do.'

Key terms

Rhetorical question: a sentence with the grammatical form of a question but used to make a statement. It can be a more forceful or effective way of making a statement. 'Have I got news for you?' is an example of a rhetorical question. It means 'I have' but it also conveys the message that it is very important or very interesting news for the person I am speaking to.

Jack may think he has defeated Ralph's argument but all he has done is defeat Ralph.

It is a common occurrence when argument degenerates into quarrelling, or when anger and frustration take over from reasoning. You have probably done it yourself. Someone makes a point you don't like, perhaps with very good reason, and you respond by criticising the person and not their argument. You may put the person down very effectively in the process, but in terms of rational argument you have failed. To use a sports analogy, you would be said to have committed a kind of 'foul', like going for the player instead of the ball. In the context of critical thinking or logic or organised debating it is regarded as a *flaw* or *fallacy*, terms that will occur frequently in this book. There is more about flaws and fallacies in Chapter 23.

Part of the message of this dark story is that the boys fail to cope – intellectually as well as socially – with the demands of living unsupervised on the island. They struggle to put arguments together, to find good reasons for the points they want to make. Their communication skills are poor, too, so that their reasoning is crude and undeveloped. The story is a vivid account of reason and communication breaking down, giving way to aggression, with violence never far below the surface.

Even in this short extract, we can see that breakdown taking place. Ralph tries, once more, to get Jack to respect the rules, on the grounds that the rules are all they have got. But this time Jack doesn't even attempt to reason. His 'Bollocks to the rules!' is not just a bad argument, it is not a reasoned argument at all. Nor is 'Shut up you fat slug!' Nor 'Who cares?' Nor is shouting and mimicry, or any other displays of anger or contempt.

Critical evaluation

The core activity of critical thinking is evaluating reasons and arguments and the conclusions that are drawn from them. We have started with a piece of very basic, primitive reasoning. As you progress with the course, you will meet up with examples of much more complex and developed reasoning, some of it sound, some unsound; some convincing, some less so. You will be asked to explain and evaluate them and say whether or not you accept the claims they are making, or the position they are defending. But you will also be expected to say *why* you accept or reject an argument, not just *whether* you do.

Before we leave the boys on the island, here is another short text to look at. It's from the same source, but at an earlier point in the debate about the beast and the ghosts, before it had degenerated into abuse. Jack, who prides himself on being the leader of the hunters, has made the following short speech:

> 'I've got the conch. I'm not talking about the fear. I'm talking about the beast.' (…)
>
> Jack paused, cradling the conch, and turned to his hunters with their dirty black caps.
>
> 'Am I a hunter or am I not?'
>
> They nodded, simply. He was a hunter all right. No one doubted that.
>
> 'Well then – I've been all over this island. By myself. If there was a beast I'd have seen it. Be frightened because you're like that – but there is no beast in the forest.'

*Source: **Lord of the Flies**, William Golding, 2002 edition, p89*

A classic fallacy: *ad hominem*

Interestingly, the practice of challenging the arguer has been recognised and written about for centuries, and is known as a 'classic' fallacy for that reason. It has a name – *argumentum ad hominem* – a Latin phrase meaning argument aimed at the person, literally at *homo* 'the man'. Usually it takes the form of sidestepping the argument itself and looking for some weakness in the character of the person who has made it. You will meet the term *ad hominem* a lot, and find examples of it in many texts. It is listed along with some other well-known 'fallacies' in the AQA Specification for Critical Thinking: section 3.1.11(a), page 16. There is more about *ad hominem* in Chapter 23, page 110.

What do we mean by 'author'?

It is important to make the distinction between the text as a whole – which is not an argument but a piece of narrative – and the argument itself which is reported in the narrative. This is *Jack's* argument, not William Golding's. Golding is the author of the narrative, Jack of the argument. Notice that 'author', like 'text', is used here in a broad sense. It doesn't just mean someone who has written a book. It means the originator of any text or piece of communication: spoken, written, drawn, compiled, etc.

You should be able to see immediately that there is reasoning going on in here. Jack is presenting a clearly recognisable argument. He is telling the assembly that, however frightened they may be, there is no beast in the forest *because* if there were he would have seen it. And he would have seen it *because* he is a hunter and has *therefore* been everywhere on the island. So he says.

The first task with a text like this is to identify Jack's argument, and to rewrite it, or reconstruct it, in a plain, uncluttered form, without the surrounding narrative and descriptive detail. For example:

> You agree that I am a hunter. I have been all over the island by myself. If there was a beast, I would have seen it. *Therefore* there is no beast.

As we saw earlier, inserting the word 'therefore' is a useful way of showing that there is a reasoned argument here. Jack gives three connected reasons for the conclusion that there is no beast in the forest. Think about the following questions:

Is it a good argument?

Do the reasons Jack gives provide the listener with strong enough grounds to accept the conclusion that there is no beast?

These are critical questions, and they are harder than they may look. Have a go at answering them when you have finished reading this chapter. Keep a note of what you thought, as we will return to this argument with some critical answers in Chapter 6 (page 24).

The structure of this book

The subject of critical thinking is not like a one-way street, where you begin at one end and finish at the other. It is more like a block that you go round many times, in different directions and from different starting points, recognising and understanding more on each trip. It is sometimes described as a spiral progression, and that is a useful way to think of it. This book follows a similar spiral path.

Parts 1 and 2 introduce the main elements of critical thinking and provide opportunities to apply them. Each topic is explored via one or more texts. The first topic, for example, centres around a debate between farmers and wildlife campaigners. Chapter 7 is based on a news article about the young royals. Chapter 8 is about graffiti, and so on.

The skills and concepts you need to learn about arise naturally out of the texts – just as 'reasoning', 'argument' and 'flaw' arose out of this chapter. But that is not the last you will hear of them. The main points are introduced and reintroduced repeatedly in different contexts. This is necessary if you are to become familiar with them and confident in applying them.

Part 3 is a critical thinking 'toolkit' that provides short, focused coverage of key critical thinking skills and terminology – you can dip in or out of this and use it for ready reference. Part 4 introduces and helps you think about how to present longer and more complex arguments.

Critical questions

Much of the content of this book is based around questions or, to be more precise, critical questions. This is hardly surprising given what was said about questioning at the beginning of the chapter. A typical critical question will ask you to say what justification there is for a particular claim, or what strengths or weaknesses there are in a given argument. You have already seen some examples of critical questioning in this chapter.

Critical questions, or tasks, fall roughly into two categories, although there is some overlap between them:

- *Analytical tasks* require you to identify and explain the reasoning found in a text.
- *Evaluation tasks* require you to assess the quality of a piece of reasoning, or the degree of justification it provides for a conclusion.

Naturally your success in answering the second type of task will depend heavily on how well you have answered the first, hence the importance of developing strong analytical skills.

There is a third task which you will also encounter:

- *Presenting your own arguments*. The idea is that by studying the reasoning of others and learning to recognise both strengths and weaknesses, you will improve your own reasoning skill and confidence.

Some critical questions will be left entirely to you to answer. Others are followed by discussion, either immediately or in the next or a later chapter. But even where there is an answer given, it is a good idea to have a go at answering the question yourself – or, better still, to discuss it with others – before reading on. That way you will be able to compare your own responses with the ones given in the book.

There are also recommended activities at intervals in the book. They come with the heading 'Over to you'. The first appears alongside. Some invite written answers, some invite discussion, some both. The more you can discuss critical questions, the more depth of understanding you will develop, because others will inevitably come up with ideas and possibilities you would not have thought of. And vice versa.

Examination questions – and answers

For exam purposes, critical thinking is divided into three assessment objectives (AOs) which correspond to the three categories of critical questions listed above. You can find out more about these AOs by reading the subject specification, and your teachers will no doubt discuss them with you as well. In short, you can think of them as:

- AO1 analysis;
- AO2 evaluation;
- AO3 your own reasoning.

The critical questions therefore have close parallels with the questions you will be asked in your critical thinking exams. This is a further reason to give the questions careful attention and, whenever possible, to attempt to answer them yourself. The practice will pay off.

One difference between the questions here and those in the exam is the time factor. When you answer or discuss a critical question in class, or as part of your individual study, you can take as long as you like over it. Indeed you *should* give yourself time to explore different angles, consider consequences, anticipate objections, and think about the wider issues.

In the exam you will have limited time. Your responses will have to be straight to the point, especially for short-answer questions where only one or two marks are at stake. You will need to identify exactly what the question requires you to do and respond with no more *and* no less – an important and demanding skill in itself. But by then you will have learned to think more quickly and more confidently, and have experience of cutting through to the essentials.

AQA Examiner's tip

Always remember that critical thinking is primarily a skill-based subject: something you *do* rather than something you *know*. And, as with all skills, it is practice, more than knowledge, that brings results.

Over to you

1 Before you move on, try to answer the two critical questions on page 6, relating to Jack's argument about the beast: is it a good argument? Do the reasons Jack gives provide the listener with strong enough grounds to accept the conclusion that there is no beast? Note that they are closely related questions. In fact, they are two ways of asking the same question – one in a very general way, the other more specific.

2 There are people who believe in ghosts. There are others who deny that any such thing as a ghost exists. There are others still who 'don't know'. Regardless of what your beliefs are, make a short list of reasons either *supporting* or *rejecting* a belief in ghosts. Organise them into a short argument. Then ask someone else in your group to critically evaluate your argument, whilst you do the same for theirs. Note this is not a debate. You don't need to exchange arguments with someone who is drawing the opposite conclusion. You need to be just as critical – perhaps even more so – if you are looking at an argument for something you agree with.

Claims, reasons and arguments

◼ Key terms

Claim: statement that is supposedly true. Claims can be factual or non-factual, and can be supported or unsupported. In an argument, the claims which are supported by other claims are conclusions; those giving the support are the reasons.

◼ Claims and beliefs

A **claim** is a statement or assertion that is supposedly true. It may actually be true, though by calling it a claim we are implying that there may be some uncertainty about it either on the part of the speaker, or the reader or hearer. If it is known to be true by all concerned, then it would be more natural to call it a fact. But a claim that is anything less than a known fact is simply an expression of belief, an opinion, or an assumption. There is more about claims in Chapter 14.

Take the following three claims.

i   Badgers are a protected species.

ii   Badgers spread bovine tuberculosis (bTB) in cattle.

iii Badgers should be culled to reduce the spread of bTB.

We can learn a lot from looking at these examples. In fact, we can learn a lot from this issue: the problem of bTB and the role, or alleged role, that badgers play in it. It has many features that show why critical thinking is so important and how its methods can be applied to difficult problems and controversies.

◼ Claim **i** is a fact. A law has been passed that prohibits the killing or harming of badgers without a licence; and a licence will only be issued if it can be shown that the animals are a serious threat to humans or to livestock. A landowner cannot shoot a badger just because he or she finds it a nuisance, as they can with foxes or rabbits. A lot of people believe that foxes are also protected, but it is not so. There are laws against hunting foxes with dogs, and laws against cruelty to animals in general, but the kind of strict legal protection that badgers have as a species does not apply to foxes. Because **ii** is a fact, you don't need to have any further reason to believe it: you either know the fact or you don't. If you don't know it, you can look it up in the statute books or on the internet and see for yourself that it exists in law. And if someone else questions the truth of it, you can prove it to them by producing the evidence.

◼ When we turn to claim **ii**, things are rather different. **ii** may also be a fact. Many farmers and vets claim that it is, vociferously. Some independent researchers agree with them. Many others, especially animal welfare groups and conservationists, contest the claim. Neither side is able to point directly to a conclusive body of evidence, and so the question remains open. There is general agreement that badgers are carriers of bTB, but to what extent they are to blame for the incidence of the disease in cows is as yet unknown. Nonetheless, **ii** is a claim of a factual kind, meaning that either it is true or it is not. It is a theory or hypothesis, rather than an established fact, but that doesn't mean that at some future point it won't be proven true – nor of course that it might be found to be false.

◼ Claim **iii** is different again. It is not a claim of a factual kind at all. It is purely a matter of opinion or judgement. It barely makes sense to say that **iii** is true or that it is false. Saying either of these things means no more than saying 'I accept that' or 'I reject that'.

These three classes of claim need to be kept distinct, and it is important to do so when you come to assess them critically, especially the second and the third. The second is an opinion on a matter of fact – a claim to knowledge. The third is a recommendation without factual content. It might be a wise recommendation or a misguided one, but it is not a 'true' or 'false' recommendation, because those words don't apply to claims of this sort.

Reasons and arguments

Unless a claim can be established as a fact in its own right, the natural thing to do is to look for reasons or arguments to convince ourselves and/or to persuade others that it is true. Many of the people who support a cull of badgers use **ii** as their reason for claiming **iii**:

> Badgers spread bTB in cattle. Therefore badgers should be culled when and where bTB is a problem.

The word 'therefore' placed in between these two sentences indicates that the first is being given as grounds for the second – **ii** as grounds for **iii**. This kind of construction is itself called an *argument*, a piece of reasoning.

We could alternatively have written the argument down using 'because' as the connective:

> Badgers should be culled ... because they spread bTB in cattle.

This is not a different argument, but the same argument differently expressed. Both are saying that if claim **ii** is true, then claim **iii** follows (logically) from it, or that **iii** is a *conclusion* that can be drawn from **ii**. In critical thinking, and in logic, arguments are often set out in a *standard form* to make plain what the reasoning is. The reason (or reasons) is placed above a line with the conclusion below it. This is like a *model* argument. We'll call it **A1**:

> A1
>
> Badgers spread bTB.
> ———————————————————
> Badgers should be culled ...

Analysing argument

Whichever way the argument is expressed in natural language, it looks the same when it is put in this standard form. It is a way of *analysing* arguments to reveal their underlying form or structure. Of course, with an argument as simple as this one, where the reasoning is already perfectly clear and unmistakable, there is little practical need for further analysis. But when you move on to longer and more complex texts, you will begin to see the value of doing it.

Here is another argument, this time incorporating the first of our three claims:

> Badgers should not be culled. They are a protected species.

Notice that this time there is no connective 'therefore' or 'because', but it is still very obviously an argument that we are looking at. **i** is clearly being given as a reason for rejecting or opposing **iii**. In relation to the previous argument, this is a counter-argument. In standard form the **counter-argument** is:

> A2
>
> Badgers are a protected species.
> ———————————————————
> Badgers should not be culled.

Standard form

A useful skill to learn is this standard way of representing an argument by putting each claim that functions as a reason on a separate line, with the conclusion at the bottom under a horizontal line.

Key terms

Counter-argument: an argument which takes the opposing view.

■ Key terms

Premise: this is another word for a reason. 'Premise' is the more technical term and is sometimes more precise. It is the word normally used in logic. 'Reason' is a plainer word for the kind of support people offer for their conclusions when they are arguing naturally. In this book and in the AQA specification both words are used, and you should use whichever you find more appropriate. It is mostly a matter of preference.

Value judgement: a judgement is an opinion rather than a matter of fact. A value judgement is an opinion about the value or worth of something, including whether it is good or bad, right or wrong, harmful or beneficial, deserving or undeserving, etc. 'Claudia paid £2000 for a hairdo' is either a fact or it's false. 'It is wrong for anyone to pay £2000 for a hairdo' is a value judgement.

■ Evaluating arguments

Are these good arguments? In other words, do they give good reasons for believing or accepting their conclusions? This question takes us to the core of what this subject is about – evaluating reasoning and responding critically to it.

We'll look at the original argument first. We can see immediately that it is a very flimsy argument. It only gives one reason, or **premise**, in support of the conclusion. And as we observed on page 8, premise **ii** is not a proven fact but simply a claim, and a contested claim at that.

Suppose, however, that you were prepared to accept the truth of **ii**. Let's imagine you have seen and studied some of the evidence and satisfied yourself that it is at least *likely* that badgers do spread the disease. Should you then accept the conclusion as well, on the strength of **ii**?

In a word, no. Even if it is true, **ii** by itself is not a *sufficient* or *adequate* reason for the conclusion. For one thing **ii** is vague. It asserts that badgers spread the disease, but it doesn't specify to what extent. A term as important as 'spread' (in this context) would need to be precisely clarified before we could begin to say whether or not it justifies the culling of a valued and protected wild species. If it means that badgers are the sole cause, and that if there were no badgers, there would be no disease; that would be one thing. If it means that they are a contributory factor – one cause among others – and that killing them off would still leave cattle at risk of TB from other sources, then obviously it is a very different matter. We need to know which it is. We need to question further.

Also, argument **A1** makes a number of assumptions. It doesn't state them, but when you think about it carefully, you can see they are needed for the argument to be at all persuasive. One assumption is that the health of cattle *has more value* than the lives of the badgers, because it is for the sake of the cattle that the badgers would be killed. For farmers, the health of cattle probably does have more value; and for the economy as a whole *perhaps* it does. For animal lovers, wildlife enthusiasts and conservationists, etc., it probably does not. Since this is a **value judgement** – a term you will encounter a lot in critical thinking – there is no single right answer to the question of which matters more. There is more about value judgements in Chapter 14, page 87.

Another assumption is that culling badgers would *work*, or that it would work better than other possible measures. You could not sensibly defend the cull if you thought it would have no beneficial effect. But it is not a *fact* that it would work. Trial culls that have been conducted so far have not been conclusive, partly because there are so many conflicting factors to take into account. Also there was an outbreak of foot and mouth disease which disrupted the trial. So even if **ii** were true, it would not necessarily provide good grounds for a cull. A cull might simply be a waste of time, money, cattle – and badgers.

Once you see that these and other assumptions are necessary to the reasoning, and that they are *questionable* assumptions, the argument becomes very much harder to defend.

■ Over to you

Think about or discuss these assumptions and try to identify one or more further assumptions that argument A1 requires.

What about the counter-argument? Is that any better? Almost certainly not. It too is extremely flimsy. For although its one premise is a *fact*, and therefore not open to question like **ii**, it is still not sufficient on its own to rule out a cull. The fact that badgers *are* protected by law does not mean that they *should* be – whatever the circumstances or the consequences. In the end, the counter-argument rests on principles or conviction rather than reasoning. You may agree wholeheartedly with its conclusion, and there is nothing wrong with that. But if you do agree with it, it is a safe bet that you agreed with it already.

It is also a safe bet that if you did *not* already agree with the conclusion, this argument would not have changed your mind. A really good (strong) argument is one that *could* change someone's mind because its reasons are convincing grounds for the conclusion. Neither of the arguments we have looked at so far come anywhere near doing that. They would leave people continuing to think as they had before, or remaining undecided if they had been undecided before.

Giving more reasons

An argument is not limited to one reason or premise. Though quantity does not ensure quality, it is often true that the more support you give a conclusion, the stronger the argument. One deficiency we saw with each of the above arguments was that they relied on just one reason apiece. That would be all right if the reason were a sufficient or adequate reason, but in neither of the two examples was the reason sufficient.

The counter-argument, for example, could have been enlarged as follows:

> **A3**
>
> A badger cull would be wrong. No one has proved badgers are to blame for bTB in cattle. They are shy, peaceable creatures who have as much right to live their lives unmolested as any other animals, wild or domestic, and they're protected.

In standard and slightly abbreviated form:

R1 No one has proved badgers are to blame for bTB in cattle.

R2 Badgers are shy, peaceable creatures.

R3 They have as much right to live as any animal.

R4 The badger is a protected species.

C A cull would be wrong.

A = argument, C = conclusion, R = reason. (If you prefer to call them premises, you could label them P1, P2, …, etc.)

Labelling or numbering the lines is optional. It can be useful if you want to refer to the claims without repeating them in full, as we have been doing with **i**, **ii** and **iii**.

Is this a better argument? Obviously there is more to it: four points instead of just one. But would it persuade someone who did not already agree with the conclusion? You will have a chance to answer this question at the end of the chapter.

Reasoning indicators

'Therefore' and 'because' and their various synonyms are known as *reasoning indicators* (or argument indicators). They show where reasoning is taking place. They don't always appear in natural language arguments because they are not always needed. If you are unsure whether or not a particular piece of text is an argument, you can try inserting 'therefore' or 'because' in front of some of the sentences to see if they make sense. If they don't, it is unlikely that there is any argument intended. You will often see this referred to as the 'therefore-test'. There is more about the therefore-test in Chapter 13. In standard form versions of an argument, the horizontal line has the same kind of role as 'therefore'.

Show the structure

Setting out the structure of an argument in this way always makes the reasoning (i.e. the thinking behind it) clearer. Doing this careful analysis often helps with evaluation – it's easier to see where the weaknesses in the reasoning are once you have made the structure clear. While the claims are connected together in a block of prose it's harder to see *how* the argument works and *where* it's not working so well. Think of it as of a mechanic pulling out the parts of a car to see where the fault may lie.

■ Summary

The purpose of this chapter has been to give a broad picture of what critical thinking is all about. We have therefore introduced a number of terms and ideas, a lot of which may be unfamiliar to you, especially if you are new to critical thinking.

Actually, it is more accurate to talk about *uses* of words than words themselves. Most of the key words used in this book are in fact ordinary, everyday words that have special, slightly narrower meanings in critical thinking and logic. The words 'reason', 'conclusion', 'sufficient', 'value' and 'assumption' are examples of words in this category. They are referred to sometimes as 'semi-technical' words because they are half technical and half ordinary. You know already what they mean. It is just a matter of learning to apply them and use them more precisely.

There are some fully technical words as well, such as 'premise', but they are rarer. By and large, critical thinking uses plain words where they will do as good a job as technical words.

If there were parts of the chapter you feel unsure of or were confused by, don't worry about it, as we will be returning to all of the ideas again in greater depth, and the important ones will crop up regularly all the way through. You are not expected to have a complete grasp of them just from first acquaintance. But what you should have is an overall picture of the kind of approach critical thinking takes to texts, and some of the language it uses.

■ Over to you

1 Write a short definition for each of the nine terms listed here. If it's helpful, also give an example. The nine terms are claim, reason, premise, conclusion, argument, counter-argument, reasoning indicator, analysis, evaluation.

It is a good idea to keep a list like this open throughout the course, adding new terms and concepts to it as you come to them. It will provide you with a useful personal glossary, and future revision aid. You'll need three columns: one for the headword, one for the definition and one for any examples. (Maybe a fourth for notes.) You should leave plenty of space between the entries so you can modify or add to them as you progress – for example with extra examples. Alternatively use a card index or database with a separate record for each headword.

2 Give your own evaluation of the enlarged version of the counter-argument on page 11.

3 Find out a bit more about the bTB debate by looking at the source material on page 13 and use the information to have a preliminary class or group discussion on the subject. (It will be the topic for the next few chapters in the book, so the discussion and reading will be useful.)

Badgers must die to halt bovine TB

First cull of the animal in a quarter of a century

*Valerie Elliott, Countryside Editor,
April 9, 2008*

The popular portrayal of the badger as a stern but shy mainstay of British wildlife was revised dramatically yesterday by orders for the first cull of the animal in a quarter of a century.

The threat posed to cattle by bovine tuberculosis – which can be transmitted by badgers – prompted the announcement of a culling zone to stem the spread of the potentially lethal disease. The decision to set up the zone, which will be in an area of Wales, was described yesterday as a milestone by officials.

Farmers' leaders in England, where bovine TB is most common, said that they hoped that Hilary Benn, the Rural Affairs Secretary, will adopt the same policy. (…)

Animal welfare campaigners accused Welsh officials last night of wrongly victimising badgers and said that the illness was brought on by modern, intensive farming. They said that on no account should the cull be extended to England.

Last year the Independent Scientific Group, which supervised trials to determine a link between badgers and the spread of bovine TB to cattle, said that "badger culling can make no meaningful contribution to cattle TB control in Britain".

Critics argue that culling trials have shown that the approach simply prompts badgers to move to new areas, spreading the disease. The RSPCA also condemned the decision and said it flew in the face of sound scientific judgment. Rob Atkinson, its head of wildlife science, said: "We are not a bunch of badger-huggers. Our opposition to a badger cull is based on solid science, not sentiment."

But Christianne Glossop, Chief Veterinary Officer for Wales, … said that "doing nothing was not an option. We know there's a link between infection in cattle and infection in badgers. … The aim is healthy cattle, healthy badgers and healthy people." (…)

Dr Glossop said that the disease was out of control and the current policy was not working. The cost to the taxpayer of compensating Welsh farmers for the loss of infected cattle had risen from £1.3 million in 1999-2000 to more than £15 million from 2007 to the end of March this year. By 2012 the cost would be £30 million if the disease continued to increase at this rate.

In England an average of 5,000 farms are being infected each year with the slaughter of some 20,000 cattle at a cost to the taxpayer of almost £100 million. Last year 21,000 cattle tested positive for bovine TB on 9,000 farms. Ten years ago there were 3,000 cases on 1,500 farms. (…)

There has been limited badger culling in the past, and gassing was common in the 1970s before the 1982 badger protection laws.

These were introduced when badger numbers were below 250,000 but the badger population today is flourishing.

Source: www.timesonline.co.uk/tol/news/environment/article3708956.ece

Working with a live text

Learning objectives:

- to begin to recognise whether texts contain reasoning or an argument

- to start to extract 'embedded' arguments from texts

- to start to identify implicit conclusions

- to judge the significance of a reason within an argument: the work it does in supporting the conclusion

- to begin to recognise more complex arguments and identify intermediate conclusions; to be able to map out arguments accordingly.

Note

The critical questions are numbered according to the chapter where they first appear.

The word 'text' is used in a very broad sense in critical thinking. In fact, it is so broad that almost any item you are given to respond to can be referred to as a 'text'. Often it will be a piece of continuous writing, of one kind or another. It can be informative, argumentative, descriptive or narrative. It could be a screenplay or transcript of an interview. But it could also be a set of data, even a graph or image. Another word you will find being used with the same sense is *document*.

Many of the texts you encounter will be, or will contain, *arguments*, but by no means all of them.

The first document we are going to work on is the article by Valerie Elliott on page 13. You will no doubt have formed some opinions of your own about the issues raised in this article. In fact, you probably had views on the issues already. Now, however, we are going to look at the text itself – closely and *critically*. That means setting aside any existing views you have so that you can consider the material in a purely objective way.

We move to our first critical question.

Critical question

3.1   Is the text an argument?

Over to you

Take a few minutes to think about or discuss question 3.1, and give your answer to it.

Response

This is primarily an *analysis* question (AO1). It is not asking you to say whether you agree with the claims, or whether you think they are justified. It simply asks whether or not the author is presenting an *argument*, as defined on page 3.

The straight answer is no. Admittedly, the author deals with a topic that generates argument in the sense of debate and disagreement, but equally clearly, she does not herself make the case for either side. The right description for this text, as a whole, is a *report*.

The neutral stance of the author is clear from the second paragraph:

> The threat posed to cattle by bovine tuberculosis – which can be transmitted by badgers – *prompted the announcement* of a culling zone … The decision to set up the zone … was described yesterday as a milestone by officials.

It continues throughout the passage. Nowhere in the article will you find Valerie Elliott's conclusion or her reasons.

This doesn't mean that reporters and journalists never take sides, or that they never present their own arguments. Often they do, especially in editorials or leading articles. But this one, on this occasion, does not. If she has views, she is not stating them or trying to win readers over to one particular view – at least not explicitly.

Embedded argument

Having said that, there is obviously reasoning contained, or *embedded*, within the text. Among the subject matter being reported are the views of different individuals or groups, and some of the grounds they have for holding and/or defending those views. This is particularly evident in the reporting of what Dr Glossop, the Chief Vet for Wales, has to say. She clearly supports the cull. She doesn't say so in as many words, but that is unmistakably the conclusion or decision that she has reached. It's a reasonable guess that she was one of the 'officials' referred to in paragraph two, who approved the decision and called it a 'milestone', but even if she was not, it is evident that she backs them. It is also obvious that the claims attributed to her in paragraphs seven and eight are among her grounds for doing so.

We can treat reported or **embedded arguments** in much the same way as we treat arguments that are presented directly. We can take Dr Glossop's implicit conclusion that the badger cull was the right decision and ask to what extent, if at all, it is justified. To achieve this, we need to answer two related questions, one analytic, the other evaluative.

> **Key terms**
>
> **Embedded argument**: where reasons for a new conclusion are presented somewhere within a text but the author has not given the argument directly, for example because they have reported or quoted from someone else's argument.

Critical questions

3.2 According to the article on page 13, what reasons does the Chief Vet give to justify the decision to cull badgers?

3.3 Are they adequate reasons?

Response to critical question 3.2

One straightforward way to answer this question is to simply reconstruct the embedded argument in the standard way, identifying the reasons and the implicit conclusion. This is not difficult in the present text because all the reasons are clustered together in two consecutive paragraphs, and the conclusion, though not stated explicitly, is unmistakable from the context.

In standard form the argument might be spelled out as follows:

1 Doing nothing is not an option.
2 We know there is a link between infection in cows and in badgers.
3 The aim (of the cull) is healthy cows, people and badgers.
4 The disease is out of control.
5 Current policy isn't working.
6 Compensation costs have risen to £15 million …
7 They will rise to £30 million …

C The decision to cull badgers was the right one.

If this is all we do, however, it is a very raw analysis: just a list of claims. Nothing has been done to suggest how reasons **1** to **7** would best support the conclusion: whether, for example, each of them is a separate reason, or whether some of them should be grouped to form *sub-arguments*. This is important because when we later come to evaluate the reasoning, we may be underestimating its effectiveness if we simply judge each premise on its own.

Clearly in this case there are not seven separate lines of reasoning. If there were, it would be a very poor argument, because not one of them on its own even begins to justify the conclusion. If they are going to be at all effective as reasons, they have to be seen to assist each other.

For example, take the very first claim: that doing nothing wasn't an option. If we treat this as a separate reason, we might be very tempted to say that it is nothing more than a statement of opinion, with no independent support. But some of the other claims do support it. If it is true that the disease is out of control *and* that present policy isn't working *and* that the costs are spiralling upwards, then – arguably – something does have to be done. You can see, therefore, that claim **1** together with claims **4** to **7** form a smaller argument within the main argument.

> **We can't just do nothing because the disease is out of control, present policy isn't working, and costs are rising.**

We can think of this as a sub-argument with an *intermediate* conclusion. But it is not the whole argument. Dr Glossop is not just arguing that *something* must be done. She is arguing that the 'something' has to be a trial cull. This is implicit in the remaining two premises – **2** and **3** – which specifically bring badgers into the equation.

It is sometimes useful to draw diagrams like this one to show the structure of an argument: how the parts of the argument support each other and lead to the conclusion. Structurally our argument could be constructed as follows:

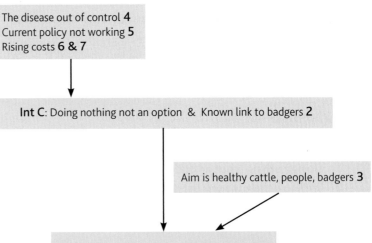

The claims in the top box of the diagram support the intermediate conclusion **Int C**. (**Int C**) + (**2**) then combine to support the main conclusion. Claim **3**, pointing out the aim of the cull, adds a possible further reason for doing it. It is a slightly puzzling claim for the Chief Vet to have made, but it could be understood as pointing out that all of the parties involved, human and animal, would gain from the cull if its aims are met.

Best interpretation

How do we know this is the 'right' analysis of the argument? We don't. We have not been given the argument directly. We had to extract it from the report ourselves: identify the reasons and the intended conclusion and put them into some form that made sense. There is no 'right' interpretation. But there is often a *best* interpretation, one that makes the reasoning as persuasive as possible. And *that* is what we aim for when we analyse a text.

But why? If as a critic my next job will be to evaluate the reasoning, why is it up to me to put the best interpretation on it first? The answer is: *because* you are about to evaluate it. 'Evaluate' doesn't just mean pick holes, score points. The purpose of critical evaluation is to *assess claims and their grounds fairly*. In the case of this article, the question you will be asking is whether the decision to cull was justified or not and, if so, to what extent? If you were to launch straight into an attack on the premises and/or the conclusion without first considering their merits, you would not be being critical in the critical thinking sense. Rubbishing arguments is not the object of the exercise. Nor is taking sides and just trying to win. That belongs to debating, and it should not be confused with evaluation. There is more about evaluating arguments in Chapters 20, 21 and 22.

Besides, if you *were* debating this issue and were planning to challenge the decision to cull, you would want to be able to say that you have dealt with the strongest arguments for it, not the weakest.

It should be clear that the interpretation we have put on the claims made in the text gives a much more effective argument than the plain list of reasons. None of the claims, on its own, gives any convincing support to the conclusion. Taken as an organised whole, they give much more.

The straw man

Giving a weak interpretation of an opponent's case so that it will be easier to knock down is known as the fallacy of the 'straw man'. It is a cheap trick rather than an example of good reasoning. For example, if you were to interpret Dr Glossop (on the strength of the article) as arguing that badgers should be indiscriminately killed *because* the public needed to see that something was being done, this would be a gross distortion of her reasonable argument that 'doing nothing was not an option'.

If you then challenged such an argument as being cynical, that might be fair criticism; only it would count for nothing as a challenge to Dr Glossop as it is not Dr Glossop's argument. It would be a straw man. Fallacies are errors in reasoning, or claims based on flawed reasoning. You will meet up with various *fallacies* as they occur in the texts for coming chapters. You can find out more about the fallacy of the straw man, and about fallacies in general, in Chapter 23, page 111.

Is it enough support? That was the third of the three critical questions considered in this chapter. It's over to you now to try answering it. Some appropriate responses will be considered in the next chapter.

Over to you

Are the reasons given by the Chief Vet for Wales adequate to justify the decision to cull badgers?

Is the reasoning adequate?

Learning objectives:

■ to distinguish between the reasoning in an argument and the truth of its premises; explain when an argument is poorly reasoned or there is a flaw in reasoning

■ to begin to recognise problems with causal reasoning

■ to appreciate the reason for adopting the principle of charity.

Critical question

3.3 Are the vet's reasons adequate for supporting the cull?

Response

On page 15 you were asked an evaluation question: whether claims attributed to the Chief Vet support the conclusion that a cull was the right decision. Two *main premises* were identified:

Main premise 1   That doing nothing is not an option,

because costs are spiralling, the disease is out of control, and current policies are not working; and

Main premise 2   That we know there is a link between infection in cattle and infection in badgers.

True or false?

You might think that the first thing to be settled is whether or not these various claims are *true*. Certainly that is a factor in evaluating *any* argument, since any argument based on false premises is obviously unreliable. However, it is not by any means the only question, for even if the premises are 100% correct, the conclusion may still not follow from them. The reasons given may be irrelevant, or there may be a flaw in the reasoning.

But there is another reason why the truth or falsity of claims is not necessarily the most important question and that is that in many cases we are unable to say whether the claims are true or false, either because we do not have the factual knowledge needed to check them, or because they are just opinions.

Both apply in this case. Unless you happen to belong to the small minority of people who have studied the factual evidence surrounding bovine disease, you won't be in any position to say whether the Chief Vet's figures are accurate, or whether the author of the article has quoted her correctly. As for her claim that the disease is 'out of control', this is at best only a judgement; it is not something you can put a precise measure on. Nor is the claim that present policies are not working. We are not even told what these policies are.

Before we even get to the crucial claim about the link to badgers – which is also an unsupported assumption – we have more questions than answers.

Uncertainty about the truth and falsity of reasons

It might seem as though we have reached a dead end, but we haven't. Uncertainty about the truth or falsity of claims does not stop us from assessing reasoning. Indeed, the right way to assess reasoning is to set aside the question of truth or falsity and to ask: *If* the premises are true, does the conclusion follow from them? For example, could it be true that the disease is out of control and costing millions, etc., *and* that doing nothing was still an option? If so, then the conclusion does not follow and the argument fails.

Does it follow?

The principal question for evaluating reasoning is to ask whether or not the conclusion *follows* from the reasons. If the reasons are true, then it is highly likely that the conclusion will also be true. Practise thinking like this by taking claims you know or believe to be false and asking what would follow from them *if* they were true.

If we take the statement literally, doing nothing obviously *was* an option. It may not have seemed a very practical or sensible or desirable option, and it may not have been the option favoured by the Chief Vet and the officials and some of the farmers, but that is not the same as saying it is not an option at all. It may even have been the best option. Sometimes doing something, rather than nothing, can make matters worse. This can be the case even when the situation is bad to begin with. You can probably think of at least one occasion when you have tried to put something right and wished afterwards that you had not.

But ought we to take the phrase 'not an option' quite so literally? Remember what was said in Chapter 3 about looking for the best interpretation, not the one that is simply the easiest to knock down. In ordinary conversation, people often say that something is not an option when they actually mean that it is not a *serious* option, or that in their opinion it would be a very *high-risk* option. If that is all that Dr Glossop meant, then the sub-argument is not completely doomed after all. If you challenged her, she might say: 'All right then, it is an *option* to carry on as we are doing, but look what it's costing; look at the risks. Surely the cost of doing nothing is just too great.' Since that is a perfectly reasonable line to take, perhaps we should give it the benefit of the doubt.

Assumptions

Next we turn to the second premise, **Main premise 2** (page 18). Even if we concede that doing nothing is not an option – at least not a realistic or sensible one – we still have to assess the next step in the argument, where **Main premise 2** is added and the main conclusion drawn. Remember that both **Main premise 1** and **Main premise 2** are needed if the conclusion is to follow. Neither is sufficient on its own.

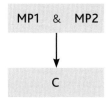

It is here that the argument meets it biggest challenge. It requires two big *assumptions* to be made: one *explicit*, one *implicit* – and both essential to the argument.

The explicit assumption is the premise itself:

> **We know there is a link between infection in cows and badgers.**

But do we really know this? 'Know' is a very strong word to use. It implies certainty. Are we to accept as *certain* that there is a link between infection in cattle and in badgers? After all, there are no grounds given for the claim; it is just asserted and we are expected to take it on trust. Should we?

Once again the answer is probably yes. There are several good reasons for this:

■ Firstly, this claim is factual in nature, not merely a matter of opinion or a value judgement. Either there is a link or there is not.

The principle of charity

Giving the author of an argument the benefit of the doubt, and looking for the best interpretation, is sometimes referred to as applying the principle of charity. 'Charity' is a slightly misleading word because in this context it has nothing to do with being kind or generous. It simply means assuming that the person arguing or giving reasons is a *rational* person and a competent user of the language. No such person would say that doing nothing was *literally* not an option, because literally it *is* an option. Any intelligent person would know that, and would not draw it as a conclusion from these premises. Under the principle of charity, we should always interpret a text on the assumption that the person making it is not a fool. Observing the principle of charity can be thought of as a way of being fair-minded, and of avoiding the error of the *straw man* (page 17).

Over to you

What is your answer to question 3.3? Should we accept the vet's claim?

Secondly, the person making the claim is an expert, an authority, and whilst that does not make anything she says automatically true, it does count for something. She is the Chief Veterinary Officer in the whole of Wales. She is undoubtedly well qualified in this field. She also has a reputation to think about and would not want to be discovered to have made a careless or false assumption about something as important as this.

Thirdly, no one appears to be denying a link. The author, Valerie Elliott, says in the first sentence of the article that bTB 'can be transmitted by badgers'. And the Independent Scientific Group (ISG) who were set up to 'determine the link' do not say that there isn't one, only that culling would make 'no meaningful contribution' to controlling the disease.

All in all, a link seems likely. (In fact, if you were to research elsewhere, you would soon find that it is generally accepted by all scientifically minded parties, though the text does not tell you it in so many words.) There is something else to take into account as well: the claim itself is actually quite a weak or cautious claim. *All* it says is that there is a link. It doesn't specify the kind of link. A link need not mean much more than that both badgers and cattle can carry the disease, which they do. This is why the Chief Vet can safely say that we *know* about it. Even if we do know about it, it may not actually tell us very much, which brings us to the real weakness in the argument.

Implicit assumptions: missing premises

As we said in the last section, there is also an *implicit* assumption connected with **Main premise 2**. What is more, it is a very questionable assumption. You have probably recognised it already; it is the assumption that the link between bTB in badgers and bTB in cattle is a *causal* link. Even more than that, it is the assumption that the cause is *from* badgers *to* cattle.

Main premise 2 does not state that the link is causal at all, only that there is a link. But it is the *causal* connection that is needed for the conclusion to follow. If there is not a causal connection, there are no good grounds for a cull. The assumption that the link is causal can be thought of as a missing premise. It is as necessary to the reasoning as any of the stated reasons, like the costs, and the failure of present policies, or the need to do something rather than nothing. In fact, it is probably more important than any of them. The whole argument hangs on whether badgers really do spread the disease to cattle, *or* (for example) whether cattle spread it to each other, and maybe to badgers as well.

This point can be pursued even further: suppose we concede that there is a causal link, and that badgers do spread bTB to cattle, it still doesn't follow that a cull would solve (or help to solve) the problem. If thousands of badgers are killed and the disease carries on spreading, nothing has been achieved, in addition to much being lost in terms of wildlife. And this is more than just remote possibility; if the ISG are right (paragraph 5 of the article on page 13), a cull would make 'no meaningful contribution'.

Cause–correlation fallacy

A correlation is a statistical link. There is a correlation between blue eyes and sunburn, but only in the sense that many people with blue eyes have fair skin, which burns more easily than dark skin. It does not mean that having blue eyes causes your skin to burn; both have a common, genetic cause. Sometimes a correlation is evidence of a causal connection, but by no means always. It is a fallacy (flawed reasoning) to 'jump to the conclusion' that because there is correlation, there must be cause. It is sometimes called the *correlation = cause fallacy*, because the two are *not* the same (so it is sometimes abbreviated to *cause ≠ correlation*).

Verdict on the argument

So the argument looks to be flawed. It commits the fallacy of assuming that because two occurrences are connected that one, in particular, is the cause of the other. So the claim that there is 'a link' is not an adequate defence of the decision to cull. There may be an adequate defence, but this is not it.

The pro-cull faction does have a possible line of defence: they could argue that because there is uncertainty about the nature of the link, a *trial* cull is needed to see if it makes a difference. The anti-cull faction could counter this by stating that the ISG have already conducted a trial and decided that culling wouldn't make any real difference.

And so it goes on. Arguments are typically part of an ongoing debate: claim, argument, counter-argument, counter-counter-argument, objection, response, new evidence, etc. It would be peculiar to find an argument that was not a response to some earlier argument and/or a target for a further argument.

As we said in Chapter 1, we are not trying to solve the problem or reach a final conclusion. We are looking critically at a particular text and assessing whether the claims made in it make a convincing case or not. To do that well, we need to be neutral and objective – whatever our beliefs or sympathies or convictions may be. The discipline needed for this objectivity is hard to achieve, especially if you do have strong feelings on an issue. But in the long run it will give you greater confidence in your own reasoning powers, and in the conclusions you draw and the decisions you make.

Strong and weak claims

'Strong' and 'weak' are semi-technical terms when used to describe claims. A strong claim is one which asserts a lot or asserts it forcefully. It is much stronger to say we *know* something than to say that we *think* or *believe* it. On the other hand, to claim that there is a link is much weaker than to claim there is a *causal* link. Obviously that tells us much more, and is much harder to prove or justify. (You are not required to use these two terms technically at AS level, but you may find them useful.)

Over to you

1 How justified is the claim by animal welfare campaigners that the cull should not be extended to England? Consider claims made in paragraphs four to six but also refer to information in paragraphs 9 to 11. Construct the best argument you can from the claims made in the document, and evaluate it.

2 The following technical or semi-technical terms were used in this chapter: implicit assumption, falsity, correlation, cause–correlation fallacy, principle of charity. Add them to your personal glossary, explain what they mean and possibly give an illustrative example of your own for each one.

5   Before we leave the badgers

Learning objectives:

- to put together strategies for evaluating argument introduced so far

- to understand the methodology of giving grounds.

In Chapter 2 we *extracted* an argument from a journalist's report on the decision to set up a culling zone, and on the bTB-badger debate in general. It was not the author's own argument. Nor was it an argument written or spoken directly by the Chief Vet. It was reconstructed from the claims attributed to her and the context in which she made them, i.e. defending the decision to introduce a cull and answering the 'critics'.

In constructing this argument, we relied on the author of the article to have reported accurately what people had said. We also looked for the best interpretation we could give to their claims. This meant grouping the claims so that they supported each other, rather than just putting them in a list dealing with them one by one.

In Chapters 3 and 4 we discussed the question of whether or not the argument was a good one: whether the claims did or did not give adequate grounds for the decision to cull. We decided that they did not.

The general strategy for evaluating the argument was as follows:

- Assume that, without good reason to doubt them, the claims were true.
- Concede that the intermediate conclusion was reasonable.
- Challenge the unstated assumption that the link with badgers was a causal one.

Giving ground

It may have seemed that this strategy was very generous, and that the argument could have been attacked on many other grounds, such as the mere *opinion* that the disease is 'out of control' or the vagueness of such a claim. You could have said it was too vague to base any conclusion on; that would, in fact, have been a fair point to make.

However, 'giving ground', conceding points that *could* have been challenged, can be an effective strategy, even if you want to give a **refutation** of the argument as a whole. For one thing, it demonstrates that you are being open-minded and fair in your assessment. For another, it saves your criticism for the most vulnerable parts of the argument. In this case it is clearly the jump from 'link' to 'cause' which shatters the argument. In challenging it, you were able to say: '*Even if* we accept all the other claims and conclusions, the argument still has this serious flaw/weakness.' It doesn't mean you do accept them all.

Giving ground is not something done out of kindness, which is why the principle of charity should not be understood that way.

Key terms

Refutation: the successful defeat of an argument, either by identifying something wrong with it or by making a better counter-argument. The word is often used loosely to mean opposing or denying something: 'I completely refute that.' In critical thinking it should be used only in the stricter (some would say correct) sense.

Long answer, short answer

In Chapter 1 it was pointed out that in the exam you would have only limited time to answer critical questions. Obviously the kind of discussion you have seen here would neither be possible nor appropriate in an exam. Much of the discussion, anyway, was to make teaching points; the actual answers to the questions need not be nearly as elaborate. An evaluative question would normally carry around 4–6 marks in an exam. An answer would need to be no more than a short paragraph, like the Specimen answer below.

Specimen answer

Critically evaluate the Chief Vet's argument

The argument is that because of high costs and other problems, something has to be done, and since we know that there is a link with badgers, a cull is the right thing to do. Even if we accept that the problems and costs are as high as the Chief Vet claims they are, and that doing nothing is not a sensible option, the argument depends on an implicit assumption that badgers are the cause of the spread of bTB in cattle and that culling them would be effective. These are very questionable assumptions, as the ISG have said (paragraph five of the article on page 13).

Although this is very short in comparison with the lengthy discussion in Chapters 3 and 4, it shows that all the relevant critical thinking has taken place and would be a good answer. Indeed, part of its strength as an answer is that it wastes no words; it answers the question exactly, and no more.

Between the lines

Before finishing with our first topic and moving on to a new one, here is a critical question of a different kind. At the beginning of Chapter 3, the following comment was made about the author of the article:

> If she has views, she is not stating them or trying to win readers over to one particular view – at least not explicitly.

The phrase 'at least not explicitly' was added in case some readers felt – you may be one of them – that the author is *not* 100% neutral, that she does tilt the article slightly one way or the other. An important part of critical thinking is reading *between the lines* as well as just assessing the literal meanings of claims. There may be subtle ways of influencing the reader whilst appearing neutral. What do you think?

Over to you

Some readers of this article have commented that there is evidence of bias in the way it is reported. Do you think this is a fair assessment of the article, or do you think it is entirely neutral? You should support you answer by referring to parts of the article or features of its presentation.

6   Was there a beast?

Learning objectives:

■ to begin to distinguish between the rhetoric and reasoning in a text

■ to understand what is meant by an implicit assumption and be able to identify more obvious cases of these

■ to identify unwarranted assumptions.

Rhetoric

In real, live arguments there is nearly always some element of rhetoric, because the natural purpose of an argument is to persuade. There is nothing intrinsically wrong with rhetoric when it is used to add to an otherwise sound argument. It is only something to be critical of when it is used to disguise an otherwise bad argument or a possible untruth.

In Chapter 1 we said that we would return to the argument about the beast in Golding's *Lord of the Flies*. It is now time to do so. To remind you, here is the original text:

> 'I've got the conch. I'm not talking about the fear. I'm talking about the beast.' (...)
>
> Jack paused, cradling the conch, and turned to his hunters with their dirty black caps.
>
> 'Am I a hunter or am I not?'
>
> They nodded, simply. He was a hunter all right. No one doubted that.
>
> 'Well then – I've been all over this island. By myself. If there was a beast I'd have seen it. Be frightened because you're like that – but there is no beast in the forest.'

And here is Jack's argument which we extracted from it:

> (You agree that) I am a hunter.
>
> I have been all over the island – by myself.
>
> If there was a beast, I would have seen it.
>
> Therefore there is no beast.

In the original text you will see that the first premise is expressed as 'Well then – ' and follows the question Jack has just asked. It is quite a clever way of saying to his audience that they have accepted his claim to be a hunter. It is more effective than simply stating it and running the risk of someone challenging the truth of it. You can see the politician in Jack!

Although this is not part of the argument itself, it is part of the persuasive technique that Jack is using. We call this kind of thing a rhetorical device (or just *rhetoric*); we need to be able to recognise it and separate it from the basic reasoning when we analyse an argument.

Critical question

6.1   We have listed the reasons and the conclusion. But what is the structure of this argument?

Response

If we look at this argument simplistically, we see that it consists of three reasons and a conclusion. That does not, however, indicate anything about its structure. For although it is very short, this is not a simple argument. It is a complex one, meaning that there is more than one step in it. This is the same as saying that there is a *sub-argument* and a *main argument*. There is also a missing premise which would need to be taken into account in any complete analysis.

The sub-argument is that *because* Jack is a hunter, and because he has been all over the island, he would have seen a beast if there was one. From that intermediate conclusion he argues that, therefore, there is no beast.

The missing premise is that he *hasn't* seen a beast. Jack doesn't say this in so many words but it is obviously implicit in his argument. If he had seen the beast, it would make the whole argument nonsensical.

We can now show the structure of the argument as follows, adding the missing premise and putting it in brackets to show that it is implied rather than stated:

1   I am a hunter.

2   I have been all over the island by myself.

C1 If there was a beast, I would have seen it.

   (I haven't seen it.)

C2 There is no beast.

Note that in this version of the analysis the intermediate conclusion is labelled **C1** and the main conclusion **C2**. There is no particular right or wrong way to set out arguments, as long as it makes the structure plain. You can explain it in your own words; you can use the conventional form. You can even use a diagram.

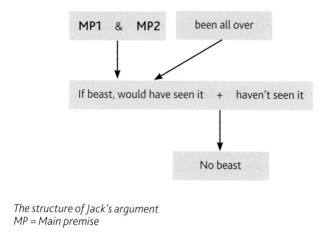

The structure of Jack's argument
MP = Main premise

As you gain experience, you will find that some arguments suit one method of analysis better than others. You will also find that some suit *you* better than others. The best way to gain that experience is to try several different techniques with the texts you work on, and to see for yourself which works best.

Critical question

6.2 Is this a good argument?

Response to critical evaluation (page 5)

This, you may remember, was the question you were asked in Chapter 1. Since then you have learned a lot more about critical thinking. But even then you probably realised that this was not a very sound or reliable piece of reasoning. If so, you were right: it is not sound or reliable. But in critical thinking the important question is *why* not.

The problems lie, not with the main argument, but with the step leading up to it, the sub-argument. What we are being asked here is to accept that Jack could not possibly have missed seeing a beast if there was one, given that he is a hunter and has been everywhere on the island. Of course, we don't know whether he has been everywhere on the island or not. We have to take his word for that. Whether or not he is a hunter is a matter of opinion. The other boys evidently accept that he is. They nodded when he asked them. Reading between the lines, it is probably closer to the mark to say that Jack *fancies* himself as a hunter and that the other boys are too scared of him to disagree. However, that is only one of the two premises in the sub-argument and the less important one.

Following the strategy introduced in previous chapters, we can afford to assume – for the sake of argument – that both of the claims are true, because even if they are, they do not support Jack's first conclusion. Not unless we make all kinds of additional assumptions about, for example, the inability of a beast (if there is one) to keep out of sight. These might include questions such as:

■ What if the beast lives underground and only comes out at night when Jack is asleep?

■ What if it is simply a clever enough beast to stay hidden when Jack is hunting? It is well known that wild animals are very good at hiding.

■ What if it just happens to be always in a different part of the island from the one where Jack is?

■ What if Jack is not as observant as he thinks he is?

These are serious possibilities and we cannot just assume they are *not* possible. In other words, Jack's argument rests on the implicit assumption that no beast could possibly hide from him. If that is *not* assumed, the first conclusion does *not* follow. And as we have seen, it is not something we can reasonably assume. It is what we call an **unwarranted assumption**.

What about the main argument?

In one way it doesn't matter whether the main argument is any good or not, since the chain of reasoning has already broken down at the first link, and therefore the main premise – that if there was a beast Jack would have seen it – is false, or at least unacceptable.

But as a matter of interest, there is nothing wrong with the reasoning in the main argument. For suppose Jack's claim that he could not possibly have missed the beast were true, and he really hasn't seen one, then from these two claims it would have to follow that there is no beast.

If there was a beast, I would have seen it.

I haven't seen a beast.

There is no beast.

Summary

Look at the specimen answer (in the margin) on Jack's argument. Would it make any difference if we knew that the conclusion was true? (Those of you who have read the book will know whether it was or not, and we won't spoil it for those who have not read it.) No, it would not make any difference. It would not mean that the argument was sound or reliable after all.

What it would mean is that the argument was *unnecessary*. The whole purpose of reasoning in the practical world is to try to find out or decide what is true and what is not. You don't need an argument for something you already know to be true.

Over to you

Thoroughly analyse and evaluate the following short argument about another much-discussed beast. Note any other similarities you can see between this argument and Jack's.

■ The Loch Ness monster is as much an object of fascination for non-believers as for believers. In fact, the non-believers probably spend far more time trying unsuccessfully to disprove the existence of the creature than we believers do in watching out for it. What is more, they have all the benefits of modern science and technology at their disposal. If there were a convincing scientific explanation, someone would surely have come up with it by now. So the odds are that there is something very much alive down there that the scientists can't account for. Anyway, what is so unscientific about a large sea creature? The oceans are full of them.

Specimen answer

Two-step argument

The argument has two steps: a sub-conclusion and a main one. The sub-argument breaks down because it assumes that Jack could not have missed seeing the beast, even if he had been everywhere on the island. This is a crucial assumption and it is almost certainly false. That means that the next step in the argument starts from a false premise and is therefore unsound.

Conclusion

In Part 1, Thinking critically, you have explored the territory of critical thinking from one end to the other. You've experienced the subject's three central activities:

■ identifying, analysing and interpreting reasoning
■ evaluating arguments
■ producing reasoned responses of your own.

Part 2 – Critical thinking in practice – will present you with a range of different texts and topics to exercise and extend your critical skills.

7 What to believe

Key terms

Sceptical: assuming or suspecting something is likely to be false until proven otherwise.

Critical: suspending judgement until sufficient evidence is presented either way.

When you read a newspaper or magazine article like the one opposite, what is your natural response?

- Do you *accept* most of the claims you find there unless there is strong reason to disbelieve them?
- Do you *reject* most of the claims unless there are strong reasons to believe them?
- Do you read with an *open mind* and neither accept nor reject anything without careful thought?
- Do you believe what you *want* to believe and reject what you don't?
- None of the above – give details.

This set of questions requires considerable honesty on your part. You would probably like to tick the third box, especially now that you have been studying critical thinking for a while. It is certainly the most critical attitude, but how often do you really do it? How often when you are reading a newspaper do you have time to consider each claim carefully and weigh up reasons for or against accepting it at face value? Probably not very often.

What about the first two answers? They stand in direct contrast to each other. The second is obviously more critical than the first. There is a single word for it: *scepticism*. A sceptic (pronounced *skeptic* and sometimes spelled that way) is someone whose natural instinct is to doubt or question, rather than to accept things or take them on trust. Thus '**sceptical**' and '**critical**' are related in meaning, although extreme scepticism – refusal to believe anything at all – can be just as uncritical as passive acceptance.

That leaves the fourth response, believing what you want to believe. This clearly is an uncritical way to respond, but if we are honest with ourselves, we probably all do it much of the time, and unless we make a conscious effort not to. It is very natural to reserve criticism for those claims which we already disagree with, and then to be lenient towards those claims which it suits us to believe. It is probably also true that studying critical thinking won't stop us from doing it. What it will do is make us aware of it so we can guard against it. Thinking critically is not so much a natural attitude as a discipline: something that takes conscious effort and practice.

Daily Mail

Prince William flies multi-million pound RAF Chinook helicopter to Isle of Wight stag do … and picks up Harry on the way

By MATTHEW HICKLEY

Most young men are happy to jump in a taxi to get to a stag do. But not Prince William. The second in line to the throne used a £10 million RAF helicopter to fly to a drunken weekend in the Isle of Wight, it emerged last night. He even stopped off in London to pick up his brother Prince Harry on the way.

Prince William now has his wings with the RAF and is continuing his training with both jets and helicopters. The RAF says that the trip to the Isle of Wight was a vital part of his training. They insisted the jaunt was "legitimate training", teaching the prince to fly over water.

But MPs and taxpayers' campaigners demanded to know why the young royals were allowed to use the Chinook aircraft as a "stag do taxi service". British troops in Afghanistan are critically short of the helicopters.

Privately, senior commanders are furious over the incident, which threatens to take the gloss off William's four months of pilot training with the RAF. They fear the stag party trip will bolster claims that the whole costly training package has been a "jolly".

William, 25, spent last week with a Chinook squadron before receiving his RAF "wings" from his father in a ceremony on Friday. Hours later he took the controls of the Chinook heavy-lift transport helicopter for a low-level sortie south to London, where he flew through the busy civilian airspace to land at Woolwich Army barracks to pick up Harry before crossing to the Isle of Wight.

A Chinook helicopter like the ones used by the RAF

The 80-minute journey – it is understood it costs more than £5,000 to keep a Chinook in the air for an hour – saved William seven hours of driving through rush hour traffic and waiting for a ferry, meaning he and Harry arrived by 4pm, ready for the start of the three-day stag party for their cousin Peter Phillips.

According to onlookers two dozen friends toured the island's pubs and clubs drinking heavily, and at one point rowdy revellers pulled down William's trousers.

The Chinook was flown back to its base at Odiham in Hampshire by an RAF crew.

The Ministry of Defence insisted the sortie had always been planned as part of William's training and included important elements of a pilot's skills. A spokesman said: "Prince William flew a legitimate training sortie which tested his new skills to the limit."

But critics reacted with anger, pointing out that the RAF's 48-strong Chinook fleet is one of the most overstretched parts of the armed forces. Only around ten are available to commanders in Afghanistan, who privately complain that operations are constantly hamstrung by a lack of helicopters.

Lib Dem defence spokesman Nick Harvey said: "This is serious kit with serious running costs. The public will not appreciate it being used as a stag do taxi service." Matthew Elliott, chief executive of the Taxpayers' Alliance, said: "It is jaw-dropping that this was given approval."

Clarence House declined to comment but senior royal sources denied that William had done anything wrong. One said: "He missed a flight last week that he needed to do as part of his training, so they rearranged the sortie. The RAF wouldn't have approved it if they weren't happy with it."

But another source said: "It isn't the first time I am afraid, and it won't be the last."

Source: Daily Mail, 16 April 2008

■ Scepticism and sceptics

'Scepticism' is the name for a way of thinking that *starts* with doubt. The idea is that knowledge can be built only on a foundation where nothing is taken for granted and everything can and should be doubted. This system is also known as *philosophical scepticism*, because it describes how many philosophers approach the theory of knowledge. Some extreme sceptics argue that nothing can be known because nothing is beyond some doubt. Critical thinking encourages a sceptical approach up to a point, but not to this kind of extreme. What you want to develop is a *healthy* scepticism.

■ Cynicism

Care is needed not to confuse scepticism with cynicism. A cynic is someone who tends to see bad in people, or who looks for explanations which assume the world is a nasty place. It is cynical, for example, to assume that all politicians are liars, all journalists write only what will sell, all police are corrupt, etc. Scepticism can shade into cynicism, but when it does it loses its critical edge and becomes a form of prejudice.

■ Over to you

Do you feel that the Matthew Hickley article is mainly objective or that it is judgemental? Find some examples or evidence in the text to support your answer. In the process of answering this question you need to think carefully and discuss what the two words 'objective' and 'judgemental' mean. Are they, for example, opposites? You can add the words to the personal glossary you started at the end of Chapter 2.

■ The document

Ostensibly this is a narrative, a news story, although what makes it 'news' is not the rather ordinary events being reported, but the fact that they involved Princes William and Harry. If any other trainee pilot had flown to a stag party, collecting his younger brother en route, it would not have hit the headlines with quite the same force. Nor would it have received the same high-profile responses from MPs and taxpayers' groups, and senior commanders and royal spokespersons. These are what the article is mainly about. In fact, considerably more of its column inches are devoted to comment and reaction than to the story itself.

The journalist doesn't openly state his views, though you may feel he makes them fairly plain. He doesn't condemn Prince William for using the helicopter, but he doesn't spare him or excuse him either. This could just be because he thought the behaviour was pretty indefensible anyway, and any reporting of it would put the princes in a bad light. Or it could be that the journalist has told it in a way which exaggerates or sensationalises. Certainly it is true that bad behaviour (like bad news) makes more interesting reading than good behaviour, especially when it is royal behaviour. So any author could have an incentive to spin the story in a way that invites disapproval or outrage in the reader.

This is not to suggest that Matthew Hickley has actually spiced up the story in any way. You must reach your own verdict on that, and you may well decide that he has reported fairly and responsibly, and that any disapproval that may come the prince's or the RAF's way is merited by their actions and not by the author's rhetoric.

Healthy scepticism means being aware that writers *may*, and *sometimes* do, give a slanted account, not an assumption that they always do. That is cynicism.

■ Whose claims are they?

There are several different kinds of claim or assertion in this document. Before we look at any of the claims themselves, something should be said about whose claims they are. We can sort them into two main categories: assertions by the author and reported assertions by other people. You may recall that in the document on page 13, which had some similarities, we also called these *embedded* claims.

The author himself tells us that most young men are happy to jump in a taxi, but that Prince William was not, and that he used an RAF helicopter to fly to a drunken party. These are his own assertions, presented directly to the reader. But he also tells us that, for example, an MoD spokesman said this was a 'legitimate training sortie'. Indeed he quotes him verbatim. This is really two claims:

> that the spokesman said the words

> that the sortie was legitimate.

The second claim is embedded in the first. The significance of this becomes obvious if you want to question the claims. It might be true that the spokesman made the assertion, but not true that the helicopter flight was legitimate. Or, though perhaps less likely, it might be true that it was a legitimate sortie but not that the spokesman said it. Or, of course, both could be true – or both false, and the whole thing a fiction. (Seriously considering this last possibility would require a high level of scepticism.)

Reported speech and uncertain sources

The claim of the MoD spokesman is in quotation marks, indicating that these were the exact words of a specific person. There are other claims that are more indirectly reported, where the author of the article has summarised or paraphrased or just referred to what was said. For example:

> … senior royal sources denied that the prince had done anything wrong.

There are some places in the text where the author has mixed direct quotation with his own report of what was said, especially when a particularly interesting or significant phrase has been used. Take paragraph 3 for example:

> But MPs and taxpayers' campaigners demanded to know why the young royals were allowed to use the Chinook aircraft as a "stag do taxi service". British troops in Afghanistan are critically short of the helicopters.

Here it becomes a lot harder to know exactly who is being quoted or reported. 'MPs and taxpayers' campaigners' is a very vaguely defined group of people. We don't know whether it was a sizeable group or just one or two. Strictly speaking, the account is true if there were just two or more, but the impression given is of a substantial number. If so, it is unlikely that they all had the same reasons for demanding answers, and even more unlikely that they all used the phrase 'stag do taxi service'. We know of one who did because he is quoted again in paragraph 11. The rest are anonymous.

You may also have wondered whether the remark about British troops being short of helicopters was something the MPs and taxpayers' campaigners raised (whoever they were), or whether it is a comment added by the journalist. What is clear is that it is making a point, especially following the words 'taxi service' as it does. What is not as clear is whose point it is. It is ambiguous, perhaps intentionally so. If you read it one way, it looks like the reason why the MPs and others were 'demanding to know …'. But it is just as possible that it is the journalist's point. If so, then it is very relevant to the question you have just answered about how objective or judgemental the article is.

As always when there is ambiguity, you must interpret the text in the way that seems most likely given the context; that is, the article as a whole.

We also know little or nothing about the 'senior commanders' in paragraph 4, the 'onlookers' in paragraph 7, or the 'critics' in paragraph 10.

There is also a convention used in paragraph 12 which is becoming increasingly common in journalistic writing:

> Clarence House declined to comment …

Clarence House is the official residence of Prince William's father and stepmother, but is also occupied by numerous servants and officials, and we don't know which of them, if any, was asked for an opinion. The sentence means that no one from the royal household said anything at all on the subject, but to assert that Clarence House had nothing to say gives the *impression* that someone there is not pleased about the situation.

Clarence House

You often find Downing Street or the White House, or just Paris or Berlin being quoted, or refusing to be quoted, in the same way.

Fact or opinion – or what?

When you are given a claim to consider, it is very natural to ask: is it fact or opinion? You were probably first asked this kind of question at primary school, in a language or literacy lesson. However, as you may have often thought then, it is not always a very simple question to answer. As we saw in Chapter 2, not every claim fits conveniently into one or the other classification. There are claims that state facts without our *knowing* that they are facts. And there are claims which are believed to be facts but are actually false. How are we to decide which are which?

What the question 'Is it fact or opinion?' really means is: which expressions are *claiming* to be facts? Or, which are **factual in kind**?. This includes opinions and expressions of belief, but only those that are about factual matters. These statements can be contrasted with claims that are not about factual matters, such as value judgements.

Several claims in the document are strongly and clearly factual. This does not necessarily mean they are facts, only that they are presented as fact. For example, the narrative account in the paragraph 5 is strongly factual.

> William, 25, spent last week with a Chinook squadron before receiving his RAF "wings" from his father in a ceremony on Friday. Hours later he took the controls of the Chinook heavy-lift transport helicopter for a low-level sortie south to London, where he flew through the busy civilian airspace to land at Woolwich Army barracks to pick up Harry before crossing to the Isle of Wight.

What makes it strongly factual is that it either happened or it didn't. Either William took the controls or he didn't. Either the aircraft stopped to pick up Harry or it didn't. They are also the kind of claims that could easily be verified or corroborated by evidence. For example, the helicopter would have a flight log, listing all its 'sorties' and all the crew members and passengers on board for each flight. By the same token it could easily be falsified. Eyewitnesses could be asked, did it happen? And the answer would be yes or no.

At the other extreme are claims which are not factual at all, but entirely judgemental. For example:

> It is jaw dropping that this was given approval.

You may agree or disagree with this claim, but you can't say in any objective sense that it is 'true'. It could never be more than an opinion, a value judgement. It may be jaw-dropping to some people, and to others it seems it was a 'legitimate sortie'. Neither would be wrong in the same way that they would be wrong if the whole story were a fabrication and the princes had actually gone to the Isle of Wight by train.

In-between claims

In between fall a range of claims which are factual in the sense that they could be true or false, but are not so easy to verify. Take the assertion that:

> Privately, senior commanders are furious …

or:

> They fear the stag party trip will bolster claims that the whole costly training package has been a "jolly".

Both these claims may be accurate reports of how *some* senior commanders feel. But who are they? The trouble with claims like these is that they are vague, hard to pin down. For a start, how *many* senior commanders are furious and fearful? And how many have to feel that way for the claim to be true? All of them? The majority? If we can't answer questions like these, how can we say with any conviction whether these are facts or not?

Also, we have to ask how it can be known that these senior commanders are privately furious. 'Privately' means that they don't let it show, they keep it secret. They don't tell a journalist on a national newspaper. That may mean it has been leaked or rumoured, or that it is just speculation. It may be very plausible speculation, but it's a long way from being strongly factual.

Claims like these deserve to be treated with some scepticism. They are not so much facts as allegations – closer to opinion than to fact.

Link

There is more about corroboration on page 66.

Over to you

Select some of the other claims in the documaent on page 29 and discuss how they should be classified.

■ Predictions

Another class of assertions is the one that includes forecasts and predictions. Generally, a prediction is a claim about what will happen in the future, or about something that is not yet known for sure. There are two in the text, one in paragraph 11:

> "This is serious kit with serious running costs. The public *will not appreciate* it being used as a stag do taxi service."

and one in paragraph 13:

> "It isn't the first time I am afraid, and it won't be the last."

Obviously a claim that something will take place or will come about cannot be factual in the same way as something that has happened or is known about already. It may *come* to be true, but at the time of making it, a prediction is always an opinion.

■ Conclusion

What we have been doing here is analysing and classifying claims with a view to understanding them more critically than we would if we were just reading casually. This will also help us assess their reliability.

This is not a negative criticism of the author or of the article. We have identified some claims that are more readily acceptable than others; and some that, by their nature, need to be treated more cautiously or sceptically.

None of this means that the author is being untruthful or misleading. There is nothing wrong with making allegations, indulging in speculation or offering opinion. It is only wrong when these are passed off as hard facts. And there is no sign of that in the article.

■ Over to you

We finish our study of the *Daily Mail* article with three critical questions.

- ■ How *justified* is the claim by 'senior royal sources' that Prince William had done nothing wrong?
- ■ What grounds have critics given for their objections? Are these strong grounds?
- ■ Comment on the choice of language in paragraph 2.

8 The writing's on the wall

Learning objectives:

- to become more adept at identifying unwarranted assumptions

- to start to increase range of knowledge and understanding of common flaws (*ad hominem*, cause and correlation, false dichotomy).

In 2007 a major controversy was generated when two young men were jailed for spray-painting a train. The newspaper article below tells the story. Read through the article now.

End of line for graffiti pests

Andy Russell

TWO train graffiti artists who were tracked by their distinctive 'signatures' have been jailed for causing nearly £13,000 damage.

Thomas Dolan, 20, and Thomas Whittaker, 18, daubed trains, bridges and other railway property throughout Greater Manchester with spray paint murals – and posted examples of their work on graffiti websites. Dolan used the 'tag' – or signature – of Krek with a caricature cat called Kreky. Whittaker used the tag of Mers, Manchester Crown Court was told.

Both men from Macclesfield were traced after British Transport Police tracked website postings of their work back to their emails. Dolan was jailed for 15 months after admitting seven counts of criminal damage and asking for 12 more to be considered. Whittaker was jailed for 12 months after admitting six counts of criminal damage and asking for eight others to be considered. They were responsible for graffiti on trains, stations and railway property.

Sub culture

Andrew Mackintosh, prosecuting, said: "Both these men belonged to a graffiti sub culture in which each artist has his own tag by which the authors identify themselves and the property they have damaged. They constantly develop and practise their tags. They tend to work in groups known as crews and put their tags on property where they could be seen by other members of their crew and by the general public."

Dolan and Whittaker belonged to a crew called FMS and often recorded their work on video and loaded them on to computer discs.

Judge Anthony Ensor, sentencing them to jail, told the pair: "This conduct has caused an unpleasant nuisance as well as disruption and expense. You are decent people who have a talent but those who scar railways and other people's property have to be deterred. This kind of behaviour is carried out for self-indulgent gratification."

Source: *Manchester Evening News*, 29 August 2007

As you can see, this is just a report; it doesn't overtly take sides. The claims made in it are mostly of an informative, factual nature. They inform the reader, for example, who the convicted men were, what they did, how they were caught, the cost of the damage, that they pleaded guilty, and the length of the sentences. The author does not offer any conclusions of his own about the rights and wrongs of giving a substantial prison sentence to two young men for what many would see as a minor offence, and what a few might even argue was no offence at all. Nor does he offer any view on the subject of graffiti itself, for or against.

This chapter looks at some of the arguments which commonly arise from this issue of graffiti, and which did arise at the time of the trial and sentencing of Krek and Mers. You may have strong feelings of your own on these issues. But remember, critical evaluation of arguments is not the same as arguing for your own beliefs or opinions. There will be a chance to do that at the end of the chapter, but first we focus on the text and such reasoning as it contains.

The text

Although the author, Andy Russell, does not venture any explicit opinions on the case, he does include quotations from two of the people involved in the trial and conviction: **a** the counsel for the prosecution, Andrew Mackintosh, and **b** Judge Anthony Ensor. Each gets a short paragraph, so these can only be small extracts of what they said or thought. Here are the extracts, followed by a pair of critical questions about them:

a

> This conduct has caused an unpleasant nuisance as well as disruption and expense. You are decent people who have a talent but those who scar railways and other people's property have to be deterred. This kind of behaviour is carried out for self-indulgent gratification.

b

> Both these men belonged to a graffiti sub culture in which each artist has his own tag by which the authors identify themselves and the property they have damaged. They constantly develop and practise their tags. They tend to work in groups known as crews and put their tags on property where they could be seen by other members of their crew and by the general public.

Critical questions

8.1 Can either of these extracts, a or b, be understood as presenting an argument?

8.2 Are either of the extracts judgemental?

Over to you

Discuss critical questions 8.1 and 8.2 and try to agree on answers of your own before looking at the responses that follow.

Responses

In the case of **a** the answer is no to both questions. This might seem surprising, as it is the job of the prosecuting counsel to persuade the jury that defendants are guilty. However, in this part of his submission there is no conclusion drawn, no argument. Nor is there any obvious trace of condemnation. Elsewhere, no doubt, he may have had much more to say, but here he is simply presenting background information in a neutral and non-judgemental manner. Perhaps he is assuming that the facts speak for themselves, and are sufficient to make the case against the men. He may also feel that by seeming neutral he will come across as fair-minded and unbiased and win the sympathy of the jury.

Alternatively, you might want to say that the prosecutor cleverly and deliberately uses terms like 'tag' and 'crew' because they will create the impression that graffiti belongs to a subculture – to the street, to young people – and that this might make the jury feel threatened and turn them against the defendants. You could also point out the way he uses the word 'property', implying that the graffiti crews and taggers are vandals. But if these are intentional uses of language, to influence the court, then they are very subtle ones.

In the case of **b**, again we would expect to find something condemnatory. After all, it is a *judge* delivering a *sentence*. Sure enough, his claims are laden with value judgement and emotive language:

> … unpleasant nuisance … disruption … decent people but … scar … other people's property … self-indulgent gratification.

Is it an argument? This is a more difficult question. There is no explicit conclusion, though there are plenty of potential reasons for an implicit conclusion. The judge does not say, in so many words, that the men deserve imprisonment or that the sentence is the right one, but something of this kind could naturally be inferred from the statements he makes.

Alternatively, you could say that the author is *explaining* his sentence or decision, rather than arguing for it.

Either of these answers would be an acceptable analysis of the passage, but before you decide which you prefer, take a closer look at the concepts of 'argument' and 'explanation' (see also Chapter 18, page 94).

Argument or explanation?

It is easy enough to state the difference between an argument and an explanation: an argument gives reasons for concluding *that* something is, or should be, the case; an explanation gives reasons *why* it is. But it is not always so easy to say which is which in practice. We have just seen an example of short text which could reasonably be described as either or even as both.

As is often the case when interpreting a text, the best clues are in the context. Here the immediate context is in the clause just before the extract:

> Judge Anthony Ensor, sentencing them to jail, told the pair: …

Taking the passage literally, the judge is not arguing *that* the men are being, or will be, sentenced to jail. He has already decided that. He is explaining *why* they are, why he has given them a jail sentence. If you read it that way, the right description of the extract is that it is an explanation for a decision, not an argument for a conclusion.

> **Argument and explanation**
>
> Both arguments and explanations can be phrased in the form of a claim followed by 'because' followed by a reason. However, with arguments the bit *before* the claim is the inference – with explanations it is the 'reason' which has been inferred.

Reason or premise?

This discussion illustrates another useful point. It shows that the word 'reason' is a general term that can be used either in connection with arguments or with explanation, whereas 'premise' is a more technical and more specific term, referring only to reasons in an argument. See also Chapter 2, page 10.

But we can see too that the judge is *justifying* his decision as well as explaining it. He could be understood as offering reasons why he considers it to be the *right* decision, why the two men *should* go to jail, why the punishment is *deserved*. Explaining and justifying amount to much the same thing when we look at it that way. The judge's words are *premises* as well as reasons why.

P1   This conduct has caused an unpleasant nuisance, disruption and expense.

P2   Those who scar railways and other people's property have to be deterred.

P3   This kind of behaviour is self-indulgent gratification.

C (implied)   This jail sentence is justified.

If you are satisfied that **C** is clearly implied by the judge's words, and their immediate context, then this is a legitimate interpretation – instead of or as well as saying that it is an explanation. If you're not sure that he is saying this, then it is safer to say it is just an explanation.

Evaluation

Fortunately, when it comes down to evaluating the reasons, the task is effectively the same whichever way we interpret the passage. The only difference is how we word the question.

A reminder

Remember, you don't have to find flaws or weaknesses in a text. Being critical does not always mean finding fault. If you consider the judge's reasons to be strong, his language appropriate, etc., then say so and say why. In fact, you should as a rule try to see the strengths in a piece of reasoning before you look for its faults. Critical thinking is as much about giving credit as it is looking for flaws.

Critical question

8.3   Is the judge's argument a convincing one? Or is the judge's sentence justified by the reasons he provides?

Over to you

Reconsider the whole text on page 35, especially the last paragraph quoting the judge's reasons for the sentence, and discuss the critical questions above. As usual in tackling evaluative questions, you will need to ask: are the grounds sufficient/adequate? Are there any implicit assumptions, and if so are they reasonable? Are there any flaws or weaknesses in the reasoning? You may also want to talk about the judge's use of language: is it appropriate? Does it match the facts? Does it disguise any weaknesses in the reasoning?

The case against graffiti

Graffiti is an issue that can provoke strong feelings. Some people love it, some hate it, and others still have ceased to notice it, as it has become so much a part of the urban landscape.

One of the claims that people frequently make about it is that it is offensive. This, of course, is not an argument; it is just a personal reaction. Nor is it an argument to say that you like graffiti, or that you find it attractive or artistic. These too are just personal opinions, not arguments.

So what reasons, if any, can be raised for or against graffiti? Here is one argument that appeared on a municipal website in the United States, where the modern graffiti culture took off a few decades ago, and where it is still considered a social and environmental problem. Ostensibly it was published as a warning, but clearly it is also answering those defenders of graffiti who claim it is a form of art.

c

> Graffiti is not art, it is vandalism. It defaces property. It is illegal when done without permission of the property owner; and – with or without permission – it is prohibited on outside walls, where it can be seen by the public.

Source: author's paraphrase

The argument

The grounds given here are that graffiti defaces property, and that it is illegal. The argument can be analysed in one of two ways: either with a single, two-part conclusion:

1 Graffiti defaces property.

2 It is illegal ... etc.

Therefore

'C   It is not art but vandalism.'

or in two steps, with 'graffiti is vandalism' as an intermediate conclusion:

1 Graffiti defaces property.

2 It is illegal ... etc.

Therefore

'IC   It is vandalism.'

Therefore

'IC   It is not art.'

The second of these looks the stronger argument, so under the principle of charity (see Chapter 4, page 19), that is the one to go for. However, there is really little to choose; and, as we shall see shortly, neither version escapes the criticism that there is at least one important and very questionable assumption – a hole, you might say – in the middle of the argument.

Here is the first critical question.

Critical question

8.4   In addition to what is stated in passage c, what implicit assumption or assumptions are made by this argument?

Response

There are at least two implicit assumptions here. The first is that anything which illegally defaces property is vandalism. This is not altogether unwarranted because vandalism is, by definition, illegal damage, and graffiti does arguably deface property, i.e. damage it. It could be countered that 'deface' is a value judgement, and it is a matter of opinion whether graffiti does *deface*. But let's allow for the time being that graffiti can be defined as vandalism, as there is another and potentially much more serious assumption underlying this text.

Over to you

Think about critical question 8.4 and try to come up with your own answer before looking at the response that follows.

You have probably spotted the other assumption already, as it is a glaring one. It's the assumption that if something is vandalism, it cannot be art; or to put it another way, that something cannot be both vandalism *and* art. Whatever we decide about the first assumption, the second one is entirely unwarranted. For however much someone may despise graffiti, however worthless they may think it is, they cannot say that the case against graffiti as art is made just by saying it is vandalism and/or that it is illegal.

Unwarranted assumptions as flaws

Saying that an argument makes an unwarranted assumption is tantamount to saying that it is flawed, or that it commits a fallacy. This particular assumption is a recognised fallacy, known as *restricting the options* or, more grandly, as a *false dichotomy*.

The *assumed* **dichotomy** here is between art and vandalism. But there is no dichotomy because there is no necessity for either to be wrong. Both can be apt descriptions. You may observe a New York subway train, painted overnight from end to end with skill and imagination, and admit: 'That is a real work of art.' That does not prevent you from condemning the artist's illegal act of spraying paint all over something that is not theirs to paint; that is, from committing vandalism.

What the assumption underlying the argument means is that you have to choose between calling some exhibit 'vandalism' or calling it 'art'. In other words, it is *restricting the options* to just two, and overlooking the third option of something being *both*. If we include the missing premise in the main argument, we can see what it is asserting and see that even if it is not obviously false, it is at the very least debatable.

A counter-example

Another way to challenge the argument is to produce a **counter-example**, in this case an example chosen to show that something can be both art and vandalism. It can be a real example or a hypothetical one. The example that follows is obviously **hypothetical** but it still makes the point.

d

> Suppose that Michelangelo had not only painted the ceiling of the Sistine Chapel but also the ceiling of another building, in exactly the same style but without the owner's permission. Suppose, too, that the owner hated painted ceilings and considered that his had been illegally defaced. Would we say that one of the pieces was art and the other was not?

Critical question

8.5 Is the text at d an *effective* counter-example? Does it present a serious challenge to the argument we are considering?

Response

Yes, it does. It may be a purely hypothetical – i.e. fictional or imaginary – scenario. But that does not stop it making the point that judging whether or not something is a work of art is independent of whether it breaks the law, infringes property rights, or causes some people offence. Just saying these things about it does not win the argument that it is not art. This imagined example helps to demonstrate that.

Key terms

Dichotomy: a pair of opposing ideas which cannot both be true or both be false. It is similar to a dilemma, which means a choice between two (usually unattractive) alternatives. Restricting the options is sometimes called a false dilemma.

Counter-example: an example chosen to show why a general statement, viewpoint or explanation is not necessarily true.

Hypothetical: something imagined to be true in order to consider what effects it might have, for example on a statement, viewpoint or explanation, if it were true.

Link

For more on false dichotomies see page 58.

The case for graffiti

It is interesting, while we are on this topic, to compare the argument against graffiti with the same line of argument in reverse. Suppose someone who is a genuine admirer of graffiti were to argue, as many people do:

e

> Graffiti is not vandalism, it's art. It takes real skill and imagination, and it brightens up drab surroundings. Rich patrons even pay graffiti artists to decorate their property …

What is revealing about this argument is that, although it is motivated by a very different viewpoint, it makes virtually the same assumption:

Nothing can be art and vandalism.

Therefore both arguments **c** and **e** suffer from the same problem. Unless you agree with the assumption, you have to reject the argument, even if you agree with the conclusion. Critical thinking, as we said at the beginning of the book, is not about what you believe but about the reasons for believing it – the grounds, the justification. Whether you are for or against graffiti, you need a better justification than either of these.

Over to you

Write your own short argument for or against the claim that graffiti is an art form and that graffitists should be treated in the same way as other artists.

Analogies

Look at the following short argument which appeared on a blog at the time of the Krek and Mers conviction for spray-painting the train. Then consider the critical question which follows it and discuss various ways of answering it.

f

> Has anyone noticed that trains, buses, taxi, etc are all covered in adverts? Why is it ok for MegaCorp to plaster its brand everywhere but it's illegal for an individual to spray/scrawl/etch their equivalent tag? Companies are given carte blanche to put their brands all over the place all in the name of money. (Julian, London, UK)

Critical question

8.6 Identify the conclusion, and describe the strategy used by Julian in the argument contained in f. Is it an effective argument?

Response

The conclusion is the middle sentence. By now you should instantly have recognised that this is a rhetorical question (see Chapter 1, page 4). The claim it is making is that if it is legal for big companies (MegaCorp as Julian calls them) to advertise on trains, etc., then it should be all right for graffitists to do the 'equivalent'. His strategy is to **argue from analogy**.

Another way you could have described Julian's method is to say that he is pointing out an inconsistency, the inconsistency being that big companies are completely free to put their brands all over the place, whereas it is illegal for individuals to do the same.

Analysis or evaluation?

Is identifying implicit assumptions analysis or evaluation? Short answer: it's both. As you have seen, you should really include important assumptions in any complete analysis of an argument. If an assumption is warranted, then identifying it doesn't inflict any harm on the argument. If it is questionable, however, it throws doubt on the reasoning and opens it up to challenges and counter-arguments. If it is completely unwarranted, then identifying it effectively destroys the argument. It is common in critical thinking to explain the flaw in an argument in terms of an implicit assumption. For example: 'It (wrongly) assumes that …' or 'The argument requires the (false/unwarranted/dubious) assumption that …'.

Key terms

Argue from analogy: analogies are comparisons. They are often used in arguments to make the point that if something applies in one situation then it applies, or should apply, in a comparable one. This strategy is called 'arguing from analogy'. The adjective 'analogous' means comparable in some relevant way; the noun 'analogue' refers to something that is said to be analogous to the object being discussed.

So to the last part of the question: does this strategy work? Is it an effective argument? Given the nature of this particular kind of argument, these questions boil down to asking whether or not the analogy is a good one, whether or not it makes a *fair* comparison.

On the surface of it, the analogy looks quite effective. An advertisement on a train or graffiti on a train, what's the difference? The public have to see them both whether they like it or not. Doesn't that make them equivalent? Not really. They have some things in common, but it is going too far to call them 'equivalent'. For a start, the advertisements are paid for and professionally executed. They are also regulated, whereas illegal graffiti is not. If the owner doesn't want them on their property or their vehicles, they don't have to have them. Adverts are legal because they are put up in approved places, with permission. And in fact, graffiti is perfectly legal too if it is done with the owner's permission; advertising is just as illegal as graffiti if it is done *without* permission. The crucial difference is not just that one is done by a big company and the other by an individual, as the author wants us to believe.

This does not mean that there are no grounds for an argument against all the advertising that goes on, and that the public have to put up with. It is not an exaggeration to say that it is plastered everywhere, and it would not be going too far to say that it often defaces the environment, as much perhaps as graffiti does. But that does not make the case for graffiti. In fact, what the author does here is to commit a fallacy known by the Latin name of *tu quoque*. Literally this means 'you too', and typically takes this form: you can do it, so why shouldn't I?

Tu quoque is not just a reasoning flaw, it is also a rather infantile form of argument, though that doesn't stop politicians from using it when they want to score cheap points. The standard answer to it is 'two wrongs don't make a right'. In this case the two alleged wrongs are the eyesore of graffiti and the eyesore of mass advertising. To point the finger at one does not justify the other. There is more about *tu quoque* in Chapter 23, page 111.

Fair or unfair comparison?

People new to this question often think, wrongly, that the mark of a good analogy is simply the closeness of the two things being compared. Therefore they often think that all you have to do to refute an argument from analogy is identify *any* obvious difference between the objects or situations being compared. Actually, however, some of the most effective analogies are between things which are very different but which have at least one *relevant* feature in common.

To give an example, let's suppose you are arguing with a friend that, whether she likes it or not, graffiti is art. To make the point, you have drawn an analogy with street music, provoking the following exchange:

g   There's no comparison.

Yes there is. Take a busker in Covent Garden, performing without a licence. Is that music?

Yes, but the busker isn't defacing property.

He's breaking the law. And you could say he's creating a disturbance, especially if you didn't like the kind of music he's

---

Key terms

Tu quoque: term used for an argument which tries to justify a wrong action on the grounds that a similar wrong action is being done by someone else.

AQA Examiner's tip

When evaluating analogies, think carefully about why the author has made the particular comparison, so that you focus on the relevant similarities between the two situations, or at least the ways in which the author believes the two situations are similar.

Over to you

An analogy was used in the Examiner's Tip on page 7. Identify the analogy being made and consider whether or not it is a good one.

playing. I mean, suppose he's very loud and not very good. That's kind of like defacing – spoiling the peace and quiet.

Then he'd get moved on. How do you move graffiti on?

You paint over it. But stick to the point. All I'm asking is one thing: Is the busker making music? Or does the fact that he is breaking the law and being a nuisance mean it is not music? We're not saying it's good music.

It's music.

Then graffiti is art. Sorry, but you've just proved it for me.

No I haven't. You can't compare the two things. You listen to music; you have to look at graffiti. Music's a performing art, painting is visual. They're not the same.

Over to you

Revisit argument **d**, the counter-example on page 40 about a hypothetical Michelangelo painting. Explain and assess the effectiveness of the analogy that it draws.

Who wins this phase of the debate? Quite clearly, you do. Your friend objects to the analogy, but her objections are irrelevant. The difference between visual art and performing art, for instance, doesn't undermine the analogy. All that matters for the analogy to work is that unlicensed busking and graffiti are both unregulated forms of expression that break the law or be a nuisance. In fact, it is the difference which makes the argument work, because in the case of busking no one ever says it's not music, whereas in the case of graffiti many do say it's not art.

Final word: a matter of principle

By no means every commentator on the case of the jailed graffitists was sympathetic towards them, or felt that the sentence was undeserved. We finish with an argument based on principle:

h

Of course they should be jailed. As with anything in life, if you don't own it, don't abuse it. I have no problem with art of any description, but it should be done on or in private property. If you don't own the property, permission should be sought. If not, you are clearly breaking the law and should be punished accordingly. If we excuse this because it 'looks nice' where do we end? It is quite simple really, the law is the law and any such deviant behaviour should be dealt with firmly, and no exceptions! (Karen, London, UK)

Critical question

8.7 Identify the author's conclusion within the argument h and outline the structure and the method of her reasoning.

Response

As the section heading suggests, this is an argument from principle. Its conclusion, asserted in the first sentence, is that the two men should be jailed. It is followed by five or more reasons, depending on how you break the sentences up:

1 If you don't own something, you should not abuse it. (This claim is grammatically a command, lending it extra rhetorical force.)

2 Art should be done in or on private property that you own or have permission to use.

Key terms

Statement of principle: a claim expressing a basic truth, rule or guideline. The mark of a principle is that it is more general than other claims. Statements of principle are therefore powerful claims, for the purposes of argument, because if we accept a general principle, then we must accept all the particular claims covered by it.

Slippery slope: the assumption that a small or moderate change or concession will necessarily lead to extremes, either directly or in stages. For example, if you give the workers the small pay rise they are demanding this year, next year it will be twice as much and they won't be satisfied until they have bankrupted the company. There is no necessity that this will follow from a moderate pay rise this year.

3 Otherwise you are breaking the law and should be punished accordingly.

4 If we excuse graffiti because it looks nice, we end who knows where?

5 The law is the law and any such deviant behaviour should be dealt with firmly, and no exceptions.

Item **5** is the strongest **statement of principle**, and the most general: '*Any* such deviant behaviour,' it says, 'should be dealt with firmly, and *no exceptions*.' If we subscribe to this general principle, and we accept that the men's behaviour was 'deviant' (i.e. broke the law), then we really have no choice but to accept the conclusion that they should be 'dealt with firmly'.

But from there the argument makes a big leap. It is one thing to say that Krek and Mers should be dealt with firmly, it is another to interpret that as meaning a custodial sentence. This would require the dubious assumption that the only 'firm' way to deal with them is to send them to prison. The word 'accordingly' in premise **3** is equally vague, and cannot be taken to imply that prison is the only or even the right solution.

A slippery slope to where?

Reason **4** is yet another vague claim:

> If we excuse this because it 'looks nice' where do we end?

But vagueness is not its only fault. It is intended to support the need for firmness and for not making exceptions, and it does so by claiming that if we do not take firm action, we don't know where we will end. The implication is that things will end badly, or that the consequences will just go on getting worse indefinitely. Yet there is no support for this, and it is generally regarded as a fallacy to argue that just because some concessions are made, however small, that they will typically lead to something much worse or more serious. The fallacy is called the **slippery slope**. It is a nice metaphor for starting something that cannot be stopped.

Over to you

Either

Working as a class (or smaller group), conduct a mock retrial of Krek and Mers, based on the text on page 35 and any further research you may wish to carry out. Participants will be needed for the roles of the two defendants, defence and prosecution counsels, judge, expert witnesses, jury members (any number).

Or

Prepare a short speech summing up for the prosecution or the defence, in an imaginary retrial.

The following technical or semi-technical terms were used in this chapter: false dichotomy, analogy, *tu quoque*, slippery slope. Add these to your personal glossary, explaining what they mean and possibly giving an illustrative example of your own for each one.

9 A scientific argument

Learning objectives:

- to separate out targets, background and counter-arguments from the main argument
- to identify and know how to respond to conditional claims/hypothetical reasoning.

Key terms

Genre: a kind of text. It has partly to do with the subject matter, but also to do with a style of writing.

The document we are going to study in this chapter is an interesting and provocative one. It is also a more demanding text than the ones you have looked at before, and it will take some careful reading to understand and interpret it critically. Its topic is science, although it is written for a non-specialist audience, i.e. readers who are not professional scientists. The **genre** is often called 'popular science' for this reason. Read the text below.

Unicellular life

People like to think that they are the most successful form of life on Earth, the result of billions of years of evolution by natural selection, forever improving the individuals that it operates on. This is wrong. Evolution is not about improving anything, it is about producing many offspring that carry copies of your genes forward into later generations. By this criterion, the most successful forms of life on Earth are the unicellular [single-celled] life-forms, micro-organisms which have been around for billions of years without ever having to change their basic form.

At every stage of evolution, successful species become superbly adapted to their ecological niches, and stay much the same. We are descended from a long line of evolutionary misfits and outcasts, the individuals who were less successful in those particular niches, and had to find new ones to occupy. Take the transition from the sea to the land. The most successful fish stayed as fish – there was no pressure for them to move on to the land. It was the less successful fish who were forced into the shallows and which found a new way of life by becoming amphibians. Then, the less successful amphibians got pushed out of the water altogether, and had to become reptiles; and so on.

All the while, simple bacteria were doing what they had always done – surviving, reproducing and filling all the available niches in abundance. Close relatives of the earliest bacteria, single-celled organisms that lack even a central nucleus in which to package the DNA of their cells, are the most abundant and widespread organisms on Earth.

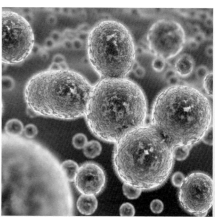

Source: *The Little Book of Science*, John Gribbin, 1999

One of the first things you should notice about this text is that it is an argument. After reading it through think about it by asking yourself the following critical questions.

Over to you

Discuss critical questions 9.1 to 9.3 and try to agree on an answer of your own before looking at the responses that follow.

Critical questions

9.1 What is the author arguing against?

9.2 What conclusion does he draw himself?

9.3 What argument does he give for the conclusion?

Responses

In common with many texts which present an argument, this one begins by identifying its target, that is the claim or belief or viewpoint that it is arguing against. The target claim is contained in the first sentence: the widely held view that we humans are the most successful species because we are the result of billions of years of improvements brought about by evolution. This is not part of the author's argument. Indeed it takes the opposite position. Its function is to provide a context for the argument that is to come.

That answers critical question **9.1**. The answer to critical question **9.2** is the very next sentence: 'This [belief] is wrong', meaning that we are not the most successful organism in the way suggested.

Critical question **9.3** is more complex. The core of the argument is that evolution is not about improving species but about reproducing (carrying genes forward to the next generation), and that *therefore* the most successful species are the one-celled micro-organisms. They have remained the same, and are the most abundant and widespread on Earth. Humans, by contrast, are descended from a line of less successful species that have had to keep adapting and moving in order to survive, as shown by the transition from sea to land.

When you add together the two sub-arguments – the greater success of the micro-organisms and the lesser success of those that have led to humans – you have the author's twin grounds for rejecting the target claim. However, you also have to note that both sub-arguments depend on the first premise, about the meaning of evolutionary success. That is why the author uses the phrase, 'By this criterion' instead of just 'therefore'.

The diagram shows the whole argument structure.

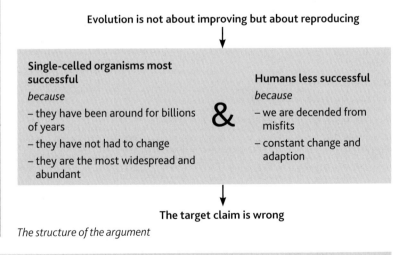

The structure of the argument

Critical question

9.4 Is it a good argument?

Response

This is an evaluation question. As always, it amounts to asking, do the premises give us adequate grounds for the conclusion?

With one proviso, which we will come to shortly, it is fair to say that they do. Certainly it is generally accepted that bacteria, etc., have been around a long time and that they have changed little in billions of years. It is also accepted by most scientists that the evolutionary pathway to humans has been one of constant change and adaptation, and that we have only been around for a few million years – a tick of the clock by comparison with the earliest life forms. From that it follows pretty conclusively that the micro-organisms have had a more successful history in terms of continuous survival.

But that is the proviso, and it is an important one. For the first premise, on which the whole argument ultimately depends, is not a matter of physical fact like the other premises, but of *definition*: what we mean by 'evolution'. John Gribbin says that evolution is not about improving anything but merely about carrying genes forward to the next generation. And then there is a further *implicit* assumption that this is how we must understand 'successful' when we are comparing different forms of life in the evolutionary context. You might well want to challenge that meaning, and argue that higher organisms, including humans and their relatives, have been successful in other ways – catching prey, using tools, acquiring intelligence, for example. If we think of success in those terms, then bacteria start to look very inferior.

But does this overturn the argument? No. It may narrow down the conclusion, but it doesn't make it wrong. This is because the author has worded the argument carefully, precisely to protect it against this kind of objection.

Conditional claims, qualified assertions

We are back to that all-important phrase, 'By this criterion'. What the author is saying in effect is '*If* we apply this criterion, *then* we must accept that we are not as successful as people like to think we are.' That neither means that we do apply the criterion nor that we are not successful in any way. The whole claim cannot be split up in that way. It must be understood as one claim.

We call such claims 'conditional' because they assert something *on condition* that something else is so. Typically they have the form 'If … then …'. They are also referred to as *hypothetical* claims or sometimes just *hypotheticals*.

It is the conditional nature of the conclusion that saves the argument from the objection that 'success' means more than just one thing. The writer is limiting his conclusion to that one meaning, and so his inference is safe. Another way this can be explained is to say that the writer qualifies what he is saying by stating the criterion he is using. It stops his assertion being too strong or sweeping, and because of that the grounds are adequate to support it.

> ### Conditional or hypothetical claims
>
> Some claims say what would be the case *if* something else were the case. These conditional or hypothetical claims come in two parts, the 'if…' part and the 'then…' part, and cannot be split into two separate claims.

If the conclusion were not qualified in this way, the grounds would not be adequate. You can see this yourself if you read the argument again, leaving out the phrase 'By this criterion' and replacing it with a plain connective like 'so'. You will see at once what a difference such a small change makes.

Right or wrong?

It is important to learn that there *are* right and wrong answers to critical questions; not always, perhaps, but very often. It is a mistake to think that your analysis or evaluation is as good as anyone else's just because it's your opinion and you can give some reasons to back it. There are good and bad evaluations just as there are good and bad arguments. (An evaluation is itself a kind of argument.)

You would not get many marks if you had said:

> This is a flawed argument because humans are successful in other ways.

The author would almost certainly agree with you that humans are successful in many ways that bacteria couldn't even dream of (literally). But he is not arguing that they are not. He has chosen to limit the argument to the context of survival and is claiming nothing beyond that context. If you interpret his conclusion as asserting more than it does assert, your analysis is at fault and your evaluation with it. It's a *straw man* (see pages 17 and 111).

Nonetheless, there are critical comments that you could make, for example:

- You may have something to say about the author's definition of evolution.
- You could question the example he uses to support the sub-argument that humans have descended from 'misfits' and 'outcasts'.
- You may want to question the use of these words to describe the species that had to adapt and find new niches.

Alternatively, you may be completely satisfied with the argument and agree with all its claims and conclusions.

Over to you

Try constructing either a *counter-argument* or a *supporting argument* in response to John Gribbin's article. If you are not studying biology as one of your subjects, you may want to find out a bit more about evolution and the origins of species, either by reading or talking to teachers or other students.

Critical thinking questions like these can be answered without specialist knowledge of the subject area, but a little research into the topics you encounter is always useful. Reading around the texts and critical questions will improve your general knowledge. General knowledge will in turn help to inform your answers to future critical questions.

Coach crash: taking the skills further

Learning objectives:

- to identify and map out the reasoning in a spoken exchange of views

- to identify and express implicit assumptions

- to recognise principles (both explicit and implied) and the role they're playing in an argument

- to evaluate principles through thinking of counter-instances

- to evaluate the use of principles through thinking of the consistency of their application and potential conflict or contradiction.

The aim of this chapter is to consolidate the skills you have acquired so far, and take them further through analysing a text featuring spoken dialogue.

Two listeners are responding to a newsflash they hear on the radio. First read the text, then attempt the analysis task that follows.

> *The Foreign Office is telling us that a tourist bus which overturned and caught fire in Egypt's Sinai peninsula earlier today had some British nationals on board. This is from the Foreign Office – we know no more than that, but when we have some more details we will bring them to you. (Radio bulletin)*

JASON: Did you hear that?

STEFFI: It's awful.

JASON: It's outrageous.

STEFFI: Accidents happen.

JASON: I mean what they said. 'Some British nationals on board'. Like that's all we're interested in. What about the other passengers? Why are British passengers more newsworthy than Egyptian ones?

STEFFI: Well it is on British news. It's the BBC after all.

JASON: I thought the BBC weren't supposed to be biased.

STEFFI: That's not being biased.

JASON: Course it is. There are probably hundreds of crashes all the time in Egypt.

STEFFI: They can't tell us about every crash that happens everywhere in the world.

JASON: Yes but why this one? It's because there were British people involved.

STEFFI: Perhaps …

JASON: I'm telling you. This is only on the news because the coach had British passengers on it. Who cares that the majority of them were from other countries? It's always the same. We're only interested in things that affect us.

STEFFI: What's so wrong with that?

JASON: It's racist.

STEFFI: It's natural.

Source: author's paraphrase

Over to you

Before reading on, have a go at answering the following questions about the dialogue, justifying your selection using the skills of analysis you have acquired so far:

1 Where exactly is reasoning taking place and where isn't it?

2 Which of their claims would you identify as reasons, and which inferences from the reasons?

3 Which if any of the participants' inferences expresses their main conclusion?

Step 1: Analysis

Even though the participants are clearly more articulate and intellectually developed than the boys on the island in the *Lord of the Flies* text, it is still difficult in an informal context such as this to clearly identify, unpick and unpack the reasoning that they are employing.

It is obvious that the two people are in disagreement, but over what precisely? Identifying exactly where their disagreement lies will help us decipher the arguments they provide.

Jason's position is fairly clear. He doesn't like the newsflash; it comes across to him as biased and racist. Steffi doesn't seem to share these criticisms, but her overall position is less clear. She is tending to counter Jason's views rather than emphasise a position of her own. This is often the way arguments in real life happen. One person puts forward a view and the other contests it.

We shall focus on Jason's contribution. So, first, is he providing reasoning? And if so, do his arguments tend towards a single main conclusion or a series of quite independent arguments, each with its own conclusion?

The answer to the first question you should have identified as yes. On more than one occasion he is putting forward a claim – sometimes in the form of a rhetorical question, but a claim nonetheless – that he either supports with a further claim or uses to support another.

To check this, let's break down what he says to reveal the reasoning.

Critical question

10.1 What is Jason's main conclusion?

Response

A good way to start is by looking for the claims which stand out as being the strongest or most in need of further support. Here are some contenders:

> What they said in the newsflash, about there being some British nationals on board is outrageous.

> It's biased.

> It's racist.

> We're only interested in things that affect us.

> This is only on the news because the coach had British passengers on it.

Already, you might be able to see some of the ways these claims fit together. If not then ask, are any of these claims reasons for holding of the others? Try the therefore-test or the because-test to see the direction of the reasoning. Is it fair to interpret one of them as being his *main conclusion*?

Of these, the first three claims stand out as being the strongest. The claims about the report being biased and racist are clearly reasons for accepting the first claim. It is likely that the first claim is therefore his main conclusion. But how does he get there?

Central to Jason's argument is an explanation that he gives for why this particular crash was reported:

> It's because there were British people involved.

This is based on the (fair) assumption or speculation that:

> There are probably hundreds of crashes all the time in Egypt.

Of which he is assuming implicitly (and no doubt correctly) that:

> These/most of these do not get reported in this country/on the BBC.

And that:

> They do not generally have British passengers on board.

Allowing these plausible assumptions or speculations, his explanation can be arrived at by inference:

> *Therefore* this is only on the news because the coach had British passengers on it.

This inference, though not certain, follows with a high level of probability from highly plausible assumptions.

So Jason can be fairly confident in asserting this as his explanation. This explanation plays a key role in his argument, as it provides the grounds for claiming the report to be both 'biased' and, worse, 'racist'. If he is correct in these judgements, then his overall conclusion that the report is 'outrageous' seems to be very strongly supported.

Step 2: Evaluation

So did Jason's arguments convince you? Or did you feel, like Steffi, that Jason was somewhat overstating his case? Having looked a little at how Jason's arguments are working, let's look at how strong his reasoning is, how good his reasons really are.

Critical question

10.2 How effectively does Jason support his view that the report is 'outrageous'?

Response

'Outrageous' is a very strong word to use. It is also very subjective. Whether or not you think something is outrageous depends on what makes you feel outraged. For this reason it would be hard to reach an objective decision on how well his conclusion has been supported.

Moreover, the word 'outrageous' is highly emotive. Words such as this, which carry a powerful sense of disgust, are best avoided when trying to reason fairly and objectively. A barrister would not get away with this kind of language in a court of law; it would be seen as **leading language**, leading the jury to agree with their point of view simply by their choice of words rather than the quality of their argument. If Jason was using the word 'outrageous' in a deliberately persuasive way, in order to convince Steffi, then he could be rightfully criticised for using an **appeal to emotion**. (There is more about this and other irrelevant appeals in Chapter 23, page 115.)

Both of these points are worth making, and would earn you credit in an exam. However, it would be unfair to dismiss his arguments simply because of their emotive tone or just because of this particular choice of words. He is, after all, genuinely annoyed about the report, and this being a live argument, he cannot help how he feels. Therefore, to be fair to Jason, let's amend his conclusion to read something like 'completely unacceptable', which is more neutral sounding but comes to very much the same thing.

Key terms

Leading language: language which carries with it an implicit judgement, and which encourages the audience to share that judgement simply through the way something has been described, rather than through reasoned argument. Note that 'leading' when used in this sense is not a technical term specific to critical thinking, but identifying where language has been used to persuade or manipulate someone's response to a question or topic is an important critical skill.

Appeal to emotion: when someone uses an emotive tone, language or imagery in order to make their case sound stronger or more persuasive; when they aim to persuade by appealing to the heart rather than the head.

A matter of principle

Most if not everyone shares the view that racism is bad; even people who hold what most consider to be racist views would probably argue that their views do not make them racist.

Of course, Jason has not stated that racism is bad. He obviously assumes this. He takes it to be a basic principle (see Chapter 8, page 43).

Identifying principles at work

The principle that racism is bad, or unacceptable, especially coming from a body like the BBC, plays an important role driving his argument.

Why 'especially' coming from the BBC? First, as a broadcaster it has certain rules and responsibilities to which people in a private conversation do not have to comply. This is a basic principle of broadcasting responsibility, which arises from the public nature of the medium (and is in fact based on deeper principles about respect and the rights of people in a civilised society).

Secondly, because of the type of broadcasting body it is. As Jason says, he 'thought the BBC weren't supposed to be biased'. The self-professed aim of the BBC is not to make money but to provide a 'public service'. As well as providing good quality programming, where bias is avoided, this includes maintaining certain standards of accuracy, decency, **neutrality** and morality, such as avoiding racism.

Therefore we now have two important principles that are relevant to Jason's argument.

> **Racism is unacceptable/wrong.**

> **Public service broadcasting bodies such as the BBC must abide by certain standards (which include avoiding bias or racism).**

Although Jason does not draw explicit attention to either of these, it is likely that they both play a role in his thinking. The first is implicitly assumed by his argument; the second underlies his claim that the BBC are not supposed to be **biased**, and gives his argument greater support.

Using the definitions, you probably decided that Jason is right to judge the report as biased. There is only mention of the British nationals on board, and it almost certainly *has* only been reported because of this. At the same time, Steffi is fairly adamant that this is not a case of bias. How can she claim this and is she justified?

Before we look at the counter-arguments, let us consider the other, stronger allegation: that there is something racist about the report itself, or about the attitude it exemplifies.

Although he doesn't say that the report is racist, he clearly implies this from the claims:

> **We're only interested in things that affect us.**

And that:

> **This is racist.**

In the conversation, Jason uses the news report as evidence for the first of these claims. Therefore, if the news report is an example of us only being interested in things that affect us, and if this attitude is racist, then it follows that the report is also to some extent racist.

■ Over to you

Do you agree that the report is 'biased'? Refer to the definitions of biased and neutral. Explain your answer.

■ Key terms

Neutrality: a person or a person's viewpoint is deemed 'neutral' if he/she/it considers both sides fairly and equally and judges them on their own merits.

Biased: a person or a person's viewpoint is termed 'biased' if he/she/it favours one side rather than another.

■ Over to you

Is Jason claiming that the report is racist? Justify your answer.

■ Over to you

Is Jason *justified* in implying that the report is 'racist'? Why? Why not?

Is he justified? A first critical comment might be that the news report is not necessarily an example of us only being interested in things that affect us; it may well show that we are *more* interested in things that affect us, but he's perhaps overinterpreting it (or overstating it) to claim or suggest that it shows that we are only interested (there is more about the *significance* of evidence and how much evidence *signifies* in Chapter 11, page 64).

But there is a deeper problem, or at least objection, to what he says. To get to it we need to go a little deeper into what is motivating Jason's views and consider whether or not this is warranted.

Going deeper

Let's look more closely at the claims, steps of his argument and reasoning that we've just pulled out:

> **We're only interested in things that affect us.**

This is a general statement, although it is not really a principle. He is certainly not suggesting that it is a good thing. In, fact he says that:

> **This is racist.**

Is he right?

Looking at the two statements above, you can probably see that they reduce down to one general statement:

> **Only being interested in things that affect you is racist.**

What did you make of it? It's certainly not a basic principle that most people would take for granted. It's also certainly not a fact. You could call it an opinion, but it might be better described as a judgement. This is because it is the kind of view or opinion which is almost certainly based on further reasons.

However, it's not immediately obvious what the reasons might be. This is partly because, as you may have identified, it is rather vague. What would count as illustrating this attitude in practice? It would seem that anyone who 'looks after number one' would have to be termed 'racist', when really all they are being is selfish, which is clearly not the same thing.

Let's apply the principle of charity and at the same time do some **clarifying**.

For a start, by 'us' and 'you', Jason clearly means people from different nationalities or races. Therefore a better expression of the statement might be:

> **Only being interested in things that affect people of your race and not people of other races is racist.**

Secondly, what is meant by 'being interested in'? It's a little bit vague. In the context, the issue is one of care or compassion. There are also varying degrees of interest (or care or compassion). These are not black or white. It's possible to be *more* interested in (or show more care for, etc.) one group than another without this implying that you are *only* interested in that group.

Let's try a softer version of the statement, which yet again is probably closer to the meaning Jason is intending.

> **Being more interested in the welfare and suffering of people from your own country than that of people from other countries is racist.**

Over to you

Comment critically on the claim 'Only being interested in things that affect you is racist'. What kind of claim is it? How might you go about defending or challenging it?

Key terms

Clarifying: giving words which have open meanings more focused, closed ones that fit the author's meaning as closely as possible as indicated by their line of argument.

Since there still seems to be some kind of reason, or general rule, motivating this belief, let's delve even deeper and ask why this might be. Presumably because:

> **All human suffering is of equal importance.**

Or even:

> **All humans deserve equal consideration.**

Here at last we have reached the bedrock of his argument. These last two beliefs, particularly the last, are the principles on which his judgements about the news report rest. Although he doesn't express them, they are behind the claim (implied through the rhetorical question) that British passengers are not more newsworthy than Egyptian ones, behind the view that being only interested in or caring about people from your own race or country is racist, and even behind the view that racism is wrong. Either version of the principle is therefore important to identify if we are really going to do justice to his argument and how he is thinking.

■ The case for the defence

Testing principles

As we saw, the claim Jason used – that only being interested in things that affect you is racist – was very easy to counter. We did this by finding a counter-instance or counter-example – a situation in this case where the claim almost certainly wasn't true. Any general statement, including statements of principle, can be tested in this way.

Through applying the principle of charity, however, we dug a little deeper to find a principle that is at least on the surface more difficult to challenge. The principle was, in its deepest form, something like this:

> **All humans deserve equal consideration.**

Although this principle sounds like one that most people would accept, you could probably still think of counter-instances. You might have felt that there are situations in which people forfeit the right to equal consideration, perhaps if they have committed a horrible crime. Or that someone who has treated you particularly well or kindly deserves greater consideration than someone who has not. How much these situations really challenge the principle is debatable (much of the study of ethics in philosophy is devoted to discussing such matters). Yet these examples do illustrate how difficult it is to find general principles about how we ought to behave that work across the board.

Conflicting principles

Perhaps the principle as we have been considering it is *too* general. Let's use a version of it which most directly applies to the context and which is closely implied by Jason's reasoning:

> **All human suffering is equally newsworthy.**

If this version of the principle at least is accepted, then Jason once again has a very strong argument.

The problem, however, is that although all human suffering might be equally important in one sense, this does not mean that it is equally *newsworthy*.

■ Identifying principles

Identifying as precisely as possible a principle on which an argument rests and clarifying an arguer's use of a principle are important skills in critical thinking. Sometimes you have to dig fairly deep to find the principle on which someone's claim, or argument, rests.

■ Testing principles

If you want to challenge or at least test a principle on which an argument rests, try thinking of possible counter-situations where the principle seems not to work. The easier it is to think of counter-examples, and the more plausible and less far-fetched they are, the less likely the general principle is to be true.

■ Over to you

Is the principle that all humans deserve equal consideration one which is impossible to counter – or are there situations where we might feel that even this general statement of principle does not apply?

What is worthy of being in the news is not just based on moral principles, but on matters of public interest. In fact, there is yet another principle that we might wish to point out. This is the principle that:

> Public service broadcasting has a duty to report that which is in the public interest.

When you include the fact that the BBC is paid for by the general public through a licence fee, it seems that the BBC has a clear obligation to inform the public of issues which they have most interest in. In which case, in situations where the public have a greater interest in the suffering of one group of people than another, then we have a clear case of conflicting principles.

This need not be racist, of course. It could simply be to do with the number of people interested or 'affected'. This is why, for example, news about the death of a famous celebrity is more likely to make the front page than someone unknown to the general public. It is not to imply that their death or suffering is less important, merely that it is less newsworthy.

One last thing. It is true that the BBC has a reputation for, and the expressed aim of, neutrality. These are noble aims and high standards. It might be failing to meet these standards, but the fact that it has failed is not really sufficient grounds for us to condemn it as being outrageous or unacceptable. Failing to meet an ideal of perfection is not necessarily grounds for condemning something quite as harshly as Jason does.

Consistent or inconsistent

Is it possible to somehow hold both principles at once? In other words, are the two principles **consistent**?

Can we demand that the BBC treat all human suffering as equally newsworthy and yet at the same time cater to the public interest?

It would seem impossible. To do so would appear to be **inconsistent**.

One possible way out of this dilemma is to argue that the two are not necessarily inconsistent; they are only inconsistent because the public happens to care more about the suffering of British people than people from other countries. We are wrong to be like this, however. We ought to care about and therefore be interested in the suffering of all people equally.

If this is what Jason thinks, then he has perhaps avoided the charge of inconsistency. However, this would then mean that it is not the *report* that is outrageous, as the BBC is only fulfilling a duty to report that which is in the public interest. Jason would have to relinquish his conclusion and turn his sense of outrage onto the general public.

It may be that Jason himself is not completely clear on the matter. The fact that he changes the target of his anger throughout the dialogue from outrage at what '*they* said' to the claim that 'we're only interested in things that affect us' could point to a possible confusion in his thinking here, a confusion that perhaps he needs to try and get clear. Otherwise one might want to ask Jason:

- Who is the source of his sense of outrage?
- Who is his target? Is it us or the media, or is it both of us together?

Unless we are clear exactly where the problem lies, it is difficult to work out how we ought to respond to him.

Key terms

Consistent: two or more statements are consistent with each other if it is possible for them to be true together, i.e. the truth of one does not conflict with/contradict the truth of another.

Inconsistent: two or more statements are inconsistent if it is not possible for them to be true together.

Conflation

There is one other area of confusion that you may have detected in what Jason is saying. This is more of an A2 point, but as it naturally arises here, it is worth illustrating it, even if you will not be expected to know it in the exam.

Jason has argued that the report has ignored the fate of the Egyptian passengers at the expense of the British ones, claiming that it is symptomatic of the fact that 'we're only interested in things that affect us'. He has then drawn the conclusion that this is 'racist'. But race and nationality are separate things, and to draw a conclusion about our attitudes to either on the basis of our attitudes to the other involves a dangerous shift of topic. It is of course possible to be prejudiced towards people of other nations without being prejudiced against people of other races, and vice versa. Shifting topic in this manner, or muddling two topics together that ought to be kept separate, is known as **conflation**. It is a flaw in reasoning.

Jason has perhaps been guilty of a common conflation: that of muddling together nationality and race.

Key terms

Conflation: when a point about one thing has slipped into being a point about something else, or when two separate things have been muddled together so that a point about one leads to a conclusion about the other.

Critical question

10.3 How effectively does Jason support his view that the report is 'outrageous'?

Response

Let's try to put some of the skills and concepts into answering this typical exam-style question.

First let's remind ourselves of the key critical points we have considered:

- the importance of clarifying or defining terms
- use of persuasive language and appeals to emotion
- reliance on principles
- conflicting principles and consistency of argument.

Don't panic that this is a lot to remember or write about. When you are asked an open question like this, you are not expected to make all the possible critical points (there are others we have not even considered). What you will be expected to do is to select one or two critical points (depending on the marks available) and make sure that you explain why each is relevant.

A question like this is likely to be worth about four marks. The specimen answer given in the margin would easily gain all the available marks.

Specimen answer

Jason's argument makes use of persuasive language by calling the report 'outrageous' and arguing that it is 'racist'. These involve an appeal to emotion, which makes his argument less effective. His argument also makes use of principles which are not always clear. It is very debatable that being 'only interested in things that affect you' makes you racist. Even if he means being more interested in people from your own country, this does not mean you do not care about people from other countries.

A final evaluation

So how well did each of the two participants, Jason and Steffi, reason? Do they both deserve the label of being *critical* thinkers?

Critical or cynical?

Beginning with Jason, his tone is certainly critical in the everyday sense of seeing the negative points in something.

But the questions he asks are critical questions, aimed at questioning the justification behind the way the news story has been presented, or its very inclusion in the news. He is also putting forward an argument. He is therefore clearly doing critical thinking.

On the other hand, his view seems a little extreme, given the alternative interpretations and explanations of what was reported and why. He is sticking very blindly to a principle without asking whether there are certain limitations to its application, under certain conditions: namely even though it conflicts with another principle that he would also presumably agree with, his principle remains absolute. If he is unaware of the potential inconsistency of his views, this is also a sign that he is not the world's best critical thinker.

Finally, it could be argued that the fact that he interprets the bias he hears as being motivated by racism suggests that he seems to have already decided that the media and their audience have this view, and then interpreted what he has heard to suit his view. Although this does not mean he is wrong, the fact that he seems to have a very strong fixed idea to which he fits his evidence means that, in this sense, he is not really being especially critical. You could say he's being more *cynical* than *critical*. (Look again at Chapter 7, page 30, for a reminder of this distinction and what it means.)

Critical or argumentative?

What about Steffi? What is her position? Does she have one, or is she just disagreeing for the sake of disagreeing? Sometimes people decide they are in the mood for arguing and disagree with everything someone else says, even if this means being inconsistent in what they themselves say. If someone is doing this, then you might decide that they are not so much being critical in the sense of being questioning or reflective, but merely argumentative.

Does this seem to be what Steffi is doing? Does she take a consistent line in her responses to Jason's argument? Is anything she is saying inconsistent with anything else she says or does she not say enough for us to judge this? Since the latter is probably true, perhaps we should give her the benefit of the doubt here. We will leave this up to you to decide.

Restricting the options

One final point about Steffi. Look at the last part of the dialogue:

> JASON We're only interested in things that affect us.
>
> STEFFI What's wrong with that?
>
> JASON It's racist.
>
> STEFFI It's natural.

Although Steffi's role in the debate is more to challenge Jason's arguments than put forward her own, there is still a possible flaw evident in her thinking.

Steffi is implying here that it's not wrong, or perhaps not racist, to be only interested in things that affect us *because* 'it's natural'. She has therefore provided an argument. Is it a good argument?

> It's not wrong (or racist) to only be interested in things that affect us *because* it's natural.

Link

For more on dichotomy see page 40.

Steffi's argument only works if we assume that if something is natural then it cannot be wrong (or racist). But this could be a false distinction. It could be (and almost certainly is) possible for something to be *both* wrong (or racist) and natural. She is therefore perhaps guilty of a **false dichotomy** (also known as *restricting the options*).

Like Jason, she is also relying on rather a vague idea. What does she mean by 'natural'? Something that is biological? Or sociological? Sometimes when someone says something is 'natural' they really mean that it is *understandable*. For example, it's natural that X wanted to hit him, he'd insulted X's family. This use certainly does not imply that the action is right, or justified. Is this the sense that Steffi is using the term? We would need to have a clearer definition in order to really assess the relevance of this comment.

Over to you

1. From the short conversation on page 49, who deserves the title of critical thinker more, Jason or Steffi? Explain your answer with reference to the questions and concepts raised in this chapter.

2. Is Jason right to say that the news report is 'outrageous'? Build a reasoned argument to justify your answer. (You may wish to refer to Part 4 on writing an argument.)

3. Record a discussion where there is disagreement between people, then play back and try out the frequently asked critical questions. (Are you capable of being honest and objective enough to admit that the other person's arguments are better?)

4. Consider the wider issue of broadcasters' or the media's responsibility. To what extent are they, or their audience responsible for the content or claim of their message? Write a reasoned argument for or against the following claim.

> If you are offended by something you hear, read or see in the media, it is the public ultimately who are to blame.

11 Benefit cheats: evidence and how to use it

Learning objectives:

- to appreciate the need for, and the role of, evidence in supporting a view

- to be able to identify evidence and comment critically on the way it is being used.

Chapters 11, 12 and 13, in which you will be analysing the document overleaf, are rather like a bridge between Units 1 and 2. Although you can expect the kinds of questions that follow in either paper, these chapters introduce skills and address questions that are closer to those you might get in Part 2. These include interpreting evidence and information, judging its significance in terms of what can and cannot be inferred from it, and forming views which are based on careful consideration of the evidence available. We will also be considering the credibility of evidence and of sources.

We shall look at how to go about developing a well-supported view on a difficult and controversial question. In doing this, we shall consolidate some of the work done on identifying and questioning the role played by principles, as well as introducing some of the skills and concepts you need when analysing the role of evidence.

At the end of Chapter 13 you will be asked to attempt a longer argument of your own, just as you have to do in the Unit 1 and Part 2 exams.

As well as the learning objectives outlined at the start of each chapter, an overarching learning objective spreads across all three chapters: to arrive at a carefully considered view on a topic and be self-critical and aware of the process by which it was acquired.

Having a view

Read the news report overleaf. This is clearly a controversial story. Controversial topics are often ones about which people instinctively have strong views.

Stop to ask yourself if you have an instinctive view on the matter. Does a lie detector test for benefit cheats sound like a good, morally sound idea to you or a bad, morally dubious one? How you answer might depend on how the question is phrased. Consider the following two questions, and compare the answers you might give to each of them:

> **Do you think that using lie detector technology might be justified in an attempt to catch criminals who cheat the benefit system out of millions of pounds that should be going to people who really need it?**

> **Do you think it's acceptable to use lie detectors on every person who rings a benefit centre just in case they might be trying to make a fraudulent claim?**

The first question is definitely what a lawyer or barrister might call a 'leading question'. By phrasing the question in this way, it makes it sound as if there is only one rational or morally acceptable answer.

You probably spotted that 'benefit *cheat*' is itself an emotive term and one that implies a strong judgement. Being labelled a cheat is not something people are generally proud of, and when combined with the word 'benefit' it creates a powerful effect, as it implies someone who cheats a system that is there to offer help or support to people. It would be very difficult to argue in favour of being a benefit cheat.

■ Over to you

As well as leading questions, there are other ways that language can manipulate and persuade. Look again at the title of the article and ask if there is anything that might influence someone's point of view about it.

However, consider this analogy. In most businesses, it is acceptable practice to try and get the best deal for yourself that you can. You are not generally called a *cheat*. An estate agent who makes the house sound nicer than it perhaps is, is not generally labelled a cheat. People don't like it, but then again, they're just doing their job. What if someone who was labelled a benefit cheat actually thought they were doing something similar? What if we called them benefit *experts*?

That may be a slightly ridiculous comparison, but it does show how careful we have to be with language and the way that implicit judgements, which might shape our view of things, can slip through simply in the way that something has been phrased or described.

Benefit cheats face telephone lie detector tests

By George Jones, Political Editor

Lie detector technology will be used by the Government to help identify and deter benefit cheats, John Hutton, Work and Pensions Secretary, announced today.

Voice-risk analysis (VRA) software, already used by the insurance industry, will be used to monitor telephone calls by claimants. It can detect minute changes in a caller's voice which give clues as to when they may be lying.

VRA analyses changes in voice frequency and performs thousands of mathematical calculations, identifying different categories of emotional content which enable it to identify genuine callers.

At the beginning of each call, the characteristics of a customer's voice frequency are sampled to establish a benchmark. This is used during a conversation as a guide for analysing changes in frequency caused by changes in emotions.

Callers will hear a standard message before they speak alerting them that the technology is being used.

If benefit staff assess the answers as suspicious, the caller may be asked to provide further evidence

to support their claim. Final decisions will still rest with staff.

The system will be piloted by Harrow Council, in north London, for housing benefit and council tax benefit claims. Mr Hutton said the "cutting edge" technology aimed to tackle fraudsters while speeding up claims and improving customer service for the honest majority.

According to Government figures, benefit fraud has been reduced from about £2 billion in 2001 to an estimated £0.7 billion in 2005/06.

Philip Hammond, Conservative work and pensions spokesman, said the Government was coming up with "more Big Brother technology" when the real problem was the complexity of the benefit system.

He said more money was lost through error, with £2.6 billion worth of benefits overpaid last year, than through fraud.

"The real reason fraudsters find it so easy to con the British taxpayer is the complexity of Gordon Brown's benefit system. We need a simpler, fairer system with fewer loopholes for fraudsters to exploit," Mr Hammond said.

Source: Adapted from www.telegraph.co.uk, 6 April 2007

Of course, it's not just the way a topic has been phrased or presented that can be emotive. Topics too can be emotive. Whether or not you use the term 'benefit cheat', the notion of someone trying to get something that perhaps they don't deserve is something that often upsets or angers people. There are other emotive topics connected to the debate, including things like the different levels of wealth and poverty among people, and even the very concept of 'lie detector' technology, each of which might influence people by appealing to their emotions strongly, and perhaps distort their thinking on the matter.

This is not to say that you should never trust or stick to your instinctive point of view. It's just important to be careful of what factors might be going into shaping it, especially when you are asked (as you will be in the exam) to provide good justification. If it turns out that your view is based largely on some kind of strong emotional fear or dislike of something, then it might be difficult to provide a strong, rational argument.

Of course, it's one thing to have a view, quite another to support it. Unfortunately, in critical thinking you will not be given any credit at all for simply having a view. It might sound harsh, but in a sense your opinion itself is worth nothing; it is the reason (or reasons) you give for your opinion that count. Nevertheless, before you go about building an argument in favour of your opinion, it is worth being careful that your opinion has not been manipulated too much by the way the topic has been presented, or by emotive issues to do with the topic itself.

> **Your view**
>
> Make sure it's *your* view and not someone else's. Persuasive language can be very manipulative. Be careful of the way a topic is phrased or presented before settling on your view, otherwise you may not end up holding a view that you actually agree with!

Supporting a view

Having considered some of the possible dangers lurking in the emotive waters of this debate, ask yourself whether or not you still want to stand by your original view. If you felt you didn't have a view on the matter, don't worry. It might be that you are the sort of person who likes to think about the matter before jumping in, or who likes to consider the evidence more carefully first. Both are signs of a good critical thinker.

If you did have an opinion, how strong an argument do you think you could give to support it? Have a go at composing one. It will probably help if you consider what issues are at stake, and whether or not there are any important principles that underlie the whole debate.

> **Over to you**
>
> Before reading on, try composing an argument for or against the use of lie detectors as outlined in the article. Then ask yourself how convincing a case you have made. Would it go some way to persuading someone who had a different view? (Perhaps you could try it out on someone else who has a different opinion.)

Reaching for principles

What principles did you identify? On the one hand, you may have identified the principle that:

> **People should not be allowed to get away with benefit fraud.**

and (consequently) that:

> **The state or government has a right or duty to try to prevent them.**

On the other hand, you may have identified something about the importance of individual liberty against the state, or the dangers of the state having too much power over the individual; for example, the principles that:

> **The individual's rights should not be threatened by the state.**

or that:

> **The state should not encroach unduly on the basic freedom or rights of individuals.**

Identifying these principles gives you a basis from which to start building an argument. If you identified principles on both sides, it becomes something of a balancing act, a judgement. If the principles clash, which of them is more important to defend and are there any possible compromise positions? This could form the basis of a more developed argument.

In this case there is a compromise position, something like the principle that:

> **The state should do everything it can to stop benefit fraud without imposing undue restrictions on basic freedoms/civil liberties.**

But where does that leave the use of lie detectors?

Principles and their limits

How did you get on with the second 'Over to you' activity on this page? You probably found it tricky. Perhaps you arrived at some basic principles about the importance of individual liberties. You could be against the use of lie detectors in principle and argue that the use of lie detectors by the state is always wrong (in the same way that many people think that torture is *always* wrong), or perhaps that such technology should only be used on people who are already suspected or are on trial for something, rather than on all callers across the board.

This is possible, although some might think that this is stretching the principle too far, that the comparison with torture, for example, is ridiculous. A clear case would need to be made to explain why this kind of technology is somehow wrong in itself. And it would be very difficult to do this without going into the specifics of how the equipment worked, which would mean departing simply from principles. It would mean looking at the facts.

As a rule, simply relying on principles doesn't often get us far when deciding on a course of action. For one thing, people can agree on principles, but disagree as to whether or not a particular action is consistent with, or goes against, these self-same principles.

Since most people are likely to agree that benefit fraud is bad and ought to be stopped and that civil liberties are also important, the key premise in an argument for or against the use of lie detectors to catch benefit fraud is going to be either that:

> **The use of lie detectors as described by the government in benefit centres, etc., constitutes an infringement of and imposes an undue restriction on civil liberties.**

Or:

> **The use of lie detectors as described by the government in benefit centres, etc., does not constitute an infringement of nor impose an undue restriction on civil liberties.**

How do we decide this?

Over to you

1. What is meant by the 'state' in this context? (Ask your teacher or another student if you are not sure.) Can you think of any other questions or issues where there is a conflict between the powers and responsibilities of the state and individual freedoms or liberties? How similar are they to the situation here? Compare and contrast them by identifying any major similarities and/or differences between them.

2. Try to construct an argument for or against the use of lie detectors as described in the article, using only statements of principle.

Using evidence: looking for relevance

What we need to do is to look at the facts of the situation. We need to find evidence relevant to the issue of whether or not the use of lie detectors is an infringement of civil liberties.

According to the article, the technology is 'already used in the insurance industry'. Assuming this is correct, what evidence does this provide for or against its use in detecting or preventing benefit fraud? The answer is none. The fact that it is used somewhere does not mean that it *should* be. It's possible that the different context has a bearing. It may also be that it is used in a different way. It might therefore be possible to be in favour of its use in one environment and not the other, against its use in both places, or for its use in both places. All four are possible and therefore the information that it is used in the insurance industry is irrelevant as evidence.

This is not to say that it might not be useful evidence for something else. It's worth remembering that evidence is never just evidence in itself; it is always evidence for or of something. Likewise, evidence is never good or bad, relevant or irrelevant in itself; it is always good or bad, relevant or irrelevant from a particular angle, for a particular theory or viewpoint.

A second problem with the information is its vagueness. It is not clear how or why it is used in the insurance industry. Are we to assume that it is used for all callers or just in cases where people are already suspected of fraud? Without this information the evidence is **vague**, which makes it harder to use effectively.

Let's try another piece of evidence. Again, we're looking at evidence relevant to the issue of infringement of civil liberties.

> Callers will hear a standard message before they speak alerting them that the technology is being used.

Here we have some evidence which is relevant. This is because, given this information, someone may feel the need to alter their view on the matter. It may well be that people may find it *preferable* that the technology is not being used secretively. It is feasible to argue that this particular use of lie detector technology does not infringe on people's civil liberties *because* they are told clearly before they proceed with the call that the technology is being used.

Interpreting evidence

You may not be happy with the argument at the end of the previous paragraph. This is because, while being told that the lie detectors are being used is relevant to the issue of whether or not people's civil liberties are being unduly threatened, it does not *necessarily* support the view that they aren't.

For one thing, it's not as though, once told, people have a choice. They may decide they do not want to continue with the call, but then they may lose their money. For many on benefits this is not an option. Similarly, they're not being asked if it's okay if the technology is being used, they're being *alerted*.

The word 'alerted' is interesting in this context. Although it is presumably meant in a neutral way, it nevertheless carries associations. Like 'warned', this *could* be interpreted in an almost friendly way, like a helpful warning. But the word can also imply a degree of threat, as when a teacher says, 'I'm warning you!'

Key terms

Vague: a statement that makes grammatical sense but whose meaning is unclear or too imprecise. This makes it hard to judge its relevance or significance in a given context.

Relevant evidence

Good/useful evidence needs to be relevant for the specific issue being discussed. Evidence is relevant if its truth has, or may have, an effect on a particular viewpoint. That is, knowing whether or not the evidence is true might affect someone's view on the matter. Evidence is irrelevant if it doesn't actually matter for someone holding a particular belief whether or not the 'evidence' presented is true.

Is the fact that people are being 'alerted' that the technology 'is being used' evidence that the government is showing consideration for people's civil liberties or not? It's difficult to say. Its significance depends on how you interpret it.

Significance of evidence

When you look at evidence, you need to consider not only its relevance, but its *significance*. What does it *mean*? In critical thinking terms, this really means asking, What can we infer from it? With factual information, just as with any other type of claim, you need to ask what conclusions follow, and how certain you can be of them.

As with any inference, inferences from data or evidence often entail a number of other assumptions. Of course, we want our evidence to have as much significance as possible. We want to be able to infer from it as much as we can, to take our thinking as far as possible. And yet in many cases, the greater the significance attached to evidence, the greater the number of assumptions that are being made. In the above example, we need to assume that people's civil liberties are not threatened by the use of lie detector technology if they are told (or 'alerted') that the technology is being used. This assumption is highly debatable, which in turn makes the significance of the evidence highly debatable.

Significance of evidence and further assumptions required: exam-style questions

There will often be exam questions about how evidence is used, what its relevance or significance is, or what conclusions can be drawn from it.

Another way of asking the same kind of thing is to ask about the assumptions that have been made about the evidence, or about further assumptions that need to be made for it to have a particular significance.

Critical question

11.1 From the information given in the document about the callers being alerted that the technology is being used beforehand, what further assumptions are needed in order to argue that the equipment is likely to be reliable?

Response

The most obvious assumptions that need to be made are that:

> People (e.g. experienced criminals or liars) cannot control, or learn to control, their voice patterns when they lie.
>
> The changes in voice pattern are unconscious and undetectable to the human ear.

We also need to assume that:

> Being told that the technology is in use will not distort the results by, for example, affecting people's voice patterns due to them being nervous.
>
> The changes in voice patterns that take place when someone is lying are noticeably different or distinct from those that take place when someone is simply nervous.

Significance of evidence

In a way, the critical question you need to ask about the significance of evidence can be summed up as *so what?* Asking this is important, whether commenting critically on the way evidence is used by others, or using evidence in arguments of your own.

Over to you

Before reading the response, have a go at answering critical question 11.1, a typical exam-style question on evidence and assumptions.

Simply identifying assumptions that are needed will get you the marks, but bear these assumptions in mind as they may help answer questions on the effects of further evidence on page 81.

Judging evidence: selectivity

One other thing to watch out for when interpreting or evaluating the use of evidence is to consider how selective the evidence is. In most situations where there are conflicting points of view, there is evidence for both sides. By selecting specific pieces of evidence, you can make either side look well supported, better supported than perhaps it really is. You therefore need to be on the lookout for evidence being used selectively, both when evaluating arguments and views of others and when formulating your own.

This presents a problem, however, and one which leads us into a very important aspect of dealing with evidence. Unless we are able to check the facts ourselves, which in some cases we are, but in many cases we are not, how are we to judge whether or not an author has been selective (deliberately or otherwise) with the evidence? It would seem we have to just take it on trust.

Not only that, but how do we even know if the evidence is correct? As we have seen, evidence is relevant for a point of view only if its truth or otherwise has an impact. If the 'evidence' turns out to be false, its relevance, and thus its significance, disappears. Yet if we are unable to verify the evidence for ourselves, which in most cases we are not, then the relevance and significance of the evidence depends entirely on the truthfulness, and accuracy, of the source.

In any situation, therefore, where the evidence (and thus the truth of the evidence) is important, but we are not sure whether or not it is true (which is most of the time), we need to think about its credibility.

Selectivity

When the supporter of a particular view presents 'evidence' in favour of their view, always ask yourself, how representative is this? Does it give the full picture or has it been chosen to help paint a particular picture?

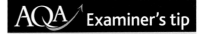 **Examiner's tip**

You may be asked to explain what support an author believes/ assumes the evidence to have for their argument, or more commonly, you may be asked to evaluate the author's use of evidence.

Table 11.1 *Evaluating evidence*

Errors to watch out for	Dangerous assumptions
Confusing cause and correlation (see also Chapter 23, page 112)	Assuming that when two things are happening together or showing a similar pattern that they are causally connected. Another version is assuming that because one thing happened after something else that it was caused by it.
Generalisations (when 'one' implies 'many' or 'some' implies 'all') (see also Chapter 14, page 87)	Assuming a sample is representative of the wider picture based only on the evidence of the small sample without further or sufficient evidence.
Predictions (see also Chapter 14, page 85)	Assuming past or current patterns will continue.

12

Benefit cheats: credibility of evidence

- ■ to be able to comment critically on the credibility of a particular statement or a source

- ■ to be aware of the factors that affect credibility and use these to answer exam-style questions.

Key terms

Corroboration: where two or more sources provide pieces of information which agree or which support each other. As in a court trial, evidence from one witness that bears out another's can strengthen the *probability* of its being true.

Credibility: the credibility of a person, a source or a claim is a measure of how likely it is to be true.

Vested interest: when someone has something to lose or gain in a particular debate or conflict (either materially or in terms of their reputation).

Over to you

Have a look at the statements given by the people quoted in the news story on page 60. Decide to what extent they are factual in kind. If they are factual, how certain can we be that they are true?

Accuracy of a report

Questions about the *accuracy* of a report are especially useful if the source appears to be neutral. Otherwise there are more important factors at stake, such as the source's motives to withhold or distort information.

When information has come to us from an external source, then we have no way of knowing absolutely whether or not the information is correct. Sometimes we are able to *verify* the information, by checking for ourselves. In most cases, this amounts to going to another source. In this case, the best we can hope for is **corroboration**, where the other source gives the same information or information which *supports* the first source. The more corroboration you find, the more faith you are likely to have in the information being correct. In other words, the more *credible* it becomes (or the greater its **credibility**).

However, corroboration is not always enough, and neither is it always possible (or desirable, as you do not have time to check every piece of information you receive). In order to proceed, we have to make certain assumptions about how credible the source is. We do this by asking key questions:

- ■ *How did the source acquire the information?* Was it first- or second-hand? If first-hand, this gives us a reason to assume the information is credible, although there are other factors to consider. If second-hand, then the credibility is only as good as the original source, and unless we are given details about the original source, there remains a question mark about its credibility for this reason.

- ■ *What factors might have distorted the picture at any point in the information being acquired?* If first-hand evidence is used, how clear a view did the person get of what they were observing? Were they in a clear frame of mind to observe accurately? Also, if the event happened a long time ago, how accurate is their recollection of what happened? Memory, as we all know, can play tricks on us.

- ■ *Does the source have a motive to be less than fully honest with the picture they are presenting? Alternatively, do they have a motive to be truthful?* The most obvious area for such motives is where the source has some **vested interest** in the situation, such as when someone claims that they did not do something that will get them into trouble. In some cases, people can also have a vested interest to be accurate or truthful, such as someone giving a statement in a court of law who can be punished for perjury. Bear in mind though that, while this kind of vested interest can strengthen the credibility of what they are saying, it depends to some extent on how verifiable the information is that they are presenting. The more verifiable the information, the greater the risk when being untruthful, and therefore the greater the likelihood that what they are saying is true.

- ■ *Is the information they have given purely factual, or has it been interpreted in some way?* If so, then you need to ask about things that may have affected the accuracy or fairness of their interpretation, such as their knowledge or expertise in the area, or their degree of neutrality or bias.

In general, you do not need to ask all these questions of every piece of evidence. The kind of questions you ask will depend on the kind of evidence it is. The best way to see this is in practice, so we'll turn again to the article on page 60.

When to talk about credibility

When using the terms 'credible' or 'credibility', notice from our definition of 'credibility' that it only applies to factual statements. If a statement is purely an opinion, it doesn't make sense to say it's true or false, just that you agree or disagree, or that it's well supported or otherwise.

This is why we use the word 'credibility' for assessing or describing evidence, since evidence, by its nature, ought to be factual in kind. In contrast, we wouldn't describe an argument as being credible.

What do we do if the evidence is itself a judgement or an interpretation? We could dismiss it as being not purely factual, too subjective. However, sometimes evidence in this form can be very useful – for example, when a coroner gives their verdict on the cause of death. Although this kind of statement expresses a judgement rather than a straightforward fact, it still makes sense to talk about its credibility. But you must then consider the knowledge or expertise of the person who made the judgement, and how well qualified they are to judge on the matter, as one of the factors in deciding on the credibility.

Remember that when we talk about credibility, we are talking about *likelihood*. A similar word is reliable. It makes sense to ask how *reliable* a particular source is. Of course, unless we have unfailing lie detector technology of our own, we can never know for certain whether or not a source is accurate. The more credible the sources, the more likely they are to be truthful, and so the more we can trust that what they're saying is accurate, truthful and reliable.

Summary

Things that affect credibility:

- where the source acquired the information (was it first-hand, second-hand or anecdotal?)
- possible distorting factors (ability to observe, state of mind of the observer, ability to recall)
- possible motives to be less than honest, or hide or distort the truth in some way
- factors that might affect the source's judgement or interpretation
- verifiability and degree of corroboration (or conflict) with other sources.

Signs of credibility:

- first-hand or eyewitness accounts, closeness to the original event (e.g. a journalist meeting and interviewing someone rather than reporting someone else's meeting)
- no reason to doubt the accuracy of what the source saw or heard, or their recollection of it
- neutrality
- relevant expertise
- verifiability of the claim (and corroboration with other reliable sources).

Remember, if you are asked to comment on the credibility of a source or some specific information, you don't need to comment on all these things, just the ones which, in the circumstances, you judge to be the most significant – those that are clear signs of strength or weakness.

Honesty of a report

For questions about the *honesty/sincerity* of a report, think whether they have a motive to be less than truthful, and if so, how likely are they to get away with it?

Credible

Use the word *credible* when talking about evidence, not about arguments.

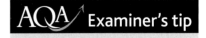

Examiner's tip

Think about the kind of claim being put forward before deciding which credibility criteria to use.

■ Returning to the text

Let's look at our article. What sources do we have? We have the article itself, written by a journalist. And then we have the people the journalist cites and quotes: the two politicians, John Hutton and Philip Hammond. Let's take these separately.

■ Critical question

12.1 How credible is the newspaper article as a source of information?

Response

A first thing to bear in mind is the kind of newspaper (or magazine or website or TV channel, etc.) that the information is found in. Some newspapers have a better reputation than others for being accurate. In Chapter 10, where we analysed a short newsflash, we commented on the high standards of reporting that the BBC aims towards. This means the credibility of the BBC is fairly high.

It is true that even the broadsheet or quality papers have their own slight political leanings and biases. However, they all aspire to be quality papers, and so have a vested interest in reporting things accurately (and the individual journalist likewise is interested in doing the same for their own career or reputation). This all strengthens the credibility of their news reporting. To judge accurately how fairly or neutrally a subject has been treated by a particular paper, you really need to look at how it is represented in a range of papers. But where this is impossible, or where you simply do not have the time to do so, you can still look for evidence of neutrality or bias in the way they have presented the story. For example, by implying things, using leading language, or giving better coverage to one side than another.

Here, apart from the title of the article (which is usually written by someone other than the journalist), the language used is mostly factual rather than persuasive, and the journalist has included comments from both sides. This indicates that he has attempted to be neutral on the subject; moreover, as a journalist on a quality paper, he has a vested interest to report things accurately in order to protect his reputation as a reporter. This again makes the document a credible source of information. When we add the fact that the stuff he has reported can probably be fairly easily verified elsewhere (assuming he wasn't the only journalist given access to the information and the documents are publicly available) then the document would appear to be a highly credible source which we can take largely at face value.

What about the other factors that can affect credibility. Is it worth asking where the journalist has got his information from?

In this case, this factor does not play a huge part in the article's credibility. From reading the report, it's unclear how close the journalist was to the people he quotes. The picture would suggest the answer is not very! (Its significance is very unclear. Who are the two men? They don't really look like people who work in benefit centres, or who might be claiming benefit.) In a different context, such as where the journalist is reporting allegations of some kind of scandal, this kind of thing might be more significant. Since these comments are presumably verifiable (they were presumably made to a gathering of journalists or press officers and are probably also quoted in other papers) and the journalist has a vested interest to report things accurately, this is not especially significant. We can fairly safely assume the comments are likely to be accurate.

What is perhaps more significant here is that the report contains summaries of, for example, what Hutton said (either in an interview or a written report). Whenever information is summarised there is a degree of interpretation going on and, of course, selectivity; the summariser has to decide what information to include and what to leave out. This means that a thorough assessment of the article's credibility ought to include questioning how carefully and fully, if at all, the journalist read (or listened to) the original text. However, once again, the journalist's apparent neutrality on the issue allows us to assume that he has given us a fair representation of Hutton's original text, therefore the fact that the text has been summarised and interpreted does not greatly affect the credibility here.

The article itself, therefore, appears to be credible, and we have no reason to distrust what the journalist himself has written.

Critical question

12.2 How credible are the two politicians in this context?

Response

The situation is different when it comes to the people the journalist cites.

When judging the statements made by John Hutton and Philip Hammond, you ought to have taken into account the fact that neither person presents a neutral viewpoint. It is clear that each has a clear position on the issue. John Hutton is responsible for introducing the policy. Not only is he in favour of it, which makes him biased, but he has an obvious *vested interest* in the policy appearing effective. If it is seen to be a good thing, then he will be seen to have made a good decision, which will presumably be good for his image and career in government.

In contrast, his opposite number, Philip Hammond, is obviously against the idea of the technology, as can be seen by his describing the lie detector equipment as 'Big Brother technology' and his comments about the real problem being the complexity of the benefit system. He is therefore also biased when it comes to this question. As an opposition politician, he is likely to feel a duty to oppose the policy, to argue that it is a bad idea. It is probably safer to describe him as being biased than having a vested interest, since he does not have so much at stake in the matter, although a case could be made along similar lines as Hutton, in that it is potentially in his interests for his opposite number's policies to fail. Either way, he is certainly not neutral, and therefore the credibility of his comments is weakened.

The more likely someone is to be biased on a particular issue, or the more they have at stake, the more careful you ought to be at taking their statements at face value. Of course, the fact that someone is biased or has a vested interest does not mean that they are lying, but it often makes it more likely. We can therefore say that the

> **Over to you**
>
> Before reading the response, consider what kind of comments you might make if asked a question like critical question 12.2 in the exam.

Biased

Sometimes someone may be biased without you (or they) knowing it. If you think that someone has used evidence selectively, or at least focused on one side of an issue unfairly, then this could be a sign that they are biased.

Specimen answer

The *Daily Telegraph* is a quality paper and has a vested interest to report news accurately because of its reputation. The journalist appears to be neutral on the topic, reporting from both sides and using mostly factual, non-emotive or non-persuasive language. This means that what he has written is likely to be accurate. The people he quotes from, however, are both biased and Hutton in particular has a vested interest to make the lie detectors seem like a good thing. This makes their comments less credible. Besides, they are not really giving information, more their opinions on things.

statement's credibility is lowered, or weakened, due to (for example) the person's vested interest. An important factor to bear in mind when considering evidence in the form of statements, then, is how *credible* they are in the context.

Let's put all this together and try to answer an exam-style question about the credibility of the information in the document. The following question would probably be worth around 3–4 marks:

Critical question

12.3 How credible is the information presented in the document?

Response

The specimen answer given on the left would easily obtain all the available marks.

Summary and exam tips

In Unit 1 of the exam, you are almost inevitably going to get at least one text which is more factual in kind, i.e. some kind of news story or report, rather than an argument or dispute. Of course, the story is likely to be about a topic where there is room for disagreement or dispute, and may even be about a dispute or disagreement itself. Assessing factual information, and its significance (i.e. how it could, should or has been used) is therefore an important skill.

In Part 2, assessing the relevance, significance and credibility of information plays a more central role, with many questions asking you directly or indirectly to do just this.

In either paper there may also be opinions or arguments quoted or embedded in the texts, and recognising these is a basic skill that you should be getting quite adept at by now.

To summarise, when evidence is used, including when people are quoted in texts, ask yourself:

- Are they giving evidence and what kind of evidence is it? (Are the statements factual in kind? How clear is the meaning?)
- What *relevance* do they – or the journalist – say (or imply) that the evidence has? (And should we uncritically accept this?)
- What *significance* do they – or the journalist – say (or imply) that the evidence has? (And should we uncritically accept this?)
- How *credible* is what they are saying?
- If it's not so much evidence but more of an opinion, do they give (or imply) reasons for the opinion, i.e. do they give (or imply) an argument? If yes, then treat it as you would any other argument – evaluate the reasoning.

All of these can be fruitful areas of comment and analysis, and are likely to earn you marks if you apply them effectively, i.e. if you make them answer the question.

Let's try them out with some of the material in the news article, by answering an open exam question about some of the evidence and the support it provides.

Critical question

12.4 Assess the support given to the use of voice recognition lie detectors by the comments from John Hutton.

Response

Hutton is associated with two comments:

> Lie detector technology will be used by the government to help identify and deter benefit cheats.

> The 'cutting edge' technology aimed to tackle fraudsters while speeding up claims and improving customer service for the honest majority.

Before we assess their significance, it is worth mentioning that neither of these are direct quotations; they have been reported by the journalist. This is something to watch out for, as sometimes when comments are reported the meaning is altered.

However, for the reasons discussed earlier, since we have decided that the article scores well for credibility, we can probably trust the comments to be an accurate – albeit simplified/summarised – representation of Hutton's views.

With this in mind, we can assess the support they give for the use of the lie detectors.

First, what kind of statements are they?

As well as the use of persuasive language in words like 'fraudsters', 'cheats' and the 'honest majority' (although since these are not direct quotes it is unclear whether this is Hutton's language or that of the journalist), the claims are not straightforward facts that can easily be verified. They describe intentions, which although they can be true or false to an extent, might not give the full picture. Moreover, they are difficult to find evidence for or against (you can always *say* something was your intention, even if it wasn't). This makes the support they provide less effective.

It is true that he is talking from his own experience and expertise, which means he had the ability to observe and the knowledge to report accurately what went on when the decision to use the lie detectors was made. However, we also know that as a politician he has to be careful about what he says and how much he reveals. And since he has a vested interest in his policies being successful and popular amongst the electorate, we know he has a motive to present them in a positive light. This does not mean that the comments are not true, just that they might not be giving the whole picture, which in turn makes their significance less clear, and the support they provide less effective.

In one sense his comments *are* relevant, as they give a good reason for why the lie detectors are to be used. Yet the support they provide is not very strong. The fact that it is 'aimed' at doing this does not mean that it will. And the fact that he says it is aimed at doing this does not mean it is.

Evidence

Never just say of a piece of evidence that its relevance or significance is *questionable* or *debatable*. Always say *why* this is the case. Otherwise you are unlikely to get any marks. Similarly, avoid just asking rhetorical questions like, but how do we know this evidence is reliable? You need to explain *why* you think it is or isn't likely to be.

Generally speaking, questioning the accuracy of the evidence is of less interest to examiners than questioning how the evidence is used, although it does depend on the question and the context (there is more about dealing with evidence, especially in the form of figures and statistics, in Chapter 29).

However, even if we accept the truth of the comments, they have little effect if you are against the use of the technology in principle; it is irrelevant how well intentioned they are if you feel that people working for the state (or anyone else for that matter) should not have these sort of powers. So, in this sense, the comments have little relevance at all.

Specimen answer

The comments only say that the technology will 'help' catch benefit fraud and that it is 'aimed' to do this, but this does not mean it will. This means the support is not very strong. There is no evidence that it has happened, just Hutton's intentions. Also Hutton is biased as he has a vested interest in making the technology sound good and not frightening to people. It was his idea to use it and he is responsible for it, so his comments are less credible.

Exam technique – selecting what to say

The question we have answered is a very open one as it allows you to talk about both the credibility of the comments and their significance. When the question is open, you can choose what angle you want to use to answer the question. Good critical comments and evidence of critical thinking, as long as they are relevant, will always get credit (although judging what is and isn't relevant is of course a core critical skill). You may be asked for more specific comments about *either* the credibility or the significance of the evidence, but if you are just asked to comment critically on the support given, then you are free to comment as you wish. Generally speaking, the more open the question, the more marks are available. A question such as this is likely to be worth around 3–4 marks, and so you would need at least two relevant points clearly explained and developed. This answer (left) would easily obtain full marks.

Let's try another type of question, using the following claim from the article (which is not attributed to or associated explicitly with John Hutton).

Critical question

12.5 Consider the following claim from the article:

> According to Government figures, benefit fraud has been reduced from about £2 billion in 2001 to an estimated £0.7 billion in 2005/06.

Suppose that this was used by a government spokesperson to provide support for the use of the lie detector technology. Comment critically on the support it gives.

Response

Again we have an open question. With this question there are three relevant ways of commenting critically:

- considering the credibility of the claim
- considering its accuracy
- considering its relevance or significance.

Any of these could be developed to make useful critical points. The following might be included in the mark scheme as indicative of good answers:

- (about the claim's credibility) The government has a vested interest in making themselves sound like they are doing a good job, which means their 'estimate' is likely to be optimistic. Furthermore, by calling it an 'estimate' they are able to give a figure which cannot be checked in the same way a more factual figure can be. *[2 marks]*

(about the accuracy of the figures) Although they are admitted as being 'estimated' and 'about', it seems very hard to know how much fraudulent activity is going on. The only way of knowing is through *extrapolating* from existing data, which involves making a number of questionable assumptions (notably a degree of generalisation). If the fraud is successful, then by definition, no one will know it is occurring. *[2–3 marks]*

(about their relevance or significance) It is not clear how or why this drop in fraud has been achieved. One might want to ask, if they have managed to cut down on fraud so much without resorting to the use of lie detector technology, do they really need to bring this in now? However, it could be that they have achieved all they can by conventional or existing methods and need to use this new technology to reduce the figure further. *[2–3 marks]*

(about their relevance or significance) One might also want to ask, if the numbers of fraud have fallen so significantly, is there still a need to pursue the policy? Evidence that a problem has diminished is not particularly useful when trying to argue for increased powers for tackling it. (On the other hand, £0.7 billion *is* still a large sum and presumably worth recovering or reducing if possible.) *[2–3 marks]*

We have therefore identified:

- problems with the credibility of the claim
- problems with the accuracy
- problems with its relevance or significance.

These are general areas to consider when you are asked to comment critically on the support evidence in the form of figures given. Of these, the second is usually the least useful. It's not enough just to say the figures may be wrong; you would get no marks for this. You would need to give a reason for why the figures may be inaccurate. It's usually easier to do this with comments about the evidence's credibility or significance.

Over to you

What are the arguments on either side so far? Set out the principles that you think support each view and also any useful evidence, explaining what the significance of the evidence actually is (how and why it is relevant or significant) including an assessment, where relevant, of its credibility. Which side to you seems stronger?

13

Benefit cheats: other questions on evidence-based reasoning

- to be able to comment critically on someone else's response to evidence or to evidence-based arguments

- to increase the range of knowledge and understanding of common flaws and reasoning errors

- to be able to spot arguments which have deployed causal reasoning and to comment critically on them

- to understand and apply the terms 'necessary condition' and 'sufficient conditions' in both analysing and evaluating reasoning

- to evaluate the effects of further evidence on a view or argument.

Responses to responses

In the exam you will get a mixture of texts. Some will be primarily informative, some will be primarily to argue or persuade, and some will be a mixture of both. You may be given short argued (or partially argued, for example where a view has been implied, or some attempt to support a view has been made) *responses* to texts. A typical example would be readers' or viewers' responses, perhaps to a comment piece or a news story. You need to be able to comment critically on these responses, either because you think they are relevant to the longer argument you need to write at the end or because the questions specifically ask you to do so.

Imagine that you read the following bloggers' responses to the article:

> What about all the fraud and tax evasion committed by big businesses? This costs the country far more than the money lost through benefit fraud. Instead they go after the little people who don't have the power to defend themselves. It's typical of our cowardly government. If they haven't got the guts to go after the big guys with lie detectors, then they should leave the little people alone! If business people can get away with massive fraud, what's so bad about some poor sod pinching a few quid down the dole office?
>
> *Blog A*

> We simply can't allow this kind of thing to happen. Our individual rights are too precious. If we condone the use of lie detectors here, what's to stop them being used in other situations? The next thing we know is they'll be using them in schools, or for stop and searches in the street. If we carry on down this road, we won't even be in a position to complain about our individual rights, as we won't even have the right to open our mouths in protest!
>
> *Blog B*

> It's about bloody time someone did something about all the scavengers out there. I bet if they knew this was happening, half the fraudsters would run a mile. Then at last they'd have to find a proper job instead of sponging off the state.
>
> *Blog C*

Over to you

Before reading our comments, think about what you might say in answer to Critical question 13.1. This being a question about the quality of an argument, you will as always need to begin by asking yourself how the argument works, which are the views that are being argued for, and what reasons are being given. Only then can you ask how good the reasoning is, or how well justified the conclusion(s) are.

Critical question

13.1 Comment critically on blogger A's response to the *Daily Telegraph* online article about the use of lie detectors in benefit centres.

Response

(We shall not exhaust the critical comments you could make about the arguments. We shall restrict ourselves to one or two points for each one, as would suffice in an exam. You may well have spotted others.)

The argument's main conclusion is 'If they (the government) haven't got the guts to go after the big guys with lie detectors, then they should leave the little people alone!' Since the argument clearly assumes that the lie detectors are only being used on the 'little people' (in the benefit centres) then its further, implied conclusion is that the intended use of lie detectors in benefit centres is unjustified.

So how well are either of these conclusions supported?

There are a number of assumptions, both explicit and implicit, that a critical evaluation of the argument might want to consider. For a start, it makes the assumption that the government are not 'going after', or trying to prevent or crack down on big business fraud; also that the greater the amount of money involved in a crime, the worse or more serious the crime, or the greater the need or duty to stamp down on it. Both of these are questionable assumptions, and so questioning these or other unwarranted assumptions would be a good way of answering the question.

There is another way the reasoning can be criticised. You may have spotted that the arguer is guilty of a *tu quoque* (see Chapter 8, page 42). The last sentence is implying, through a rhetorical question, that it is not so bad for someone to 'pinch a few quid down the dole office' *on the grounds that* business people 'get away with massive fraud'. This is effectively saying that because someone else is doing something very wrong, it's okay for someone else to do something less wrong. But two wrongs don't make a right. The 'fact' that business people *also* commit fraud, albeit on a larger scale, is not a reason for saying that people committing benefit fraud are not doing something wrong.

Let's imagine a slightly more closed question about blogger B's response.

Open and closed questions

In an exam you will be asked both closed and open questions. Closed (i.e. specifically targeted) questions are those such as 'Identify an implicit assumption blogger A's argument is making' or 'Identify a flaw in blogger A's argument' or an even more explicitly targeted question such as 'Identify an example of a *tu quoque* in blogger A's argument'. More open questions are those such as 'Comment critically on blogger A's argument'. When the question is open, it is up to you what you choose to say, and any relevant critical comments will be credited. Note that if the question is an open one, then you do not have to use the technical name for the flaw you identify, as long as you explain what is wrong with the reasoning.

The argument assumes that if lie detectors are introduced in benefit centres then this will start off a chain reaction of events which lead to us having no rights at all. This is not necessarily true. It is possible that they could be the only place they are used.

Critical thought

The metaphor of erosion, which is often used with reference to civil liberties, is worth considering briefly. Is it a good word to use and an effective metaphor, or unfair use of persuasive/leading language? 'Erode' conjures up images of damage, often irreparable, from harsh and constant hostile forces (such as wind and rain). But compare it to, for example, when cliffs are eroded; can the damage to individual liberties be undone? And if the process starts, must it continue?

Technical point

The words 'consequences' and 'implications' mean very much the same thing, although 'consequences' means specifically to do with cause and effect, whereas 'implications' can also mean things that follow logically. For example, it is an implication of winning the lottery that your relative financial status is changed greatly. A consequence could be that you go on a spending spree. Implications are more certain than consequences. Consequences sometimes depend on other factors. But don't worry; if you happen to muddle the words, you will not lose any credit. In many cases the two are interchangeable. We shall stick to the word 'consequences' for the time being. You can do the same if you like.

Critical question

13.2 In what way is the argument made by blogger B flawed?

Response

> You may recognise the flaw in the argument here as a *slippery slope* (see page 44). Note that the question does not ask you to name the flaw (although you would earn one of the two marks for doing so). The specimen answer would gain both marks.

On page 62 we asked you to try to construct an argument against the use of lie detectors using only statements of principle. Part of the purpose of this was to show you how difficult this is, and therefore to show the limitations of general principles and the need for combining these with specific evidence. However, you may have managed to arrive at some basic principles about the importance of individual and civil liberties, and the dangers and implications of eroding them. There are important and convincing arguments along these lines. Just be careful not to resort to a slippery slope: don't let the erosion become a landslide.

Thinking causally: consequences, implications ... and slippery slopes

When thinking about actions (including whether to do or not to do something) it is important to consider the consequences, or implications. Doing this in advance means thinking hypothetically: what would happen if ...? This is the very essence of rational behaviour; rather than just going on an impulse, you think about the consequences first.

The problem is that most situations are too complex for us to be able to work out exactly what the consequences are going to be. Not only that, but people sometimes get carried away with their thinking, assume a little too much in what they see as possible consequences, and before they know it, they've gone rushing off down a slippery slope.

The trick is to think carefully about whether what are projected as consequences really are, whether they are inevitable or merely possible. There is a big difference between the two, especially when there is a whole chain of consequences, each of which has been assumed to be inevitable when in fact it isn't.

Using consequences to challenge an argument or point of view

When considering arguments, in particular those recommending actions and what to do (or not do), you shouldn't only consider how well supported they are, but what the consequences are.

Someone may give a good, convincing argument, but the consequences may be worrying. Of course, just because the possible consequences are undesirable does not mean you should ignore the argument. Sometimes you just have to deal with the consequences. Sometimes, however, these might be so severe or significant that they overweigh the argument itself.

Thinking of the possible consequences of an argument or point of view could help you to respond to arguments in the exam, in particular when judging them against your own position in the longer question at the end. They can also be used to answer 'comment critically on' questions if you see a dangerous consequence of a view being put forward.

Sometimes the consequences of an argument can go against, conflict with, and even contradict explicit or implicit parts of an argument. This is more of an A2 thing, but identifying where this is the case will gain credit all the same.

Just watch out for slippery slopes.

Necessary and sufficient conditions

When thinking about consequences, it is sometimes helpful to think about the relation between cause and effect. There are different ways that something can cause or lead to something else. Some causes are just contributing factors that may or may not have been *necessary*. For example, someone may have been influenced to choose a particular career path by a book they read when they were younger, but they may still have chosen that career anyway. We cannot say for certain that reading the book was a **necessary condition** for their having made the career choice they did.

If we can be certain that something is a necessary condition for something else to happen, we can infer that if it doesn't happen, then the consequence will not happen either. People often use this principle in order to argue that we shouldn't do certain things *in order to avoid certain undesirable consequences*. This is fine as long as they have correctly identified a necessary condition. The problem is that this is not always so easy to do.

Another problem is the fact that something may be a necessary condition but that does not mean it is *sufficient*. What this means is that, while something might be a necessary condition for something else to happen, it does not follow from this that if the necessary condition happens, the consequence will also happen. For example, it might be a necessary condition for you to succeed in an interview in order to get into a particular university, but this does not mean it is a **sufficient condition**. You might interview well but not get the grades they require in your A levels. That is because, while succeeding at an interview may have been a necessary condition, this does not mean it was a sufficient one.

If we can be certain that something is a sufficient condition for something else to happen, we can infer that if it *does* happen, then the consequence *will also* happen. People often use this principle in order to argue that we *should* do certain things *in order to bring about certain desirable consequences*. Once again, this is fine as long as they have correctly identified a sufficient condition. And once again, this is not always so easy to do. (Try, for example, thinking what *would* be a sufficient condition to get offered a place at a particular university.)

Sometimes it's much easier to identify sufficient conditions than necessary ones. For example, having a nasty infection is a sufficient condition for feeling tired or lousy, yet it's by no means necessary. Other times it's much easier to find one or more necessary conditions than a sufficient one. For example, in order to catch a cold, you have to be exposed to the cold virus, but this does not mean you will definitely become infected.

The crucial point is this. Any argument which encourages a course of action in order to prevent something undesirable or bring about something desirable needs to have correctly identified the necessary and sufficient conditions for their conclusion to follow with any confidence, safety or security. If the arguer cannot be confident of this, then they ought to be careful how they express their conclusion. The safest thing to say is that, as a result, the consequence 'might' or 'might not' happen, but this is much less impressive or persuasive-sounding than saying that it *will*.

Key terms

Necessary condition: that which needs to take place for something else to happen; without it, the other thing cannot occur.

Sufficient condition: that which, if it does take place, is enough to make sure something else happens; with it, the other thing must occur.

Over to you

Occasionally a condition can be both a necessary and a sufficient condition at once. Another, more common scenario is for a group of necessary conditions together to be sufficient for something. Can you think of examples of either of these situations?

The fact that a condition is necessary does not mean that it is sufficient, and vice versa. If the argument assumes that a cause, or group of causes, is either necessary or sufficient when it isn't (or might not be), then it is making unwarranted causal assumptions and you can say so.

Let's apply this way of thinking to answer the following open question about blogger C's argument:

> It's about bloody time someone did something about all the scavengers out there. I bet if they knew this was happening, half the fraudsters would run a mile. Then at last they'd have to find a proper job instead of sponging off the state.

Critical question

13.3 Comment critically on blogger C's response to the *Daily Telegraph* online article about the use of lie detectors in benefit centres.

Response

Here is a specimen answer, which uses the concept of necessary and sufficient conditions very effectively to provide a thorough assessment of the argument.

Specimen answer

The argument uses a lot of emotive language but it is not very well reasoned as it assumes that stopping someone claiming benefit fraud is a sufficient condition for getting them to 'find a proper job', when in fact it isn't. People might have other illegitimate incomes and just use the benefits as an extra. Stopping the benefits might not be enough to make them need to find a job. However, this does not destroy their argument completely as this is not the only reason the argument gives, but an extra, positive consequence of using the lie detectors. There is still some support provided by the first sentence, but the argument is much less strong.

Thinking causally

Causal thinking and assumptions are areas where people get in the most muddle, so watch out for them. There are usually plenty of marks available in exams for identifying problems with causal thinking and assumptions that have been made. Watch out for arguments that confuse necessary and sufficient conditions. If you think an argument has done this, then the argument is probably flawed for this reason. Avoid slippery slopes in your own arguments by looking carefully at the facts of the situation, and by thinking carefully about the causal connections you are making, in particular whether or not you have correctly identified necessary and sufficient conditions.

Before leaving necessary and sufficient conditions, let's have another go at responding critically to blogger B's argument:

> We simply can't allow this kind of thing to happen. Our individual rights are too precious. If we condone the use of lie detectors here, what's to stop them being used in other situations? The next thing we know is they'll be using them in schools, or for stop and searches in the street. If we carry on down this road, we won't even be in a position to complain about our individual rights, as we won't even have the right to open our mouths in protest!

Critical question

13.4 Comment critically on blogger B's response to the *Daily Telegraph* online article about the use of lie detectors in benefit centres.

Response

Here we have an argument which is arguing against doing something in order to avoid an undesirable outcome, in this case our total loss of individual rights. This might suggest it is assuming that the something we need to avoid doing is a necessary condition for the consequence.

But notice that it is not expressed in this way. Blogger B's argument is saying that we shouldn't have lie detector tests, because if we do, then this nasty consequence will occur. Therefore it is not assuming that the lie detector use is a necessary condition for the slide to losing our rights, but a sufficient one.

Since it has assumed that it is a sufficient condition for the predicted unpleasant consequence, this is enough to argue that we ought to avoid doing it. It doesn't need also to assume that it is a necessary condition. There may be other ways of losing our human rights, but since this path inevitably will lead to this outcome, we need to avoid going down it.

The specimen answer in the margin on the right expresses these ideas as an answer to an exam question, similar to the answer about blogger C's argument.

Specimen answer

The argument makes a lot of questionable causal assumptions. Each step in the reasoning assumes that doing something is a sufficient condition for the next step to occur, but this is very unlikely. It is very unlikely that, for example, allowing the government to use lie detectors in benefit centres to catch benefit cheats is a sufficient condition for the government to start using them in schools or on the streets.

Effects of further evidence

Another type of question you may be asked in the exam is to consider what impact additional evidence has on a claim, point of view or argument. Although the form of the question is slightly different, the skills are essentially the same. You need to consider the relevance and significance of the evidence, should it be true, on the claim, point of view or argument in question.

We have seen how to judge the relevance or significance of evidence for a particular claim. It's slightly trickier when judging the impact of evidence on an argument, as an argument necessarily contains more than one claim, and could contain a number of claims as well as further implicit assumptions.

You therefore need to decide what part of the argument the evidence affects, what *kind* of effect it has, and what effect *this* has on the overall argument. For example, it might completely destroy one of the reasons, but the reason might not be essential for the conclusion to follow if there are other reasons which remain unaffected.

Ways further evidence might affect an argument

Here are some ways that further evidence may affect an argument:

- **Undermine some of the evidence:** instead of asking what conclusions can be drawn from the evidence, we ask if the conclusion or conclusions that have been drawn still stand.
- **Conflict with one or more of the reasons:** as always when there is a problem with a reason, we need to ask how important a role that reason plays in the argument – to what extent the conclusion relies on it.

Additional evidence

Assessing the impact of additional evidence on an argument is actually one of the hardest skills in critical thinking, because of the number of skills it tests. However, one thing you do not need to do is consider the credibility of the evidence, as the question is asking what effect the evidence *would* have *if* the evidence happened to be true. It's a hypothetical question, so we don't worry about whether or not the evidence is true. Just what its effect *would* be if it were true.

■ **Go against an implicit assumption:** this is more difficult; it depends on you having identified this assumption first.

■ **Give a separate reason for why the conclusion is not true:** you have to weigh the significance of this new reason against the original ones.

Put this into practice by imagining that you had come across an announcement from the government stating that if the technology proves effective in the Harrow benefit centre, they will consider introducing it to other centres across the country. Assuming this announcement is true, what effect, if any, will it have on any of the three bloggers' arguments on page 74?

The obvious argument to consider is blog B's, which sees the introduction of the piloting of the technology in the Harrow centre as very much the thin end of the wedge. The argument is based on a series of 'If ... then' statements which are all hypothetical. As we have seen, for the reasoning to work, each hypothetical claim needs to have identified a sufficient condition in the 'If ' part of the sentence for the consequence, the 'then' part, to be sure of following. Yet as we have also commented, these assumptions are highly doubtful. We certainly cannot be sure of them.

This piece of evidence would seem to be relevant to this concern, and perhaps even strengthen one or more of the 'If ... then' claims which assert the real possibility of a dangerous slide towards losing our individual rights and liberties.

But how much effect would it have? Although the author of the argument would no doubt see this as confirming their worst fears, the argument would still have a slippery slope, and its conclusion would be largely unjustified. The evidence would certainly not count *against* their argument; it would go no way to falsifying or undermining any of their claims, but it would not do enough to verify them either. It could still be true that the government are planning on adopting this technology across centres nationwide, but false that this means they will start using it everywhere.

What if you came across a statement to the effect that should the technology be effective in benefit centres, the government aim to introduce it in other public service areas, such as in disputes over the payment of council tax bills?

Here the evidence *would* seem to strengthen blogger B's argument. The assumption they had made – if lie detectors are allowed to be used here, the government will start using them everywhere – which had seemed very unlikely, is starting to look less so. *With* this evidence, what had seemed an unlikely causal connection begins to look more plausible. And yet it would still, we would hope, be some way off being a sufficient condition.

So the evidence would definitely strengthen the argument, although the argument is still a bit slippery. The author would need a lot more evidence to show that they really had identified a series of sufficient conditions to bring about their conclusion. The trouble is, when this had happened, the argument's horrible prophecies would have come true.

Over to you

1 Here are some other pieces of evidence, some real, and some merely hypothetical. Treating each one as if it were true, ask what effect each might have on any of the arguments on page 74. Explain your answer.

a Harrow benefit centre announced that they had identified 126 cases of benefit fraud through the use of the technology in the first three months of using it.

b The number of new benefit claims since the technology has been used has reduced by around 20%.

c Similar technology has been in place for more than five years in the British insurance industry but has never become widely used due to doubts about its accuracy.

d Skilled liars do not show signs of stress.

e The stress patterns when people lie are very similar to/ indistinguishable from those when people are nervous or excited.

2 Assuming again that the pieces of evidence happened to be true, what conclusions, if any, do they support about the effectiveness, or otherwise, of the lie detector technology in catching benefit cheats? What further assumptions in each case need to be made?

3 Assuming again that they are true, could any of the pieces of evidence be used to support either an argument for or an argument against the general introduction of the use of lie detectors in benefit centres nationwide? How would you use them? What further assumptions would you need to make?

Get writing!

Now you can try putting all the materials and skills together from the last few sections into writing a longer argument like the kind you will have to write in the exam. Here is the question you are to take on.

Critical question

13.5 Do you think the use of lie detectors in benefit centres is a good thing?

Write an argument in which you either encourage or oppose this policy, making use of any helpful evidence, and making clear what principles you think are most important.

Before you start

Table 13.1 may be useful for gathering material and building some better, more extended points, especially if you are always being told to develop your points more. Using the material in the original argument, as well as the pieces of further evidence which you have just been considering (and which you can assume for the purpose of the argument are from a reliable source), select pieces of evidence for either side and consider what significance they have to the claims and arguments for or against the lie detectors. We have started it by making a couple of suggestions ourselves. You may wish to ignore these and select your own, or add them to further ideas of your own. You could include the same material on either side, and see which side develops into a better argument.

The comments and significance columns are the most important ones. They are where the development of your points takes place. How well you use your information and develop your points will affect the quality of your argument.

This is a very laborious way of doing things, and would be too time-consuming to do in the exam. But even if you don't actually write a table like this (which we do not recommend in the time you have), this table *does* represent the kind of thought processes you ought to be going through.

Over to you

1 Have a go at writing an extended argument in answer to critical question 11.1 using the information, evidence, and principles discussed in Chapters 11 to 13 and any others that you have identified. (Part 4 of this book on writing an argument provides further guidance.)

2 Sometimes people are just frightened of new technology. How rational is the fear of new technology? Write an argument (200–300 words) in which you argue that in general, people are/are not too frightened of technology.

3 Research into the reliability of truth-testing technology over the years. Can you find any important evidence to argue either for its overall reliability or overall usefulness?

Table 13.1 *Sample to show gathering of material for an argument*

Material for	Comment/significance	Material against	Comment/significance
The number of new benefit claims since the technology has been used has reduced by around 20%	Shows that the technology is acting as a deterrent to potential fraudsters, assuming …	The number of new benefit claims since the technology has been used has reduced by around 20%	If this is supposed to be evidence in its favour, the significance is unclear. How do we know what caused the reduction in claims and that they were all or mostly fraudsters? May have been normal honest people frightened off by the new technology. May be another reason for this correlation (correlation not cause)
		More money is lost through error than through fraud	The government should be focusing on improving the system before using technology like this. If they are principally to blame, they have less right to use these measures which assume that the public are at fault rather than them (Is this a *tu quoque* or not?)
Harrow says the technology has identified 126 benefit cheats in three months since May	Clear evidence that the technology is effective, and a desirable outcome, assuming that this is an unpleasant crime that we need to cut down on – stops money going to the wrong people	Harrow says the technology has identified 126 benefit cheats in three months since May	Danger of generalising. Harrow may not be representative of benefit centres. One 'successful' result does not prove anything; it could have been chance or coincidence

14 Claims and assertions

Learning objectives:

■ to classify claims.

■ About the critical thinking toolkit

Chapters 14–23 of the toolkit relate to Unit 1, the Foundation unit of the AQA specification. Chapters 24–29 relate to Unit 2, the Information, inference and explanation unit.

■ What is a claim?

A claim is a particular kind of sentence. It is similar in meaning to 'assertion' or 'statement'. 'Stating', 'asserting' or 'claiming' something all mean roughly the same.

A property that statements, claims and assertions all have in common is that they can be described as true or false, or at least that you agree or disagree with them. This distinguishes them, for example, from questions or commands. If someone says to you, 'Clean the car!' that is a command. It would make no sense to reply 'That's true' or 'I agree', or to say that it's *not* true or that you *disagree*. You may refuse, by saying 'No I won't' or 'Clean it yourself'. You may say it is an unreasonable or inappropriate command, but that is not the same as saying the command itself is untrue.

Similarly, a question is neither true nor false. If you were asked 'Have you cleaned the car yet?', you might say 'No' or even 'No, and I'm not going to'. But it would be irrational to say the question was false or wrong. Questions, commands, requests, etc., do not have the property of being true or false.

Claims do. And, because they do, you can respond meaningfully by saying 'I agree with that' or 'I disagree with it.' You can say you don't believe it, or that you question it, or that you accept or reject it.

You can give other claims to support it, or to persuade others to accept it. When you do that you are producing an *argument*. Or you can give reasons for not accepting it, in which case you are making a *counter-argument*.

Claims are the building blocks of reasoning and argument.

From a grammatical point of view, 'statement' is the term for sentences which make claims. A more technical term is 'declarative sentence'. A *declarative* sentence is one which declares or asserts something, as distinct from an *imperative* (which commands) or *interrogative* (which questions – think of interrogation).

> I have cleaned the car. (statement, declarative)
>
> Have you cleaned the car? (question, interrogative)
>
> Clean the car. (command, imperative)

In practice, of course, claims are not always in the form of complete grammatical sentences. The single word 'yes' may perform the same function in answer to a question. For example:

> Have you cleaned the car?
>
> Yes. (I have cleaned the car)

Sometimes, too, a question can be used to assert something rather than ask something. It is known as a *rhetorical question*. For example:

> Do you really think I've got nothing better to do than clean your wreck of a car?

See also 'Giving reasons' in Chapter 1 (page 4).

Fact or opinion?

One of the first and most natural questions to ask about any text is whether the claims it makes are stating fact or expressing opinion. This may seem a simple distinction, but when you come to think about it critically, it is anything but simple.

A fact is a claim that is *true*. The trouble is, we don't always *know* whether a claim is true or not. Therefore it is quite possible to express an opinion that *happens to be* a fact but without your knowing it, or without being sure of it. And it is quite possible to state what you believe to be a fact, and be mistaken. It is even possible to state something that you know to be false. In all of these cases you are making claims, but it is a lot less clear which are facts and which are opinions.

Matters of fact and matters of opinion

There are some claims that are not even *matters* of fact. If I say to you, 'The car needs cleaning,' that is not factually true or false. It depends on what you mean by 'needs'. Some people feel the need to clean their cars every week; others leave them for months and don't think it matters. Therefore it is a matter of opinion, rather than fact, whether a car needs cleaning at any particular time or not. Another word for it is *judgement*. People make judgements. Circumstances make facts.

On the other hand, if I said, 'It hasn't been cleaned for a year,' that would be a matter of fact. It is either true or false, depending on when it was last cleaned, i.e. the circumstances. If it is true, it could be used to support the claim (or judgement) that the car *does* need cleaning, and that would be an argument. However, it would still be a matter of opinion whether it is a strong enough argument or a good enough reason. To strengthen the argument, you would really need to add a further claim such as:

> Every car needs cleaning at least once a year.

But that too is a matter of opinion, not of fact. We begin to see now why this distinction between fact and opinion is so central to analysing and evaluating reasoning.

Kinds of claim

Claims are not all of one kind. They fall into many different categories which it is useful to understand and recognise. On page 85 you will find a reference list giving some of the more useful labels that can be applied to claims, and which will help you when evaluating the texts in which they occur.

Note, however, that many of these categories overlap, so that you will often find that the claim you are considering or discussing belongs to more than one. This is quite normal with any sort of classification. Claims, like any other objects, can have more than one description. The skill is in giving the relevant one.

One or more?

A single sentence can contain more than one claim, joined by connectives such as 'and', 'because', 'if ' (or 'if … then'). Such sentences are called *compound* or *complex* sentences and need special consideration. For example:

> The car needs cleaning and it's your turn to do it.

> The car is filthy because you didn't clean it when you said you would.

> It will rust more quickly if it isn't cleaned regularly.

Reference list: kinds of claim

Statement of fact or factual statement

As we have seen, just because something is *presented* as a fact, it is quite possible for it not to *be* a fact. Nonetheless, we need to be able to recognise when a speaker or writer is making a claim to fact, or intending something to be taken as fact. If we are in any doubt about its truth, and want to draw attention to this doubt, we can always call it an *alleged* (or *presumed* or *supposed*) fact. Normally when we say that an author is *stating a fact*, or making a *factual statement*, this is what we mean.

Prediction

Predictions are claims, usually about the future, or about something which is not yet known for certain. Strictly speaking, a prediction is always an opinion at the time when it is made, even if it is a very well-justified opinion. If I put a stick in the ground on a sunny day and 'predict' that its shadow will shorten in the morning and lengthen in the afternoon, I am not going to be proved wrong, because my prediction has such strong scientific grounds, including the fact that it has *always* happened in the past, and the explanatory fact that the earth constantly turns on its axis (making the sun appear to move across the sky). What makes it a prediction is that it is about the future, and – theoretically – the future will not necessarily be the same as the past. (The laws of physics *could* have changed in the night!)

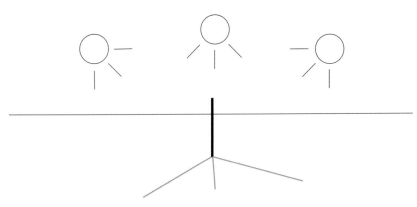

Predictions are claims about the future: in your opinion, how will the sun's shadows fall today?

Explanation or causal explanation

An explanation is a claim about why something happens, or *why* it's the way it is or what causes it. For example:

> A shadow shortens in the morning and lengthens in the afternoon because the earth turns on its axis.

This is a complex sentence. To be justified, as a whole, it must be true that:

A   A shadow *does* shorten in the morning AND does lengthen in the afternoon.

B   The earth *does* turn on its axis.

C   B causes or explains A.

Hypothesis

A hypothesis is a claim that is put forward for consideration, to be tested or investigated. It is more than just a guess, and indeed many hypotheses are so strongly supported by evidence that in practice we treat them as facts. Others less so. It is a hypothesis that global warming is taking place, but it is not yet a generally accepted fact. It is also a hypothesis that the earth turns on its axis, making the sun *appear* to orbit the earth. Once this was not just regarded as a hypothesis but as a *crazy* hypothesis, and people were often punished for openly subscribing to it. But since the time of Copernicus it has been so well tested that no rational and informed person would question it.

Definition

A definition is a claim about what something is, its distinguishing characteristics. A definition is also the meaning of a word, as found in a dictionary or glossary. For example:

> A shadow is an area that is not illuminated because light is intercepted by a solid or opaque object.

This is not like a scientific fact (or hypothesis); it is just a claim about what the word 'shadow' means in English. Definitions can be very important when evaluating arguments, because the success of the reasoning may depend on the way in which a particular word is understood.

Recommendation

A recommendation is a claim or suggestion about what should be done, how someone should act, what policy should be adopted. It is often recognisable by inclusion of expressions like 'should', 'must', 'ought to' or 'it's time that'.

> It is time that the European nations agreed on a binding timetable to tackle climate change by increasing taxes on fuel.

This is a recommendation. It is an opinion rather than an objective fact. You can say that you agree with the recommendation, or that you disagree, but neither would make it 'true' or 'false'.

Recommendations are often found as the conclusions of arguments: 'We must do X because …' or 'These are the facts, so Y is the way forward.'

Value judgement

A value judgement is a claim that something is good or bad, desirable or undesirable, virtuous or wicked, etc. It is called a *value* judgement because it is a claim about the alleged value, or worth, of something – or the absence of it. For example:

> The reluctance of some world leaders to face up to the threat of climate change is a disgraceful dereliction of duty.

What makes this a value judgement is the use of 'disgraceful'.

Generalisation

A generalisation is a claim that covers many particular cases or examples. It is a generalisation that students are lazy. It may be true of one or two particular students, known to the person making the claim; it may even be true of a great many. But provided there are some students who are not lazy, this is an unacceptable generalisation, and therefore a false claim. Not all generalisations are false, of course. As we have seen, it is perfectly acceptable to say that shadows (in sunlight) lengthen in the afternoon, because they all do.

Over to you

1. Investigate the words 'theory' and 'conjecture' and compare them with 'hypothesis'.

2. An 'allegation' is a certain kind of claim. What is distinctive about it?

3. How would you say a 'statement of principle' differs from other kinds of claim?

4. Find three examples of claims that make value judgements, and three contrasting claims that do not.

5. Discuss this question. Are all claims, in the end, just opinions?

Identifying arguments and their conclusions

We use *arguments* to put reasoning into words. As we saw on page 3, 'argument' has a number of meanings, so what we really mean here is *reasoned argument* (as opposed to quarrelling, for example). Argument of this kind consists of at least two components: one or more *reasons*, and a *conclusion* that supposedly follows from them. We have to say 'supposedly' because some arguments that we have to deal with are not very good ones, and the conclusion does not always follow from the reasons. But a bad argument is still an argument, just as a false claim is still a claim.

■ Inference

The conclusion and the reasons (or *premises*) are claims. However, just putting two or more claims together does not necessarily produce an argument. The claims have to be related in a particular way, and not just by subject matter. This relation is called *inference*. In an argument, the conclusion is an inference (i.e. it is *inferred*) from one or more of the other claims. Do not confuse **imply** with **infer** (though it is often done). We can say that one claim (call it P) implies another (call it Q), or that someone is implying Q by asserting P. But it is incorrect to say that 'P infers Q', or that someone who asserts P is 'inferring Q'. The correct way to say it is that Q is *inferred from* P.

Key terms

Imply: to mean something without actually saying it, e.g. 'You didn't invite me but you implied I was welcome.' To say one thing from which another follows logically or naturally, e.g. 'Telling me to pack warm clothes implied that it would be cold where we're going.'

Infer: to take one claim or assertion as grounds for a second, and to draw the second (as a conclusion) from the first.

For example, here are two claims: a statement of (alleged) fact **1**, followed by a prediction **2**:

1 Worldwide demand for oil is soaring.

2 Fuel prices will continue to rise.

Neither **1** nor **2** is an argument; they are just claims. Nor do **1** and **2** together necessarily add up to an argument. For us to say that **1** and **2** formed an argument, it would have to be clear that one of the two claims is being offered as grounds for the other, or (which is the same thing) that one is being inferred from the other. For example:

3 Worldwide demand for oil is soaring, so fuel prices will continue to rise.

or:

4 Fuel prices will continue to rise because worldwide demand for oil is soaring.

Argument indicators

There are two broad sets of connectives that indicate the presence of reasoning, or argument. The first group – so, therefore, consequently, thus, hence, for that reason, etc. – are used to flag up the *conclusion* in an argument. (They are also called *inference indicators*.) The second group – because, for, since, given that – signal *reasons*, or *grounds*.

Grammatically speaking, the words 'so' and 'because' belong to a class called *connectives*. In examples **3** and **4** they also function as *argument indicators*. It is fairly obvious why.

■ Texts without indicators

However, not all texts contain such helpful clues. Suppose **1** and **2** just appeared with no connective, just a full stop between them:

> Worldwide demand for oil is soaring. Fuel prices will continue to rise.

Is this an argument? Yes, but that doesn't necessarily mean that the author meant it to be an argument. In fact, we don't know what the author meant, because there is no contextual information available.

Saying that this is an argument means that it could be. The first claim *could* be understood as grounds for the second – not perhaps as very strong or persuasive grounds, but at least as one of a number of reasons that could be given for predicting a rise in oil prices. It is because of this that it made sense earlier to place 'so' or 'therefore' between them.

The 'so' or 'therefore' test

Inserting an appropriate argument indicator in this way is a kind of test as to whether a string of claims can form an argument or not. If the insertion results in nonsense then it is clearly not an argument. The test also tells us which of the claims is the conclusion and which is the reason (or reasons), so that in the process of *identifying* an argument we are already beginning to *analyse* it as well. For example, the test would tell us that if the above pair of claims is understood as an argument then **1** must be the reason and **2** the inference. Why not the other way round? Because '**2** therefore **1**' would be such a strange argument that no rational person would make or accept it:

> Fuel prices will continue to rise, *therefore* worldwide demand for oil is soaring!

Where an argument consists of one or more facts and a prediction, as many arguments do, it is the facts which typically support the prediction, not the other way round. Similarly, when one of the claims is a recommendation, it is the recommendation that is likely to be the conclusion. Take the following related argument:

> We should make research into alternative fuel sources a number one priority. World demand for oil is soaring, and natural deposits are getting harder to find with every day that passes.

Because the first sentence is a recommendation, as indicated by the 'should', we don't really need the therefore-test to identify the conclusion. Nonetheless, it confirms the matter:

> World demand for oil is soaring, and natural deposits are getting harder to find with every day that passes. *Therefore* we should make research into alternative fuel sources a number one priority.

Try connecting the sentences the other way round, and the result, though not ungrammatical, is not an argument – at least not an argument that anyone would recognise or take seriously:

> We should make research into alternative fuel sources a number one priority. *Therefore* world demand for oil is soaring, and natural deposits are getting harder to find!

Over to you

Decide, for each of the following, whether it could be understood as an argument and, if so, identify its conclusion:

a   Biofuel is at present the front-runner in the race to come up with an alternative to mineral oil, especially in America. The trouble with biofuel is that it replaces food crops, and food in many parts of the world is more important than fuel.

b   The trouble with biofuel is that it replaces food crops, when many people are still dying of hunger. There is a real danger that biofuel will create more problems than it solves. There is only so much land that can be farmed, and populations are growing not shrinking.

The anatomy of an argument

■ to analyse argument to reveal its structure.

In this chapter we are going to look at some standard patterns of arguments, in order to gain a clearer understanding of the underlying *structure* of reasoning. We will call them **S1** for Structure type 1, **S2**, etc.

■ Simple arguments

Simple arguments have a single conclusion and one or more reasons – also called premises – which directly support the conclusion. If there is just one reason, the structure is always the same.

If there are two or more reasons, then we have to ask whether each one is separate, or whether some or all of the reasons work together and depend on each other. This is the beginning of argument analysis. Each arrow can be thought of as a *line of reasoning*.

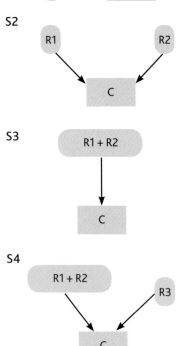

In type **S2** structures the reasons are separate, making two or more parallel arguments for one conclusion. If you took **R1** away, there would still be an argument from **R2**, though it may not be as good. In type **S3** there is a single argument, but with two (or sometimes more) reasons that depend on each other in their support of the conclusion. Here, if you took one premise away, the argument would be incomplete. **S4** is a mixture of types **S2** and **S3** (see examples below).

■ Complex arguments

In many structures, two or more simple arguments (or 'sub-arguments') are linked together to form a complex argument – a *'chain of reasoning'*.

In **S5** **C1** is an *intermediate* conclusion, supported by **R1** and **R2**. **C2** is the *main* conclusion, supported directly by **C1** and indirectly by **R1** and **R2**. In **S6** there are *two* intermediate conclusions (**C1** and **C2**) which support the main conclusion (**C3**) with the help of a separate, direct premise (**R4**). An intermediate conclusion is both a conclusion *and* a premise for a further conclusion.

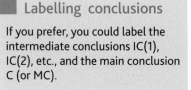

■ Labelling conclusions

If you prefer, you could label the intermediate conclusions IC(1), IC(2), etc., and the main conclusion C (or MC).

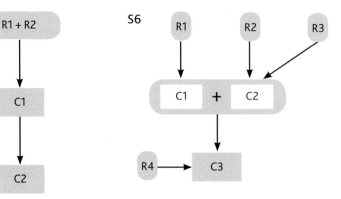

Examples

The following short texts provide examples (let's call them **ES1**, **ES2**, etc.) of each of the six structures shown on the previous page.

ES1 Heath Ledger (who played the Joker in *Batman*, *The Dark Knight*) made a good film great. He really should get the Oscar.

ES1 has one reason, one conclusion.

ES2 Ledger seems to have got right inside the twisted mind of the cartoon character. And he is terrifying in the part. He deserves to pick up the prize for Best Supporting Actor.

ES2 gives two independent reasons leading to one conclusion.

ES3 The Oscars are a sham. They are controlled by Hollywood, where everything is sham.

Again in **ES3** we find two reasons, but this time they are not separate.

ES4 The Oscars are a sham. Winning one of those silly statuettes has nothing to do with the quality of the performance. What's more, they are controlled by Hollywood, where everything is sham.

ES4 is the same as **ES3** but with an added reason. There are two 'strands' of reasoning, leading to the same conclusion.

ES5 The Oscars serve an indispensable purpose because they generate the massive media interest without which the film industry could not survive. So, whether we like it or not, we should put up with this annual charade if we want to keep going to the cinema.

This argument has two 'steps' (rather than strands). First we have a sub-argument with two connected reasons and an intermediate conclusion. From the intermediate conclusion the author then draws the main conclusion.

ES6 The whole purpose of tipping waiters is to reward them for the quality of service they give to the customer. So, if it is done at all, it should be entirely discretionary and should go straight to the pocket of the individual who has earned it. But in many restaurants today a percentage 'service charge' is automatically added to the bill. It is used to pay wages and boost profits, so that it is neither discretionary nor given to the individual. Considering all this, it is time we stopped paying tips altogether. It is a socially demeaning custom anyway.

In **ES6** there are initially two strands of reasoning, *each* leading to an intermediate conclusion. These in turn combine to support a further, main conclusion (**C3**), which is then supplemented by an additional, separate reason (**R4**).

These are just a few examples of the many (practically countless) patterns of reasoning that arguments can follow. Also, because they are artificial models of argument structure, they don't have much of the untidiness that authentic, real-life texts have. However, by studying the models, and seeing how they work, it will help you to analyse and interpret 'live' arguments when you return to them.

Over to you

Complete the analysis of texts **S1** to **6** by listing and labelling the claims R1, R2, C1, etc., to match the structural diagrams on page 90.

17   An argument, or not an argument?

The principle of charity

You may recall that in the introduction we talked about the 'right' interpretation of an argument being the best interpretation – the strongest or most convincing – and that this is known as applying the *principle of charity* (see Chapter 4, page 19). If a text can be interpreted either as a bad argument or as something else that makes better sense, then under the principle of charity you should not insist that it is an argument.

As well as being able to recognise and analyse arguments, it is also necessary to be able to say with confidence when a text is *not* an argument. As we have already seen, a single claim or assertion on its own cannot be an argument. But even a sequence of claims is not an argument unless one of the claims is a conclusion and the other, or others, are reasons.

Take the following example:

a

> A rigorous training regime is essential for anyone expecting to achieve real success in athletic sports. Even in a purely intellectual contest like chess, regular physical exercise will improve performance.

This is not an argument. It is easy to see how it might be *part* of an argument, but as it stands, it consists of nothing more than two related assertions. The therefore-test confirms this; it shows that neither of the two claims could reliably, or even sensibly, be inferred from the other. The claim that athletes need to train rigorously every day does not give us any grounds for believing that chess players will benefit from physical exercise, even though it is probably true. Similarly, the first sentence does not follow from the second, though it too is almost certainly true.

But why do we say that **a** is not an argument, rather than saying that it is a bad, or illogical, or *flawed* argument? What is the difference between a bad argument and a *non-argument*? The answer is that we call it what would make the best sense out of it. As an argument it does not make sense; it would be *baffling*, and if we thought its author meant it as an argument, we would have serious doubts about his grasp of English. On the other hand, it makes perfectly good sense as a pair of observations or pieces of advice. If we wanted a suitable connective to link the claims, 'and' or 'but' would fit much better than 'so'. And neither 'and' nor 'but' is an inference indicator.

■ Compare a 'bad' argument

Sometimes, of course, there is no choice but to interpret a sequence of sentences as argument, even when it is very poor or absurd. Suppose someone tried to reason as follows:

b

> There is a popular belief that alcohol diminishes the ability to think clearly and logically. This can't be right. Russia has the highest proportion of chess grand masters per head of population in the world, and yet Russians are renowned for their consumption of vodka.

Although there are no inference indicators, it is clear, from the shape of the text alone, that the author is using the correlation between vodka drinking and success at chess as twin reasons to challenge the 'popular belief'. Abbreviating **b**, and applying the 'therefore-test':

Russians excel at chess. Russians drink vodka. *Therefore* it can't be right that alcohol diminishes the ability to think ...

This is a grotesquely flawed argument. Nonetheless, it is hard to see any other way to interpret it or any other kind of connective which would make better sense in place of 'therefore'.

Reported argument

What should we make of the next example?

c

> Although the researchers conceded that in general alcohol and sport don't mix, they denied that it had no advantageous effects. They cited increased self-confidence and reduced sensitivity to pain as two of the ways in which alcohol consumption can remove psychological barriers to performance. They also noted the incidence of alcohol use in precision sports such as shooting and fencing, where it was found to reduce both excess anxiety and hand tremor and in some events it is banned for that reason.

Is this an argument? As a whole, no. It's a report or piece of narrative. But it would be a very unobservant reader who missed the argument that is in there. In Chapter 3 we introduced the idea of 'embedded' argument (see page 14). This means that the argument is indirect or reported, rather than plainly stated, so that part of the job of analysis involves *extracting* it from its existing context.

Extracting this argument into an abbreviated, standard form, we can identify the following reasons and a conclusion:

1 Alcohol consumption can remove psychological barriers to performance.

2 It increases self-confidence and reduces sensitivity to pain.

3 Alcohol is used in precision sports where it reduces anxiety and tremor.

4 It is banned in some events because of this.

C Alcohol has some advantageous effects.

Note that this is not the argument of the text's author. It is the *researcher's* argument. The author of the text is reporting it. The conclusion and reasons are not stated directly in the text, but they are in the extracted version. For example, the report tells us the researchers 'denied that [alcohol] had no advantageous effects'. This amounts to saying, as the conclusion **C** does, 'alcohol has *some* advantageous effects'.

It is very common for arguments to be found in this reported form. We can analyse and evaluate them just as we can analyse and evaluate any argument. It just means doing a bit more work first, and care in remembering whose argument it is.

Over to you

1 Using real sources – newspapers, magazines, websites, recorded speech, etc. – *collect* one or more samples of each of the following: a good argument, a poor argument, a non-argument, a reported or 'embedded' argument.

2 Working as a small group discuss, analyse and evaluate some of the samples, and try to agree on the right way to classify them into these four categories: a good argument, a poor argument, a non-argument, a reported or 'embedded' argument.

3 Complete the analysis of argument c above by commenting on its *structure*.

18   Argument or explanation?

Learning objectives:

■ to distinguish between inference and explanation.

It is very easy to mistake argument for explanation, and vice versa. Grammatically and linguistically, they are often indistinguishable, especially since they typically share the connectives 'because' and 'therefore'.

Suppose, for example, I am the school basketball coach, and I tell you that your friend Joey has been dropped from the team. 'Why?' you ask, 'He's a good player.' 'Yes,' I say, 'But he hasn't been coming to training.' What I have given you is not an argument, even though I am providing a reason. It is an explanation:

> **A**   Joey has been dropped because he hasn't been coming to training.

Or:

> Joey hasn't been coming to training. *Therefore* (that's why) he's been dropped.

In **A** it is clear that I am not inferring, or trying to persuade you, that Joey has been dropped. I am not even *claiming* that Joey had been dropped; I am presenting it as fact, as something that needs no support. Nor are you contesting it. You're asking *why* he had been dropped, not *whether*. And I am telling you why, not *that*.

However, it does not require much in the way of change to turn an explanation into an argument. Suppose instead someone used the same reasons to *predict* Joey would be dropped, or to recommend that he *should* be dropped. Then it is a claim that is being made and the reason becomes a premise. The following is an argument:

> **B**   Joey hasn't been to training so he ought to be dropped.

Explaining a decision

The distinction between argument and explanation becomes a bit more complicated when what is being explained is a decision or intention. Suppose, as coach, I had said:

> **C**   I have decided to drop Joey because he hasn't been to training, and coming to training is a condition for being in the squad.

Here 'I've decided to drop Joey' is a sort of fact. In giving a reason, I am not inferring that I have made the decision but explaining *why* I have made it, for anyone who wants to know. And I am giving two reasons.

In a case like **C** I am also *justifying* my decision. You can evaluate the explanation by asking the question, Is it a *good reason* for dropping Joey? This, too, makes some explanations look and feel very much like arguments. A lot of care is needed when deciding which is the right description.

Causal explanation

In **A** and **C** the claim that Joey has not been attending training is not only given as the explanation for his being dropped, it is also given as the *cause*.

Reason or premise?

Remember that in an argument we can call the grounds either 'reasons' or 'premises', and that 'premise' is simply the more formal, technical term. Explanatory reasons, like that given in **A**, should not be called premises because there is no inference being made. 'Premise' is only appropriate when you are talking about a supporting reason in an argument.

Cause and explanation are effectively the same thing here: if you know the cause, you can give an explanation. They are two sides of the same coin and are often combined to form the single term *causal explanation*.

Causal explanation naturally plays a big part in scientific reasoning and enquiry. A classic example is the account that Newton gave for objects such as apples falling to earth:

D

> This apple fell from the tree on to the ground because the apple and the earth have mass, and all objects with mass exert an attractive force on each other, known as gravity.

This is a causal explanation, not an argument. The falling of the apple is not in question. It is a **phenomenon**, something that has actually happened and been observed, and about which there is no argument. The claim that there is a mutually attractive force called gravity is a reason why the apple fell, not grounds for claiming *that* it did.

Predictions

Explanatory reasons become arguments when they are used to support a claim about which there is some uncertainty or difference of opinion. For example, predictions, forecasts, warnings, etc., are not phenomena; they are claims about the future. Newton's theory of gravity not only explains why the apple fell, but gives us grounds for predicting that *any* two objects which have mass will come together if nothing else is restraining them. The following is an *argument*:

E   All objects with mass exert an attractive force on each other. So, if Asteroid X passes close to the earth next year, it will be pulled towards the earth and may collide with it.

Historical explanation

History is another subject in which causal explanations play a significant part. Historians are not simply recorders of fact; they are also concerned with the reasons why events happened, for instance why the First World War broke out when it did or, once it had broken out, why it lasted so long.

Key terms

Phenomenon (*plural* phenomena): a fact or occurrence which is directly observable to the senses. (The word is also used, conversationally, to mean something extraordinary or amazing. That is not the sense here.)

Over to you

1   Coffee contains caffeine, which is a powerful stimulant. Use this statement as a reason in (a) an explanation and (b) an argument.

2   Which one of the following can most appropriately be called an argument and why? Why are the others not arguments?

   a   There was a cholera epidemic in the 19th century which killed a third of the city's adult population.

   b   Measures to improve sanitation and the quality of drinking water were introduced in Britain from the late 1800s onwards, so that cholera ceased to be the deadly threat to public that it had been.

   c   The charity Water Aid deserves everyone's support. Cholera is a scourge in some developing countries and without clean drinking water it will remain so.

3   From your general knowledge, or from reference sources, give two explanatory reasons for the outbreak of war in 1914. You could visit the library, go to websites such as **www.firstworldwar.com/origins/causes. htm**, or just Google 'causes of the Great War' or 'WW1'.

19 Assumptions

Learning objectives:

■ to define 'assumption' and consider implicit assumptions in arguments.

The next few pages deal with one of the most important concepts in critical thinking: that of assumption. It is often presented as a difficult concept, both to grasp and to apply. This is partly because it is a semi-technical term with more than one meaning or use: an ordinary, everyday use and a more specialised use in critical thinking. However, so long as you are aware of this, and are clear which sense you are using it under, assumptions need not give you the problems that many students complain of.

Assumption in the ordinary sense

In its everyday sense, an assumption is simply an unsupported claim or belief, something that you take to be true without necessarily having any grounds for it. Like all unsupported claims, it *may* be true, but unless you know that it is true, or can prove its truth, someone can always challenge you by saying 'You don't know that, you are just *assuming* it' or 'You've no grounds for saying that, it's just an *assumption*'.

So far, no problem. We all understand the word when it is used in this broad sense. We use it that way all the time. The important thing to remember is that when you say something is an assumption, you are not saying anything about its actual truth or falsity, but about whether it is known or simply taken for granted.

Assumptions as premises

Typically, in an argument, the initial premises – the starting points, if you like – are assumptions. They are the grounds on which other claims are based, but they themselves are stated without grounds.

Here is a simple but illustrative example:

> 1   Blackpool has no cathedral, and a city has to have a cathedral. So Blackpool is not a city.

The two sentences joined by 'and' are the premises. Both premises (**P1** and **P2**) are required for the conclusion to follow, giving the argument the structure shown in the following diagram.

If the premises are both true, the conclusion that Blackpool is not a city is indisputable, making **1** *logically* an excellent argument. But **P1** and **P2** are just *assumptions*, for the reasons we have given, so unless we can say with confidence that they are both true, we can only give this provisional evaluation of the argument.

Assumptions as missing premises

We turn now to the second, more specialised use of 'assumption', to mean those premises which are missing from an argument but are nevertheless essential to it. When used this way, 'assumed' means something like 'taken as read' or 'understood'. It is very common in natural language arguments for the speaker or writer to leave out some of the reasons simply because they 'go without saying'.

To get a clearer grasp of all this, look again at example **1** above. We said that logically it was a very good argument, because if its premises were true, the conclusion must also be true. However, it is not a very natural argument. Someone who reasoned like this would sound like a robot. If, in real life, they wanted to argue that Blackpool was not a city, for the reasons given in **1**, they would probably shorten it by leaving out one or other of the premises; it doesn't much matter which.

> 1a Blackpool has no cathedral, so it's not a city.

or:

> 1b Blackpool is not a city. A city has to have a cathedral.

Although both premises in the original **1** have to be *true* for the argument to succeed, that doesn't mean that both have to be stated explicitly for the argument to be understood. We don't think when we read **1a** or **1b** that the argument is flawed because it's incomplete. Instead we fill in the missing piece ourselves, almost without thinking about it. We take it as *assumed*.

Another way of saying this is that by arguing *from* one of these premises to the conclusion, you unavoidably *imply* the other one. **1a** *implies* that cities must have a cathedral. Similarly, **1b** implies that Blackpool does not have one. For these reasons we call the missing pieces *implicit assumptions*.

It is safe to say that most real-life arguments rely on some kind of assumption over and above those that are explicit. Sometimes there are several such implicit assumptions underlying the reasoning.

Considering assumptions: a worked example

Suppose I wanted to add my voice to those that have argued recently for a harder driving test and a prolonged learner period on the grounds that (1) young drivers who have recently passed the existing test pose more of a danger on the roads than older or more experienced ones and that (2) the existing test only assesses skill; it doesn't assess readiness, i.e. responsibility and maturity, which are needed on today's hazardous roads.

(1) and (2) are assumptions in that they are unsupported. I therefore decide to strengthen my case by adding a sub-argument to support (1), using information found on a reputable website:

> Car insurance intermediary the A&A Group found that younger drivers were almost twice as likely to make a car insurance claim resulting from an accident.
>
> Analysing its figures for 2003 to 2005, the group found that 38 per cent of 17- and 18-year-old drivers had made a car insurance claim, compared to 20 per cent of those aged 25 or older, making it more difficult for drivers to obtain cheap car insurance in the future.

(www.expressinsurance.co.uk)

The diagram below summarises my argument.

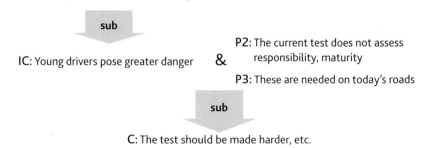

P1: 17–18 years old are twice as likely to make insurance claims …

sub

IC: Young drivers pose greater danger　**&**　**P2:** The current test does not assess responsibility, maturity

P3: These are needed on today's roads

sub

C: The test should be made harder, etc.

With the supporting evidence (**P1**), my first main reason is no longer just an assumption. It is an inference – an intermediate conclusion – based on statistics, not merely my say-so. **P2** and **P3** remain assumptions, but they are fairly safe assumptions. The current driving test clearly doesn't test maturity and responsibility; it is not that kind of test. And the need for maturity and responsibility behind the wheel (**P3**) is more or less self-evident.

That takes care of the explicit claims in my argument. But what about implicit assumptions. Are there any, and if so, do they matter?

Yes there are and yes they do. In the sub-argument, from **P1** to **IC**, it has to be assumed that the number of insurance claims made by a class of driver is a reliable indication of the level of danger those drivers pose. If this additional assumption is not made, **IC** does not follow from **P1**. Be sure that you understand this, as it is a crucial point.

Similarly, in the main step there is an implicit assumption that making the test harder and the learner phase longer would improve a driver's 'readiness' in a way that the current test does not. If this is not assumed, **P2** and **P3** give no good reason for recommending these changes.

You may consider these assumptions to be perfectly reasonable. If so, then you can give this argument a positive rating. But can you accept them wholeheartedly? The assumption behind the main argument needs particularly careful thought. *Is* there a test that could realistically assess someone's 'maturity'? A wise and critical policy-maker would want to answer this question before rushing into an expensive (and possibly pointless) overhaul of the present system.

Meanwhile, you must answer it before you accept or reject my argument. You must also look to see if there are any other implicit assumptions that might affect your evaluation.

Stating the obvious

One reason why it can be difficult to spot assumptions is that they often seem so obvious. You might have thought, when you were reading the previous paragraph, 'Well, *of course* you have to assume that insurance claims are an indication of dangerous driving. The author more or less says that. And *of course* as well the proposed changes would have to increase a driver's readiness in some way. These things go without saying.'

But the author doesn't *actually* say them. And yes, you would be quite right that they go without saying, that's why we call them implicit rather than explicit.

But being obvious doesn't make them any less important. As you have just seen, it can be just as important, for evaluating an argument, to consider the seemingly obvious, unstated premises as it is to assess the stated ones. An argument can look wonderful on the surface, then when you realise what it is assuming, you think, 'Wait a minute. I'm not so sure.'

Here is another example. You have seen this bit of reasoning already. It is the last part of example **6** in Chapter 16 (see page 91).

> It is time we stopped paying tips altogether. It is a socially demeaning custom.

There are two assumptions here. One is the explicit claim that tipping is demeaning. The other, which is implied but not stated, is the *general principle* that we should stop doing things that are socially demeaning. This may seem too obvious to need adding, especially if you agree with it. But if you don't agree with it, you cannot accept the premise as grounds for the conclusion. Indeed you could oppose the argument by challenging the assumption, for example by saying 'Not everything that is socially demeaning should be stopped. So that on its own is not a reason to stop tipping.'

If you want to include an implicit assumption in a standard analysis, you can add it in brackets, or label it, to show that it is not a stated premise:

P Tipping is a socially demeaning custom.

A (We should stop doing things that are socially demeaning.)

_____

C It is time we stopped paying tips altogether.

Back to Blackpool for the last word

Identifying assumptions that are implicit in an argument is part of the work of analysis. But the purpose of doing it is to assist evaluation. That is what makes it such a valuable critical tool.

Go back to argument **1a** at the beginning of the chapter (see page 97).

Blackpool has no cathedral.
_____

Blackpool is not a city.

The single premise is true: Blackpool does not have a cathedral. So, as it happens, is the conclusion: Blackpool is a town, not a city. People may therefore be surprised to find that the argument is *unsound*.

Here is why. We know there is an essential missing premise, which is that all cities must have a cathedral. If that were true, the argument would be fine. But it is not true, a real urban myth! There are over a dozen British cities without a cathedral, for instance Preston, which was recently given city status despite not having a cathedral. (There are also several towns that have cathedrals but are not cities. That is not directly relevant here, but we'll come back to it at a later point when it will be relevant.)

So, although the explicit claims are both true, the argument rests on a false assumption. It draws the right conclusion, but unfortunately for the wrong reason. Therefore we must reject it.

Over to you

1 Have a group discussion. The argument for changing the driving test makes at least two implicit assumptions. Remind yourselves what the assumptions are and discuss whether or not they are acceptable, and what effect they have on your assessment of the argument.

2 Joey hasn't been to basketball training, so he is certain to be dropped from the school team. You met an argument similar to this on page 94. What assumption or assumptions does this argument make?

3 There is a popular belief that alcohol diminishes the ability to think clearly and logically. This can't be right. Russia has the highest proportion of chess grand masters per head of population in the world, and yet Russians are renowned for their consumption of vodka. This is another argument you saw earlier in the book. Analyse and evaluate it, commenting critically on some of the assumptions that it makes, explicit and implicit.

Evaluating argument (1)

Evaluation means judging the quality (value) of something. In critical thinking we evaluate the quality of reasoning that we find in texts. We look at claims and try to decide whether they are justified. We look at arguments and try to assess whether they are good ones or bad ones.

But 'good' and 'bad' are very open terms, and need to be qualified. We need to be able to say what we mean by a good argument. That is what this chapter, and the two following ones, are about.

What is a 'good' argument?

Many textbooks (including this one) tell you that a good (strong, effective, reliable, etc.) argument is one in which the reason(s) offer *adequate* support for the conclusion. That's all very well, but doesn't really take you very much further down the road, because the question 'What is *adequate* then?' is waiting round the corner.

Another way to approach the question is to ask, what do I want from an argument? The answer is *assurance*. I want to be assured that if the premises are reliable the conclusion will be equally reliable. Ideally I want the conclusion to be certain. But certainty is a tall order, and much (if not most) of the time we have to settle for something less.

There are a range of standards or criteria by which we need to judge arguments, and selecting an appropriate standard is one of the first steps to a fair evaluation, i.e. to deciding what is *adequate*. Some conclusions have to be established with absolute certainty, some with near certainty, others as simply likelier than not.

Standards of proof

In some situations the standards are set for us, for example by the law or by parliamentary rules. In a criminal trial, the jury are instructed to return a verdict of guilty only if the prosecution case (i.e. their argument) has proved guilt to the point where it is *beyond reasonable doubt*. The defence merely has to argue that there is some room for reasonable doubt, so what is adequate for the defence is very different from what is adequate for the prosecution. The reason for these two different standards is that in UK law (and in many other countries) it is seen as more unjust to convict someone wrongly than to acquit someone who may be guilty. So, as you hear repeated in every criminal trial, the 'burden of proof is on the prosecution, not the defence'. You may have some views on this imbalance, but that is the law and those are the rules. If you were evaluating a legal argument, as you will if you are ever called for jury service, you have to bear these standards of *adequacy* in mind and judge the arguments accordingly.

In a civil case (e.g. a dispute over money) both sides are treated equally, so the verdict is decided 'on the balance of probability'. If A's case is found to have a 0.6 probability of being right and B's 0.4, then A wins and B pays. A probability of 0.6 is nowhere near being beyond reasonable doubt, so in a civil case you must observe different standards of adequacy again.

Judging by the consequences

In many contexts (weather forecasting, for example) a conclusion can only be drawn with some degree of uncertainty. How much uncertainty you are willing to accept depends on the consequences. For example, hearing a favourable weather forecast on the radio may be adequate grounds for recommending a trip to the beach, but not for concluding that it is safe to cross the channel single-handed in a small boat. The adequacy required varies in accordance with the severity of the consequences, should the conclusion be wrong.

Deductive reasoning and validity

There is one special class of reasoning that we call deduction. Deductive arguments do offer certainty, provided they are *valid*. What 'valid' means, when applied to deductive reasoning, is that if the premises are true, the conclusion is inescapable: it cannot be false. If an argument does have true premises and it has (or even *could* have) a false conclusion, it is invalid – by definition. So evaluating a deductive argument is an all or nothing affair. It's either valid or it's not. It guarantees certainty or it doesn't.

One of the best places to see lots of examples of deductive reasoning is in a book on logic. The trouble with the examples you find in logic books is that they rarely look anything like the arguments you use or come up against in real life, so for critical thinking you can only learn so much from them. What logic does tell us, however, is what it means for an argument to be valid, and since deductive validity is the highest evaluation that you can give an argument, it is helpful to know a little bit about it.

Here are two examples of the sort of deductive arguments that logicians use to illustrate validity:

1   All Italians are Europeans. Mussolini was Italian. Therefore Mussolini was European.

2   If two or more of the directors vote for the merger, then it will go ahead. At least two of the directors are voting for the merger. Therefore the merger will go ahead.

You can plainly see, in each of these examples, that if both of the premises are true, the conclusion must be true too. That makes the arguments deductive and valid.

Soundness

This simple definition of validity states only that *if* the premises are true, the conclusion is guaranteed. But that is a big if. If the grounds for any argument are known or found to be false, then obviously we have to reject it, however valid or persuasive its reasoning may be. The perfect argument is one that is both valid and has true premises. We call arguments that meet both these conditions *sound*. Like validity, soundness has both a general meaning and a technical one. Here it is being used with its technical sense.

In the first example, **1**, the premises *are* true, so we can say that this argument is both valid *and* sound, using both terms in the strict sense. In the second example, we don't know if the premises are true or not. We can't satisfy ourselves that the argument is sound, but we can still say that it is valid.

The term 'valid'

We use the word 'valid' to describe other things besides arguments, train tickets for example. If your ticket has the wrong date on it or if it is for a different journey than the one you are making, then it is invalid, i.e. faulty. The term is often used in a loose way about claims, objections, proposals, excuses, etc. And it is often used about arguments that are *not* valid (in the strict sense of being faultless), but more as a sort of general term of approval. There is nothing wrong with this; it is perfectly legitimate English. But if you want to use the words 'valid' or 'validity' in critical thinking, you need to exercise a bit more care. You should *either* stick to the strict sense or make it clear that you are using it non-technically.

Inference and deduction

Be careful not to use 'deduction' when you simply mean 'inference'. An inference is any reasonable conclusion that is drawn from a text or observation or piece of evidence. A valid deduction is a special kind of inference, as you have seen – one that is certain.

Natural deductive arguments

Both **1** and **2** are *good* arguments. Their reasons are certainly adequate since they establish the conclusion beyond question. However, as we've said before, they are not natural. In natural contexts you would never argue like this, because for ordinary communication it is not necessary to dot all the i's and cross all the t's.

That doesn't mean people never use deduction in everyday situations. They do, but it tends to be disguised by having parts missing. You can imagine a conversation in which someone asks their history teacher if Mussolini was a European. She replies:

1a Of course Mussolini was European, he was an Italian!

The *underlying* reasoning here is the same as in **1**, but with one premise missing, or *assumed* (see Chapter 19, page 96). We see again why implicit assumptions are so important when interpreting and evaluating natural arguments. If we judged **1a** by its single premise, we would have to say that it did not adequately support its conclusion. If we take into account the obvious implication that Italians are all Europeans, then it is entirely sound.

The same goes for **2**. You can imagine someone e-mailing a colleague about the merger and saying:

2a Derek and Sarah are both voting for it. So the merger is on.

Assuming that Derek and Sarah are directors, and that only two votes are needed, this argument is as valid as **2**. However, you would have to know something about the context to understand why Derek and Sarah's votes are adequate grounds for the conclusion.

Unsound arguments

We have seen that **1a** and **2a** can be interpreted as deductive arguments by adding in the assumptions or contextual information that underlie them. You must of course be careful that the assumptions you identify really are implied. You can't put words in an author's mouth to suit the evaluation you want to give. You must analyse it fairly, applying the principle of charity (see Chapter 4, page 19) and then judge whether it succeeds or fails.

Look again at this example, borrowed from Chapter 19. Here we'll call it **3**:

3 Blackpool isn't a city: it has no cathedral.

Is **3** a deductive argument? Yes, because it clearly relies on the implicit assumption that all cities have or must have cathedrals.

> A (All cities must have a cathedral.)
>
> P Blackpool has no cathedral.
> _____
> C Blackpool is not a city.

Is **3** valid? Again, yes, because if all cities did require a cathedral, the conclusion would follow inescapably.

Is **3** sound? No. As you discovered at the end of Chapter 19 (or maybe knew already), the assumption is false. And since the assumption is essential to the deduction, the conclusion cannot be trusted, even though it happens to be true.

Contrast the next one, which does have true premises and a true conclusion.

4   All English cities have populations above 7,000. Canterbury has a population of 40,000. Therefore it's a city.

Is it sound? No. This argument is invalid. The fact that all cities in England have populations above 7,000 does not mean that all towns with such populations are cities. In fact, most are not, including Blackpool. So it is really quite irrelevant that Canterbury has 40,000 inhabitants. It certainly does not establish that Canterbury is a city.

It makes no difference that, *in fact*, Canterbury is a city. It's true, but this line of reasoning does not make it so. In fact, if you substitute Blackpool for Canterbury, you can see at once that the reasoning is invalid by definition – it has true premises that lead to false conclusion.

5   All English cities have sizeable populations. Blackpool has a sizeable population. Therefore Blackpool is a city. (Wrong!)

Summary

A fully fledged deductive argument is capable of giving total support to its conclusion, provided the reasoning is *valid*. However, fully fledged arguments are unlikely to be found in natural contexts.

Often a natural argument can be understood as a deductive argument by recognising one or more assumptions that it is relying on implicitly.

If an argument can be passed as valid and you are satisfied that its premises are true or acceptable, then you can give it 100% positive rating. The word for that is *sound*.

Over to you

Consider the following examples from previous chapters, and for each one decide whether it can be understood as a deduction. If so, also decide whether it is valid and/or sound.

a   Joey hasn't been to basketball training, so he is certain to be dropped from the school team.

b   There is a popular belief that alcohol diminishes the ability to think clearly and logically. This can't be right. Russia has the highest proportion of chess grand masters per head of population in the world, and yet Russians are renowned for their consumption of vodka.

c   It's time we stopped tipping waiters. It's a socially demeaning custom.

d   The Oscars serve an indispensable purpose because they generate the massive media interest without which the film industry could not survive. So, whether we like it or not, we should put up with this annual charade if we want to keep going to the cinema.

e   Fuel prices will continue to rise, therefore worldwide demand for oil is soaring.

21 Evaluating argument (2)

Learning objectives:

- to evaluate non-deductive arguments
- to assess adequacy of reasons.

Non-deductive arguments

You should not infer from the previous chapter that all arguments have to be deductive to be any good. A relatively small proportion of the reasoning we use can properly be described as strictly, i.e. deductively, valid. There are many arguments that are not strictly valid but which are still perfectly adequate for the kind of conclusion they are intended or needed to support.

Take the following example. It's the kind of speech you might hear at a board meeting:

> The best bet for the company financially is to go for the merger. The quarterly figures show that we have some major monetary problems which in the current economic climate are likely to worsen. The corporation which wants to take us over is our biggest competitor. They're in better shape than us and if we try to go it alone they are quite capable of putting us out of business. Mergers tend to result in an immediate rise in share prices, attract investment and make it easier to cut costs. What are we waiting for!

Source: author's own

The main argument is that the merger is our best bet and/or that we should not hesitate to go for it (the first and/or last sentences). The rest are the reasons, eight of them in all, since some of the sentences consist of two or more claims strung together.

It is perfectly possible that each one of the reasons is true, yet the conclusion could still be wrong. For example, it may well be the case that the competitor company could put the weaker one out of business, but not that they would. (It may be a very honourable company, unlikely perhaps but not impossible.) Similarly, it may be true that mergers *tend* to have good outcomes, but this one may turn out to be the exception. You can't just assume that what could happen will happen, or even that it is likely to happen.

This all means that this argument cannot be passed as fully valid, according to the above definition of validity. The merger is not *necessarily* the best bet, and a wait-and-see policy *might* be a better one.

Yet you would not want to write off the argument. It gives strong financial reasons for a merger, and it would be foolish of anyone to dismiss it lightly. It is hard to think of a strong counter-argument in purely financial terms. And all it is claiming from the argument is that the merger is the 'best bet', not that there is no risk at all. You might well want to say that the reasons were adequate in the circumstances, even if the outcome is not a certainty.

What would be a mistake would be to reject this argument because it was invalid. Validity does not apply to arguments that are not, and don't even pretend to be, deductive. If you insist that an author is claiming to have deduced a conclusion when all he or she is doing is providing some supportive reasons, then you are not observing the principle of charity.

And if you do it so as to make it easy to refute the argument (by writing it off as invalid), you may be setting up a *straw man*, i.e. criticising it for failing what it is not even attempting (see Chapter 3, page 17).

The right approach to this argument is to assess how strongly the recommendation is supported. Ask, do the reasons give adequate grounds for going ahead with a merger?

Analogy

A very common method of argument involves the use of *analogy* to make or to challenge some point. An analogy is a comparison. Two typical patterns of reasoning using analogy are these:

> I am claiming X because it is *like* Y, and Y is widely accepted.

Or:

> You are saying it's all right to do X. But you wouldn't say that about Y, and Y is *just like* X.

The first approach is using the analogy with Y to give positive support for X. The second is using the analogy to challenge the rightness of X.

For example:

> Banks and credit card companies charge their customers a fee if they are late with a payment or if they accidentally exceed their lending limits. They say it's a fee, but really it's a fine – a fixed penalty, like a parking ticket. But unlike other fees – fines, debts, whatever – the banks can just help themselves to your money whether or not you agree. They should not be permitted to do it. Anyone else who claims you owe them money has to demand it from you, and take you to court if necessary. That way you at least have a chance to challenge them. Not the banks: they just take it out of your account. It's the same as you owing me £50, and you saying you don't, and me slipping it out of your wallet when you are not looking. If I did that, I'd be a criminal.

Source: author's own

Critical assessment of analogies

First of all, what is the conclusion of this argument? It comes midway into the text: banks should not be able to just help themselves to a customer's money. And the reasoning is that if others did the same, they would be breaking the law. This is presented as a comparison between what the banks do and an individual helping himself or herself from a wallet.

The right general description of this argument is that it is an *argument from analogy*. The evaluative questions you need to ask are, therefore:

- Does the analogy work?
- Is it a fair analogy?
- Is it adequate to convince someone that what the banks do is wrong?

These are ultimately for you to decide, but it is not just a matter of your opinion; there are certain guidelines which you need to follow.

It is not enough to just say the two examples are not the same, even though those are the words used in the argument. Of course, there are big differences between deducting money from a bank account and stealing it from a wallet. For a start, one is illegal and the other is not. But you can't just throw the analogy out by identifying one or more differences.

In the relevant respect

This is the phrase you need to remember when judging the fairness of an analogy. The above argument is not just making a *general* comparison. It says that deducting money from an account is 'the same as' stealing from a wallet, but *only in the respect that* they are both done without the loser's agreement. If you think they are the same or very similar, in this relevant respect, then you can give the analogy and the argument a positive rating. If you think that, even in the relevant respect, there are differences, you would identify this as a weakness or flaw.

Over to you

1. Complete a critical evaluation of the above argument, focusing particularly on the analogy it employs.

2. Find and collect two or three arguments from the usual sources – newspapers, magazines, websites, blogs, etc. – that rest on an analogy and evaluate the effectiveness of the analogy in each one.

3. Write a short argument of your own that uses analogy as a method of reasoning. You can choose the topic, but if you want a suggestion, try the subject of wheel-clamping, for or against.

22   Evaluating argument (3)

Learning objectives:

- to understand why consequences should be taken into account when evaluating arguments.

Consequences

An effective way of evaluating some arguments is by considering their consequences. A conclusion may look quite acceptable when you look only at the reasons *for* it, but can turn out to be less attractive when one or more of its consequences are considered.

Thinking about consequences requires more imagination and lateral thinking than some other aspects of critical thinking. You have to go beyond the text and introduce possibilities that you have thought of yourself.

For example, in Chapter 21 you examined an argument against banks charging customers directly for late payments, etc. (see page 105). Using an analogy, it argued that the banks were effectively committing theft and should not be permitted to do it. Let's suppose you accepted the analogy as being fair, i.e. comparable in the relevant respect, and hence the conclusion too. It's a conclusion many people would at least sympathise with, especially if they have had such charges made on their accounts. It's a common enough experience for cash-strapped students, for example.

However, sympathising with a conclusion is not the same as critically evaluating an argument. Weighing up the positive and/or negative consequences *is*. One consequence of ending the practice might be that there would be no incentive for people to pay on time or to remain within overdraft limits. If this in turn led to people getting deeper in debt than they already were, it could be considered a harmful consequence. Another likely outcome would be that banks would find other ways of raising the money they get from the charges, and the costs of sending out warnings and reminders, of taking persistent offenders to court. These may amount to more than the current charges and could hurt all customers, not just those who currently offend. And so on. You may well decide, when you have thought about these possibilities and estimated how likely or unlikely they would be, that things are better left alone. It could be a case of the old saying, out of the frying pan but into the fire.

Setting a precedent

One important kind of consequence that can arise from the acceptance of an argument is called setting a *precedent*. This is similar in meaning to setting an example, which then has to be followed. For instance, if you allow one person to do something, you can set a precedent for others to expect the same treatment. Because of this, some precedents are often called dangerous.

The danger of setting a precedent is particularly relevant in law, because justice requires that everyone is treated alike. You cannot justly acquit some people for a certain crime and convict others for similar offences. Interestingly, the subject we have been discussing recently threw up an example. A small number of customers took their banks to court for charging what they (the customers) claimed to be excessive charges. They won their case, *setting a precedent* for millions of other people who had had similar charges imposed. It cost the banks a fortune.

You could call that a desirable or an undesirable consequence, depending on your viewpoint. But either way, the job of evaluating the argument is not really complete until the consequences, including the setting of precedents, have been highlighted and thought about.

Over to you

Discussion

Many Scottish people argue that Scotland should be granted independence from the UK and become a separate nation in its own right. They give many reasons for this recommendation. Leaving the reasons aside, discuss their argument from the point of view of its *consequences* and the desirability or otherwise of those consequences.

23   Flaws and fallacies

Learning objectives:

■ to name, describe and assess common flaws.

Flaw or fallacy?

Ordinarily a *flaw* is a fault of some kind. You would call a crack or scratch on a glass a flaw. If someone is greedy or careless or quick-tempered, you might say it was a flaw in their character. A flaw in an argument is something that weakens or detracts from it in any way.

'Fallacy', though closely related, is a stronger and more specific word, referring to the reasoning *itself*. A fallacy is rather like a breach of the rules, something that invalidates an argument or makes it illegitimate. (You can also call the argument itself *a fallacy* if it is invalid or fallacious.)

No treatment of evaluation would be complete without mentioning flaws and fallacies. An argument is *flawed*, or *fallacious*, if the conclusion does not follow from the reasons, whether the reasons and/or conclusion are true or not. Or, which is the same thing, it is flawed if the reasons are inadequate for the conclusion: if they give it insufficient support.

For example, go back to the argument in Chapter 20 about cities and population size:

1   **All English cities have a population greater than 7,000 and Canterbury has a population of 40,000. So Canterbury has got to be a city.**

If you remember, this was an example of an *invalid* deductive argument. Therefore, if anyone did argue in such a way, they would be committing a fallacy.

Formal fallacies

To be more precise, the argument in **1** is a *formal* or *logical* fallacy (formally or logically flawed). That means the fallacy has nothing to do with the truth or falsity of the premises, all of which on this occasion are true. What is wrong with the argument is that, although all English cities *do* have populations of 7,000 or more, so do plenty of English *towns*. So, although Canterbury is a city, the reasons don't mean it has 'got to be'.

The form of the argument can be shown by taking out the particulars of the claims and replacing them with letters, like you do in algebra.

All As have B. X has B, so X must be A.

It's this *form* that is faulty whatever particulars you put in. (Try it and see.) It's flaw has nothing to do with the content, only with the pattern of reasoning.

Here are two more formal fallacies:

2
> If the report in today's *Times* is true, the Secretary of State will have to resign. But since there is no truth whatsoever in the story, she won't. She'll survive.

3
> If the report was true the Secretary of State would obviously have to resign. And she *has* resigned, so there must be some truth in the story.

In **2** we are told only that the Secretary of State will have to resign if the story *is* true. That is inadequate to show that she will survive, for the simple reason that there might be another completely different reason for which she might have to resign anyway.

In **3** we are also told that *if* the story is true she would have to resign, but also that she has resigned. But this doesn't mean the story *is* true, because she might have resigned for some unrelated reason.

Informal fallacies

As a rule, formal fallacies affect only deductive arguments, or argument which can be understood as deductive. But there are many informal fallacies that can be found in any kind of argument, deductive or non-deductive. The big difference is that with informal fallacies it is the meaning and content of the claims that determine whether the argument is flawed or not, not just the pattern of reasoning.

> Chewing gum should be banned, like it is in Singapore. The streets there are not just free of all those millions of hideous grey patches, but of litter of any kind. The trouble with chewing gum is that it doesn't end there. Young people – and not only the young – see the disfigured pavements, and it blunts their senses. They smoke in doorways and strew the ground with their filthy fag ends. Kids grow up thinking, 'Why should I care? What's the point of me taking my rubbish home or looking for a waste bin?' Soon the streets are littered with discarded food trays, empty cans, broken glass, shopping trolleys, and the walls are covered in foul-mouthed graffiti. It breeds a culture of hostility and violence, and before you know it, you have gangs roaming your neighbourhood.

Source: author's own

And all because we didn't ban chewing gum!

This example is exaggerated to make the point. But people do argue, sometimes quite sensibly, that comparatively minor issues can develop into major ones with serious consequences. This line of reasoning becomes fallacious, though, when it goes too far, or when it makes the assumption that the chain of events is inevitable or unstoppable. That is why the name 'slippery slope' is so apt. The idea is that once you are on it, you keep going all the way to the bottom.

But this argument exhibits another flaw as well. It assumes that there is a causal connection between first the chewing gum on the pavement, then the litter, and finally and less plausibly, the hostility and violence. One of the names for this fallacy is *false cause*, or mistaking a correlation for a cause. The correlation is between the signs of an uncared for environment and the antisocial behaviour. There are plenty of sociologists who would agree that they are related. But there are no grounds for the assumption – implicit in the invented newspaper article above – that it is the litter that causes the behaviour. It is just as likely, in fact a lot more likely, that it is the other way round. Or that both have a common cause, say poverty or unemployment, or a number of factors combined. So, even if you think it would be nice to get rid of chewing gum, this argument doesn't justify banning it.

Multiple flaws

You can see from all this that a single argument can have more than one flaw, or at least more than one way of saying what the fault is. Note, too, that very often a flaw can be described in terms of an *assumption*, if the assumption is one that is dubious or questionable or *unwarranted*.

Whether we describe this argument as a slippery slope or as a cause–correlation fallacy or as making an unwarranted assumption, we have identified one or more of its weaknesses correctly.

Arguments are fallacious

Be careful in critical thinking not to refer to claims or beliefs as fallacies, though people do use the word that way in conversation. They might say, 'It's a fallacy that all cities have a cathedral.' Technically that is not a fallacy at all but a *falsehood*. It's only a fallacy if it is a faulty argument.

Name or description?

Many fallacies have special names. Some of these are very old names, dating back to medieval or even classical times, because they have been known about and catalogued for a very long time. This is why many of the names are Latin words or phrases: Latin was the language in which scholarly work (including logic) was done in the Middle Ages. They are often called the *classic fallacies*.

Names are useful pegs to hang concepts such as fallacies on, but don't be afraid to explain the faults you see in an argument in your own plain language. It will earn as many marks, more sometimes than simply supplying the name, because that is evidence that you can see and understand the flaw for yourself. Even if you do recognise a flaw by its name, it may earn you extra credit if you also explain why it is a flaw. This, for example, would be a good evaluation point to make about the argument above:

> The text contains a slippery slope argument, by claiming (absurdly) that not banning chewing gum can lead by cause and effect to gang violence.

Some classic fallacies

The reference list on the following pages is based on the list of classic fallacies in the AQA specification for Critical Thinking Unit 1. It is not a complete list of every kind of flaw or fallacy you will find in arguments, but it is a significant proportion. Most importantly, it does contain all the flaws and fallacies that you are expected to know – by name, description and example – for AS examinations.

You might be asked, for example, to identify a slippery slope argument in a particular text. For that you will obviously have to know and understand what a slippery slope is.

Alternatively, you might be given a text and asked to identify a flaw in it, or to say whether there is a flaw, and if so, what it is. For this type of question, it's up to you to say what the flaw is. You can either give the name (preferably with a short explanation as well) or just a description of the fault in your own words.

Reference list: flaws and fallacies

Ad hominem

This form of reasoning – if you can call it that at all – involves challenging the author of an argument, or holder of a belief, rather than dealing with the claim or the reasoning itself. (The Latin name means literally 'at the man/person'.)

For example:

> So Dr Morley opposes 24-hour opening hours for pubs because he says it has encouraged binge drinking among young people. He claims that the licensing laws should go back to what they were before the government foolishly extended them. But he himself has a reputation as a heavy drinker, which completely discredits his argument.

Source: author's own

Clearly the doctor's drinking habits do not discredit his *argument*, even if the author thinks that they discredit him. Because Morley drinks, it doesn't mean that the new laws *don't* encourage binge drinking, as he is arguing.

It should be noted that challenging the person is not always fallacious. If, for example, an argument is that the someone is being inconsistent, it could be relevant to bring aspects of his personal past into the arena. For instance, if Dr Morley was also on record as having supported the case for 24-hour super-casinos, despite worries over increased gambling, it would be fair to argue that he could not have it both ways. But even this wouldn't make either of the two arguments *individually* less acceptable.

Tu quoque *or justifying one wrong by another*

This is similar in some respects to *ad hominem*, in that it usually brings something personal into the debate. You will be familiar with the expression that two wrongs don't make a right. The same goes for arguments as for actions.

We see regular examples of this when governments respond to criticism by accusing the opposition of similar occurrences when they were in office. *Tu quoque* literally means 'you too'. However, it is no less of a fallacy when expressed in the third person:

> It's wrong for the opposition to call this bill a 'stealth tax' when they themselves introduced all sorts of taxes by the back door.

This might be grounds for saying that the opposition are being hypocritical, but on the question of whether or not it is right to call the bill in question a stealth tax, it is entirely irrelevant. If it is a stealth tax, i.e. a hidden or disguised tax, then it's correct to call it that, regardless of whether the previous government also levied such taxes or not.

False dichotomy/limiting the options

These are two names for the same fallacy. A dichotomy is a division into two contradictory ideas or claims, call them **A** and **B**. For example, there is dichotomy between **A** lying and **B** telling the truth (as you believe it to be); you cannot be doing both. And if you are not doing one, you must be doing the other.

But it is a fallacy to argue that if **A** is not true then **B** must be, if in fact there are other options available. What is being presented is a false limitation on the *options*.

In Richard Dawkins' book *The God Delusion* there is a section in which the author assesses one of the arguments for creationism or intelligent design (ID), as opposed to Darwin's theory of evolution by natural selection. (As the title suggests, Dawkins sides with Darwin.) The ID argument in question is that human life with all its complexity couldn't have come about purely *by chance*, so it must have been designed. Dawkins counters this argument by observing that natural selection is totally different from chance, so that really there are three possibilities, not two. The argument as it stands therefore commits the fallacy of limiting the options, or false dichotomy.

By raising this point we are not saying that either Dawkins or the creationists are right or wrong. It is no part of this book, or of critical thinking generally, to declare a verdict in this or any other controversial issue. What critical thinking *does* permit us to say, is that Dawkins is right in his evaluation of this particular argument. It is flawed.

Straw man

This is a colourful name for misrepresenting or distorting an opposing viewpoint or argument in such a way that it is easily put down. Imagine two people arguing about whether or not mixing, as performed by DJs using turntables and pre-recorded tunes, is music. And imagine, as well, that one of the two has just said that a musical instrument is simply a machine for making sounds, and that what makes it music is what you do with it, what you create and compose, not what you do it on. Decks and discs are sound-producing machines, just as electric guitars and drums are. Used skilfully, all three *can* make music, so person P contends.

Person Q replies:

> So you are saying that all I have to do to make music is switch any machine on. Out will come music. There, I switched on the food mixer. Dance to that, why don't you?

If P really had argued that way, it would have been a very weak argument. However, he didn't. You may still not be convinced by the argument P did make, but you would have to admit that it made a stronger case than Q gave it credit for. Q is guilty of setting up and knocking down a straw man.

Slippery slope

This consists of assuming that something relatively small will inevitably lead to something more serious or to extremes, either directly or in stages. We examined an example at the beginning of the chapter (see page 109). Here's another:

> We can't permit students to take off their ties and jackets in summer, or before you know it, they will be coming to school in nothing but a pair of shorts.

Cause–correlation and post hoc fallacy

The fact that two events have both occurred, or two facts have emerged, does not mean that one has caused the other, and it is a fallacy to assume, with no other grounds, that it has.

This is often referred to as the cause–correlation fallacy (or correlation = cause). We saw an example in Chapter 4 (see page 20).

When the reason for assuming a causal connection is simply that one event has followed another, this is also known as the *post hoc* fallacy – short for *post hoc ergo propter hoc*, meaning 'after this so because of this.' For example, if the phone rings and a moment later there is a knock on the door, obviously no causal connection can be assumed. Yet people often do make such reasoning errors. For example, take this argument from a local paper reporting on a football match:

> The home supporters got behind their team in the second half and started cheering them on instead of whingeing at them. Consequently they played much better and turned a 1–0 deficit at the interval into a 2–1 win at the final whistle. What a difference a crowd can make!

Source: author's own

The implicit assumption here is that the crowd's cheering made the team play better, ignoring the equally likely explanation that the team's improved play gave the crowd something to cheer about.

Overgeneralisation/anecdotal evidence

This is a very common reasoning error: the use of a small number of instances – sometimes just one experience or observation – to draw a general conclusion. For example:

> Manchester is a crime-ridden city. Both times I've been there I've been mugged.

This is a gross generalisation from just two particular cases. It is anecdotal evidence and is inadequate to support the conclusion.

Begging the question or circularity

An argument is fallacious if it assumes what it is going to draw as the conclusion. This is called begging the question, or arguing in a circle. For an example, read the following imagined blog:

> If people have to speak a foreign language to be understood they will take the trouble to learn it; if they don't, they won't bother. This is why the British are so bad at foreign languages. In just about every country in the world you can find someone who speaks English, whereas foreigners coming to the UK can't expect to find people speaking theirs. So it is not that some people are better at languages than others: it is all down to needs-must.

The author concludes it is necessity that makes people learn languages, and give two examples to support this claim. Then, in just slightly different words, she draws her first claim as her conclusion. Hence she has argued in a circle – begged the question.

You may feel puzzled enough to ask, given this example: '*What* question?' True, it is not a very self-explanatory name for the fallacy. It may be a little clearer if you think of the argument as *answering* a question; in this case the question is, are some people better at languages than others? The answer is no, they are not; and that it's just a matter of necessity. But one of the reasons given to justify this answer is it's all a matter of necessity. The author has 'begged' the question.

In his useful reference book *Thinking from A to Z*, Nigel Warburton defines begging the question as 'assuming the very point that is at issue'. This may further help to clarify what it means.

Confusing necessary and sufficient conditions

This is a common reasoning error. Just because something is necessary for some outcome does not mean it is also sufficient. For example:

> The engine won't run unless fuel is getting through. So all you have to do to start it is clean the fuel line.

According to the speaker, fuel getting through is necessary for the engine to run, but it may not be the only fault. Therefore it is not *sufficient* for the conclusion, and the argument is fallacious.

Similarly, the fact that something is sufficient doesn't mean it is necessary too. For example:

> A worn seal would cause a leak, so if you've got a leak then one of the seals must need replacing.

A worn seal would be a *sufficient* condition for a leak to occur, but is not a *necessary* one; a split pipe, or something else entirely, could have been the cause.

Ad hoc *reasoning*

When a claim has been made, and a legitimate objection raised, there may be no rational option but to revise the original claim. What is not acceptable is adding some special proviso, just to suit the argument, and then trying to say that the original conclusion still stands.

Take the argument that fishing is harmless fun for all concerned, based on the premise that fish experience no pain. Then suppose that convincing evidence is provided that fish do feel pain. It would be *ad hoc* reasoning to switch to the claim that fish don't feel pain *like humans do* and still argue that fishing is harmless fun.

In a recent court case a prosecution witness described the vehicle used in a burglary as 'a black van with white writing on the side'. The counsel for the defence asked if he could be sure it was black and sure about the writing, because if he couldn't the evidence was questionable. Yes, said the prosecution witness, he was sure. The defence counsel even showed him a picture of a dark green van with no writing on the side and asked, 'Could this have been the van?' 'No, the one I saw was definitely black,' replied the witness. The defence counsel then told him that the van in the photograph belonged to the accused man. The witness thought for a minute then added that it was dark and raining, that a green car could look black in street lights, and that streaks of rain could look like writing.

What is the matter with this? The matter is that when it suited the witness to be sure, he said he was sure. When a little later it suited him better to say he was not so sure after all, he gave *ad hoc* reasons for the possibility that he was mistaken – i.e. the dark and the streaks of rainwater.

Warburton (see above) calls these '*ad hoc* clauses' and defines them as 'clauses added to a hypothesis to make the hypothesis consistent with some new observation or discovered fact'. Once again, this is a helpful way to understand a not very helpful name. The Latin phrase just means 'to this'. Think of 'this' as being the point the speaker wants to make, and his reasons as being directed *to* this, in this case fallaciously.

Argument from ignorance

Argument from ignorance takes lack of evidence as grounds for denying something, or lack of contrary evidence as ground for asserting something.

For instance, the fact that there was no proof of a link between mad cow disease and CJD in humans was often cited (fallaciously) as grounds for declaring beef safe to eat.

Note that this would be fallacious even if, in fact, beef had been safe to eat. It is not the claim that is fallacious, it is the reasoning.

Confusion/equivocation

Sometimes an expression is misused, or used in a purposely confusing or ambiguous way. This is also known as *equivocation*, especially when the same word is used with different meaning in the same argument. It may result from ignorance or it may be a deliberate ploy to mislead.

Supposing someone reasoned:

> The average family has 2.4 children and the Burton family is about as average as you can get. Therefore the Burtons must have either two or three children.

The arguer would be guilty of equivocation and the argument would be fallacious because it depends on the two uses of 'average' being the same when clearly they are different.

This is a transparent example, used to illustrate a point, and most people would see through it. But used cleverly or subtly, equivocation can be much harder to recognise.

Appeals

Arguments often make some *appeal* in support of their claims, for example to authority, popular/majority opinion, emotion, sympathy, precedent, etc. These are not necessarily fallacious, but they may just be ways of persuading rather than genuine or valid reasons for a conclusion.

For example:

1

> Ask any motorist whether they would rather keep their cars or have cheap, efficient buses and trains instead, and they will choose their cars. The right policy for the government must therefore be to put road building at the top of the agenda, and put public transport on the back burner.

Source: author's own

2

> The Battle of Britain was the most heroic episode in world history. For, as Churchill said, 'Never have so many owed so much to so few.'

Source: author's own

You need to be able to recognise when an appeal is being used as a persuasive device and assess what weight, if any, it adds to the argument. In **1**, for instance, it is of little account what the majority of motorists want in deciding what is 'right policy'.

In **2** the appeal to the authority of a great historical figure does not make the claim any truer; nor does it warrant the definition of heroism that is implicitly assumed. The strength of **2** is rhetorical rather than logical.

24 Forms of data and methods of analysis

Learning objectives:

- to distinguish different ways of presenting data.

Unit 2: Information, inference, explanation

We turn our attention now to Unit 2 of the AQA specification, in which you will be applying your critical skills to texts presenting *information* and *data*, including statistical data.

The aim of this section is to explain methods of communicating, analysing and summarising numerical information and to introduce techniques which may be used to help understanding as well as to draw conclusions from and explain such data.

Each chapter deals with an element of data analysis and interpretation. Various specific techniques are introduced which will help you to read information more quickly and methodically. Given that a large part of the data is numerical, each chapter contains a number of short tasks or questions which will give you practice at analysing and assessing data sources.

There are three main forms in which numerical data is usually presented. These vary in the amount of information given and the ease of access of the information. The figures in the examples below refer to road accidents in towns and rural areas in Scotland, graded according to their seriousness.

Tabular

The data is first given in the form of a table (**Table 24.1**). This is usually the best way to show all the data, and for this reason is almost always included in formal reports. The meaning of the data, however, is not always obvious and some further analysis or other means of display will often be necessary to highlight and clarify any conclusions.

Table 24.1 *Degree and location of road injuries in Scotland, 1998*

	Fatal	Serious	Slight	All severities
Town	116	1,883	8,746	10,745
Rural	223	1,434	4,117	5,744
Total	339	3,317	12,863	16,519

Verbal

Where it is required that the main points of the data are emphasised, this may be done as a verbal summary, for example:

> Of 16,519 injuries due to road accidents in Scotland in 1998, 339 were fatal. Although only one-third of the injuries were sustained on rural roads, these accounted for two-thirds of the fatalities.

This is the sort of summary which might be used in an executive summary of a report or in a newspaper article. The verbal summary contains four numbers. How much of the original table can you reconstruct from these four numbers?

Quite a lot of analytical work has already been done in reducing the table to this form, where just a few interesting facts are picked out. The writer has made judgements on what are the most important facts shown, chosen these numbers and converted them into a form (simple fractions) which is easily understood.

Graphical

One way of showing the data graphically is given in this graph.

A graph like this, if presented alone, leaves the reader to make judgements. Graphs are often used in scientific reports or newspapers, usually along with textual descriptions, because they provide a faster way for the reader to absorb the information. In fact, **Fig. 24.1** contains all the information given in **Table 24.1**, and **Table 24.1** could be reconstructed from it. However, if we wanted to perform more analysis on the data (especially if it was more complex), we would be better starting off from the table as this is the original source.

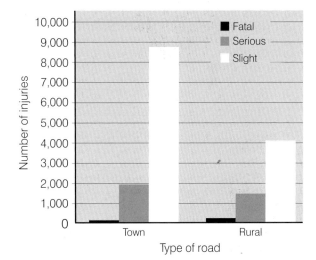

Fig. 24.1 *Number and degree of injuries by road type in Scotland, 1998*

Over to you

1. Simplify Table 24.1 by grouping some categories. What effect does this have on the information given?

2. Summarise the data in Table 24.1 using percentages, either as another table or as a short descriptive statement.

3. Draw other graphs to illustrate the data. Can a line graph or a pie chart be used? Can the data be combined in a different way to produce a bar chart?

4. Write short passages which summarise and/or describe some aspect of the information.

5. The information in the table is already a summary or selection of the data which could have been gathered. What other pieces of information would enable us to analyse what is happening here more thoroughly?

25 Extracting information from data

Learning objectives:

■ to read tables and extract information.

The simplest task we can do with data is to extract a value or a combination of values. Although this is a relatively straightforward skill, it is one which is very important for critical analysis. This skill is to select the important information from a mass of data, much of which may be irrelevant. It is useful, for example, when buying a new computer: you may look at specifications of several makes and models and want to choose from only those which have speeds or capacities above a certain value.

Table 25.1 is a typical example of data in tabular form. It gives weather statistics for a location in Australia between 1985 and 2002.

Table 25.1 *Statistical weather data*

	Temperature		Rainfall		Other daily elements	
	Mean maximum temperature (°C)	Mean minimum temperature (°C)	Mean rainfall (mm)	Mean number of days of rain greater than or equal to 1 mm	Mean number of clear days	Mean number of cloudy days
Jan	30.4	24.9	253.8	12.2	6.8	7.3
Feb	30.1	24.9	328.0	14.3	4.5	10.1
Mar	28.8	24.0	228.3	15.3	6.0	8.3
Apr	27.1	22.6	208.1	15.4	4.4	8.8
May	24.8	20.8	135.5	12.8	7.6	8.6
Jun	22.4	18.4	106.2	10.7	11.2	6.8
Jul	21.9	17.6	67.1	6.7	11.9	5.8
Aug	22.9	18.1	49.7	6.0	12.6	4.9
Sep	25.4	19.8	24.1	3.5	14.1	2.2
Oct	27.6	21.8	49.9	5.3	13.4	3.9
Nov	29.1	23.3	92.9	6.1	10.6	5.1
Dec	30.0	24.4	200.9	8.6	8.1	7.2
Annual	26.7	21.7	1,764.4	116.9	111.2	79.0

Specimen questions

Try the tasks below, which all require slightly different skills.

1. What is the average maximum temperature in July?

2. Which month, on average, has the fewest cloudy days?

3. For how many months does the mean rainfall exceed 200 mm?

4. Which month has the biggest difference between the mean maximum temperature and the mean minimum temperature?

Chapter 25 Extracting information from data

Answers and explanation

1 The average maximum temperature in July is 21.9°C. This may be taken directly from the appropriate cell in the table. This is the simplest task and requires just the *selection of the appropriate value*.

2 The fewest cloudy days are in September (2.2). This time we needed to *search* the 'cloudy days' column for the smallest value.

3 The third selection skill is a *count*. This is similar to the search, but as we scan down the relevant column, we are counting all the values above or below a certain value. In this case we are looking at the 'mean rainfall column' and counting how many values are above 200 mm; there are five such values.

4 This also requires searching but also some *processing* of the data. The answer cannot be found directly from the table. We are looking for the maximum difference between columns 2 and 3. You may be able to do this by carrying the numbers in your head, but if not, it is relatively straightforward to note down these differences: January 5.5°C, February 5.2°C, March 4.8°C, etc. We find the greatest difference falls in October and November (5.8°C).

Questions like these help to familiarise you with the different forms of data you may find yourself faced with. You might also be asked to do similar tasks using graphical data. All four of the skills above can be applied to a graph. Some, like finding the minimum, can be much easier on a graph.

Over to you

Extracting information and drawing simple inferences from the data in Table 25.1, answer the following.

1 In which months was the mean rainfall more than the monthly average?

2 Draw a bar chart showing the numbers of clear and cloudy days each month. Count the number of months where the number of cloudy days exceeded the number of clear days. Is this easier to find from the graph or from the table?

3 If you wanted to take a holiday at this location, which would be the best month? List your criteria for the weather: temperatures between 24 and 27°C are reasonably comfortable, choose the maximum number of cloudy days, etc. Explain your reasons for your choice.

Comparing data in different forms

Learning objectives:

- to compare tables and graphical data.

Table 26.1 *Breakdown of fuel costs*

Item	Price (pence)
Petrol fuel duty	48.35
VAT (17.5%)	14.90
Refinery costs	31.75
Forecourt costs	3.00
Forecourt profit	2.00

The same information can be presented in different forms. A table can be converted into a pie chart or bar chart, a chart into a line graph, a graph into a written report. However, some forms of representation suit particular kinds of data better than others. Also, different forms of representation draw attention to different features of the information. A line graph shows changes or trends. A pie chart shows proportions or fractions, and so on.

Table 26.1 represents the breakdown of the cost of £1 worth of petrol bought at a UK service station in August 2007. It then bought around 1 litre.

The most appropriate way to represent this visually is obviously a pie chart. Three attempts have been made below but only one of them represents the data correctly. Which is it?

Normally, to produce a pie chart you would have to convert the data into percentages, but as these are fractions of £1 there is no need. 1p is 1%. Pie charts sometimes have the percentage printed on the segments; this one does not, so you have to estimate which is the most accurate.

Fuel duty is the biggest proportion, followed by refinery costs then VAT. This is shown correctly in charts **B** and **C** but not in **A**, so we can eliminate **A**. Next we must check the sizes of the segments. Fuel duty is nearly 50%. This is correct in **A** and **B** but not in **C**, so we can eliminate **C**. That leaves **B**, which on inspection can be seen to have segments of the right size.

- Fuel duty
- VAT
- Refinery costs
- Forecourt costs
- Forecourt profit

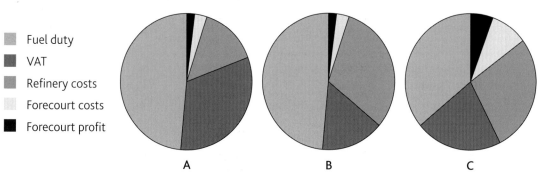

A   B   C

Over to you

The same data could also be converted into other forms or summarised in words. Choose an appropriate alternative to the table or the pie chart and convert the data again. You will not be required to draw graphs formally in a critical thinking exam, but it may sometimes be suggested that you sketch a graph from a table or report to reveal significant patterns or proportions to assist you with the question.

27 Summarising information and drawing conclusions

Learning objectives:

- to convert and interpret raw data
- to draw reliable inferences.

Given a mass of data from a survey or from a report, it is often necessary, or at least useful, to simplify and summarise this information. This enables you to recognise effects or patterns more easily, and from these you can draw conclusions.

We are going to take a relatively complicated data set and reduce it to forms which can be more easily digested or give us clearer information. **Table 27.1** represents GCSE results for a certain sample of students.

Table 27.1 *GCSE results for 2004–07*

	2004/05		2005/06		2006/07	
	Boys	Girls	Boys	Girls	Boys	Girls
Total number of pupils	321,540	311,874	329,266	316,665	330,024	318,728
5+ A* to C grades	167,844	193,674	179,779	202,982	188,444	210,360
5+ A* to G grades	283,277	288,483	290,742	293,865	296,362	298,329
Any passes (1 or more)	311,572	305,637	320,376	311,282	325,734	316,816

Table 27.1 is typical of the way data is presented in reports. It is not entirely raw since it has been subject to some processing; the numbers in the different student categories and in grades A* to C, etc., are given separately. We now have a *three-way table*, i.e. one that looks at three variables: year, gender and grades achieved. As is stands, it is very difficult to see any patterns in the data. Before looking at the analysis below, you may like to think how you would go about reducing this data to the point at which patterns can be seen. The sort of questions in which we might be interested are:

- Do boys perform differently from girls?
- Have success rates changed over the years?

Percentages

Answering both these questions would be a lot simpler if instead of raw numbers you had percentages (**Table 27.2**). By careful inspection of **Table 27.2**, we can see that the results for girls are consistently better than for boys for all comparisons made.

Table 27.2 *GCSE results %, 2004–07*

	2004/05		2005/06		2006/07	
	Boys	Girls	Boys	Girls	Boys	Girls
5+ A* to C grades (%)	52.2	62.1	54.6	64.1	57.1	66.0
5+ A* to G grades (%)	88.1	92.5	88.3	92.8	89.8	93.6
Any passes (%)	96.9	98.0	97.3	98.3	98.7	99.4

Cumulative values

However, this may not be the full story. The data for grades in both tables is *cumulative*, meaning that each row also includes the result from the previous row plus additional results. A to G grades include the A to C grades as well as D to G grades, and 'any passes' includes those students getting 5+ A to G grades.

If we want to look at all variables separately, we must split the qualification levels (by subtracting data in the bottom two rows from the one above) as in **Table 27.3**. We can now see that the girls do better by getting more of the higher grades; in the lower two grades there are higher percentages of boys.

Table 27.3 *GCSE results %, 2004–07*

	2004/05		2005/06		2006/07	
	Boys	Girls	Boys	Girls	Boys	Girls
5+ A* to C grades (%)	52.2	62.1	54.6	64.1	57.1	66.0
5+ A* to G grades, but not 5+ A* to C (%)	35.9	30.4	33.7	28.7	32.7	27.6
Any qualification less than 5+ A* to G (%)	8.8	5.5	9.0	5.5	8.9	5.8

One variable at a time

We can learn more still from these figures by looking at only one variable at a time. To do this, we must be a little careful how we handle and interpret the data. As the percentages were calculated separately for each year and for boys and girls, we cannot simply add the boys' and girls' percentages together. We must go back to the original data and calculate sums and percentages from that.

So, to look at how results may have changed over time, we must add the boys' and girls' results together. (**Table 27.4** shows the actual numbers and the percentages calculated from them.)

This shows that the percentages of top grades have risen at the expense of the lower grades. Other qualifications show little change. We can do the same thing to compare boys and girls directly by adding over the three years (**Table 27.5**). This confirms the findings about boys and girls we looked at before.

Table 27.4 *GCSE results for 2004–07*

	2004/05	2005/06	2006/07
Boys and girls			
Total number of pupils	633,414	645,931	648,752
5+ A* to C grades	361,518	382,762	398,804
5+ A* to G grades, but not 5+ A* to C	210,243	201,845	195,887
Any qualification less than 5+ A* to G	45,449	47,051	47,858
Percentages			
5+ A* to C grades	57.1	59.3	59.3
5+ A* to G grades, but not 5+ A* to C	33.2	31.3	31.3
Any qualification less than 5+ A* to G	**7.2**	**7.3**	**7.3**

Table 27.5 *GCSE results for 2004–07*

	2004/05 to 2006/07	
	Boys	Girls
Numbers		
Total number of pupils	980,830	947,267
5+ A* to C grades	536,067	607,016
5+ A* to G grades, but not 5+ A* to C	334,313	273,661
Any qualification less than 5+ A* to G	87,302	53,056
Percentages		
5+ A* to C grades	54.7	64.1
5+ A* to G grades, but not 5+ A* to C	34.1	28.9
Any qualification less than 5+ A* to G	8.9	5.6

Basic arithmetic

Don't be alarmed by the mathematics. It is basic arithmetic: × + − ÷ %. And calculators may be used if necessary. You will not be asked to process large masses of data in the exam, but you do need to understand how different ways of presenting data relate to each other and to the original, raw figures. Seeing how the processing is done and practising it yourself on different sets of data will help you draw reliable conclusions when the time comes.

A general rule

If in doubt (and if it is available), always go back to the raw numbers. Averages, percentages, etc., can give misleading information if you are not sure how to interpret them.

Drawing reliable conclusions: inference

So, having analysed this data, what conclusions (or inferences) can we draw from it? Some of the statements we have made above can be expressed as follows:

- Between the academic years 2004/5 and 2006/7, a higher percentage of girls obtained A* to C grades at GCSE than boys did.
- The percentage of A* to C grades obtained by pupils rose between the academic years 2004/5 and 2006/7.

There are a lot of similar statements we could make, but these represent the main points shown by the data.

Don't jump to conclusions

You will, perhaps, notice that these statements are very carefully worded. They do not say:

Girls do better at GCSE than boys.

or:

GCSEs have become easier over the last three years.

Yet these are the sort of thing you often see in newspaper headlines. The first of these statements is too general; for all we know, the boys might get all the grade As and the girls all the grade Cs. The second goes much too far and draws conclusions from the information that, at the very least, requires additional support or assumptions and, as it stands, may actually be incorrect.

There is one further area of which we need to be aware. When statistical data is reported, it is often based on a sample rather than on the entire possible population. The data above is different from this as it reports the results for all pupils. However, if we had only taken the results of 100 randomly selected pupils each year, we could have drawn up similar tables which would, almost certainly, have shown the same trends.

When statisticians analyse such data, they make their conclusions with such statements as 'we are 95% confident that the girls obtain more A* to C grades than the boys'. The reason for this is that a sample can never exactly represent the whole population. We may be unlucky in drawing the sample so that it includes a disproportionate number of boys with good results. The bigger the sample, the more reliable the results, and this is what the scientists are expressing by giving a percentage level of confidence which is based firmly on mathematics. So, if the tables above had been based only on a sample, we would not have been able to draw the first of our conclusions in the form shown. We would have had to modify it with either 'in our sample girls obtained higher grades' or 'we are 95% confident that girls obtain higher grades'.

This is a cautionary tale. The analysis above shows that great care must be taken both in handling and analysing data, and especially in assessing the conclusions which may be drawn from it. This is no different in principle from drawing a logical conclusion from a written passage or being aware of what assumptions have to be made to draw such a conclusion.

Over to you

Analyse Table 27.6, simplifying and summarising where possible. What conclusions can be drawn from the data given?

Table 27.6 *Fat intake from various foods*

| | Percentage of fat and energy derived from: | | | | | | | | | | | | |
| | Liquid and processed milk and cream | | Meat and meat products | | All fats | | Fresh and processed fruit and vegetables | | Cereals including bread | | Total intake per person per day | | Percentage of food energy derived from fat |
	Fat	Energy	Fat	Energy	Fat	Energy	Fat	Energy	Fat	Energy	Fat (g) (kcal)	Energy	
United Kingdom	11.2	10.4	22.6	14.7	27.6	10.7	8.3	15.3	17.1	35.7	73	1,722	38
England	11.1	10.3	22.5	14.6	27.7	10.7	8.3	15.4	17.1	35.8	73	1,727	38
Wales	11.4	10.5	23.3	15.2	28.6	11.1	8.0	15.1	16.5	34.8	73	1,713	38
Scotland	12.4	11.1	23.7	15.6	24.4	9.5	8.3	14.4	17.5	35.6	71	1,660	38
Northern Ireland	12.9	11.5	22.9	14.9	31.4	12.3	7.0	15.8	16.5	35.0	76	1,775	39

28   Explanations and hypotheses

A question which crops up frequently in critical thinking, especially in relation to statistical information, is this:

What would explain the findings?

There is, as we'll shortly see, a connection between drawing inferences from a piece of information and offering an explanation for it. But the answer to one is not the answer to the other.

For example, the discovery in Chapter 27 that the percentage of students getting five A* to C grades has risen by 4.4%, whilst the percentage getting lower grades has fallen, does *not* justify the inference that GCSEs are getting easier, even though, *if it were true*, it would explain it. The reason why we cannot infer it is that this is not the only plausible explanation. Another possibility is that the standard of teaching has improved. Another is that students are working harder. Another is that target-setting by the government is working as an incentive. Possibly it's a combination of two or more of these. Perhaps it is none of them.

So the claim that the exams are getting easier – which is the one that the media seem intent on headlining – is no more justified than any of the others. Just because this *would* provide a credible explanation *if* it were true, doesn't mean it is true.

What we can call this explanation is a *hypothesis*. (If you want to remind yourself what this is, go back to Chapter 14, page 86.) It's potential to explain *does* justify calling it a hypothesis, because a hypothesis is not being proclaimed a fact. It's a possibility, often a strong one, often deserving further investigation. But it is always less than certain. Only with further investigation and evidence could we discover whether or not exams *are* getting easier – something which, to date, no one has succeeded in doing.

■ Assessing explanations: plausibility

The question introduced at the top of the page does not say anything about the quality of the explanation. Some explanations are obviously better than others. One quality that is required for a good explanation is *plausibility*. The question would therefore have more critical edge if it asked:

What would be a *plausible* explanation?

Let's turn now to the second main finding from Chapter 27: that a higher percentage of girls in the sample got 5+ A* to C grades than boys, and a higher percentage of boys got the lower grades. Look back at the data, especially **Table 27.3**, to refresh your memory of the details. We ask the questions:

What hypotheses does this support?

What, if true, would plausibly explain it?

One serious hypothesis is that girls work harder than boys. This would explain the discrepancy, but as we have seen, that doesn't mean the hypothesis *is* true or that it is *the* explanation. However, suppose an alternative suggestion was that an extreme feminist organisation has been secretly doping boys on the nights before their GCSEs to make them sleepy and confused!

Well, if this were true, it would be an explanation. But it is hardly what you would call plausible. We would naturally say that the first explanation was the better one, and therefore a stronger hypothesis. Indeed, the second is completely *implausible*; it is in the realm of fantasy and mad conspiracy theory.

Best explanation

If we can say that one explanation is the only possible explanation, then we really do have strong grounds for inferring it from the findings. However, it is rarely if ever possible to rule out any other explanation for some finding. If, for example, girls are simply more intelligent than boys, that would explain the results just as well as the hypothesis that they work harder. Boys might work harder than girls and still fall behind in the exams.

However, we can sometimes say that one explanation is *better* than others, and if it is significantly better, that will give support for the inference, even if it doesn't prove it conclusively.

Explanation and cause

Explanation and cause are closely related concepts. Saying that X is the cause of Y is tantamount to saying that X explains Y. However, as we have just seen, we have to be careful here not to jump to conclusions. Just finding a possible explanation, even a *plausible* explanation, does not mean we have identified the cause. Again, all we have is a hypothesis.

Consider the following text, which is typical of writing you often find in newspapers:

> A survey of business executives with high blood pressure has shown that they drink 25% more spirits on average than those with blood pressure in the normal range. The report concludes that such people should reduce their intake of spirits or they will risk early heart attacks.

Source: author's own

Before reading on, you might like to critically consider this information, especially the implications of the first sentence and whether the conclusion is valid. Could other conclusions be drawn, or reasons given for the observation?

Correlation and cause

By now, when you see these two words together, warning bells should ring. If they don't, look again at Chapter 23, page 112. The conclusion stated in the second sentence assumes not only that a correlation has been identified – between high blood pressure and drinking – but also that one of these has caused the other. However, here lurks danger! One variable can only be said to be the cause of another if all other possible reasons for a relationship between the two have been eliminated. (We saw this in Chapter 27.)

But in practice, this is almost impossible; the number of possible reasons for something happening can be enormous, even infinite. The detective Sherlock Holmes famously said: 'When all else has been eliminated

Over to you

Discussion

Look once again at the two statements summarising the findings in Tables 27.1 to 27.5. Between the academic years 2004/5 and 2006/7, a higher percentage of girls obtained A* to C grades at GCSE than boys did. The percentage of A* to C grades obtained by pupils rose between the academic years 2004/5 and 2006/7.

1. Consider some of the possible explanations which could be given for each of these statements.

2. In each case try to decide which of the hypotheses provide the best explanation and why.

3. Suggest lines of investigation which might provide further evidence to support some of the hypotheses.

4. Just for fun, try to think of a totally *implausible* explanation for one or both of the findings.

… whatever remains, however improbable, must be the truth.' That is all very well in fiction, but in reality it is not a practical proposition to eliminate every possible alternative.

Let's suppose that the researchers who came up with this finding simply measured the spirit intake of those executives with and without high blood pressure, not taking into account any other factors such as family history, diet, etc. In this case how valid is it to conclude that intake of spirits causes high blood pressure? The answer is that it is not valid at all.

If we have two observations, A and B, which *correlate* with each other (beyond all statistical doubt) there are still three possible conclusions we can draw:

- A causes B (e.g. drinking spirits causes high blood pressure).
- B causes A (e.g. high blood pressure causes some people to drink).
- A and B have a common third cause (undefined in the example).

It can be very difficult to determine which is the right one of these options scientifically. It takes careful experimental design and choice of subjects to eliminate other possible sources of variation. For example, if the high blood pressure/heavy drinking subjects are, on average, older than the remaining group, *age* might be the common cause. To eliminate this, we must only compare groups which have a similar age profile.

Another feasible explanation for the results is stress at work, both increasing the incidence of high blood pressure and inclining the executives to drink.

Over to you

1. In Australia a correlation has been noted between ice cream sales and shark attacks on swimmers. Does this mean that you should not swim after eating an ice cream? Why or why not?

2. Benford's law states that in lists of numbers from many real-life sources of data, the leading digit is distributed non-uniformly. According to Benford's law, the first digit is 1 almost one-third of the time, and larger numbers occur as the leading digit with less and less frequency as they grow in magnitude, to the point that 9 is the first digit less than one time in twenty (from Wikipedia).

The frequencies of leading digits, according to Benford's law, are as follows:

Leading digit	1	2	3	4	5	6	7	8	9
Frequency (%)	30.1	17.6	12.5	9.7	7.9	6.7	5.8	5.1	4.6

This at first seems a strange result; surely you would expect the first digits to occur completely randomly. Can you give any explanation for this? Can you find any data on which it can be tested?

Consider a population of rabbits in which there are 100 in the first year and they double each year. Look at the first digits of the number of rabbits for several years (this can be done easily on a calculator or a spreadsheet).

Find some lists on the internet – populations of cities, lengths of rivers, etc. – and look at whether the numbers follow Benford's law. List possible explanations for your results. Can you think of any examples which do not follow this law?

29 Basic maths

Learning objectives:

■ to review basic mathematics used in Critical Thinking Unit 2.

Percentages

The use of percentages often leads to problems, not least because the way they are used in the media is often confused and, in particular, the way percentages are interpreted is not always correct.

In fact, percentages are very simple, and there are easy ways of handling them which enable anyone, even with a very basic level of numeracy, to understand them.

How to calculate a percentage rise

Sometimes you have to calculate the percentage change in a value. Suppose your car insurance premium was £400 last year and it has gone up to £460. What is the percentage rise? The simple formula for this is:

$$\text{percentage change} = \frac{\text{actual change}}{\text{original value}} \times 100$$

In the car insurance example above:

$$\text{percentage change} = \frac{460 - 400}{400} \times 100 = \frac{60}{400} \times 100 = 15$$

This process can easily be reversed. If the premium of £400 is to be increased by 20%, we can calculate the new value as:

$$\text{new value} = \text{old value} \times \frac{100 + \text{percentage change}}{100}$$

or, in the example, **new value = 400 × 120/100 = £480.**

Combining percentages

Let's see now what happens when we start combining percentages. If we are adding or subtracting, it is easy – the percentages can just be added or subtracted. For example, given the following pieces of information:

15% of the population are aged 10 or less.

10% of the population are aged between 11 and 20 inclusive.

We can state with confidence that:

15 + 10 = 25% of the population are aged 20 or less.

This is easy and quite obvious, so we can use it to illustrate the 'actual numbers' method, restating the two pieces of information given above:

Out of 100 people in the population, 15 are aged 10 or less.

Out of 100 people in the population, 10 are aged between 11 and 20 inclusive.

So we now know that out of 100 people, 15 + 10 = 25 are aged 20 or less. This is 25 hundredths or 25%.

Multiplying percentages

Multiplying percentages is not difficult but requires care. Suppose we are told that 30% of all cars are red and that 60% of red cars are owned by women. How do we find out what percentage of all cars are red ones which are owned by women? We clearly cannot just multiply the two numbers together; this would be $30 \times 60 = 1,800$; percentages can never add up to more than 100.

What we must do is remember that percentages are hundredths. Then we know that 30/100 of cars are red and of these, 60/100 are owned by women. Thus:

$$30/100 \times 60/100 = 1,800/10,000 = 18/100 \text{ or } 18\%$$

are red cars owned by women.

This requires a little more arithmetic and a knowledge of how to use fractions. However, for those who are uncomfortable with this, there is an easier method. We *return to actual numbers*.

In 100 cars, 30 are red (30% or 30 hundredths of 100). We also know that in 100 red cars, 60 are owned by women so in 30 red cars, $3 \times 6 = 18$ (6 in every 10) must be owned by women. So out of our original 100 cars, 18 are red and owned by women. This is 18% and we did not need to use fractions.

Example of the use of percentages

Finally, we will look at a slightly more complicated example to put all these things together. This is one which even well-educated members of the medical profession can find confusing but, by looking at it sensibly, is actually quite simple.

Suppose a patient has had a test to diagnose a certain condition: call it G15. Such tests are rarely 100% correct. The doctor knows that 1% of the population has G15. If the patient has it, there is a 90% chance that the test will be positive. However, if the person does not have it, there is still a 10% chance that the test will be positive.

The patient has tested positive and asks the doctor what the chances are that they have G15.

At first, it does not seem very straightforward how to analyse this mass of data. Try to answer the question directly using the data in percentages and you will see this for yourself.

However, this is where the 'actual numbers' method comes into its own. Consider 10,000 patients. On average, 100 will have G15, 9,900 will not. Of those who have it, 90%, i.e. 90 people, test positive. Of those who do not have it, 10%, or 990, people will test positive. So out of $90 + 990 = 1,080$ positive tests, 90 will have G15. This is 8.3%. Few people would have guessed such a low number from the original percentage data. The figures can be summarised in a 2×2 table (**Table 29.1**).

Table 29.1 *Diagnosis test: two-way table*

	Have G15	Do not have G15	Total
Test positive	90	990	1,080
Test negative	10	8,910	8,920
Total	100	9,900	10,000

Graphs: different types and when to use them

Graphs can be used to present information in such a way that it can be absorbed quickly and easily. A wide range of graphs appear in scientific reports and in newspapers. Often these days they are dressed up in all kinds of clever styles, like 3D effects and shadows, but basically graphs fall into four types.

Bar and column graphs

Bar graphs (or charts) can be drawn either horizontally or vertically (the latter are sometimes called column graphs). **Fig. 29.1** and **29.2** show examples of both formats. Bar graphs usually represent counted data which can be grouped into various categories. **Fig. 29.1** and **29.2** show the results of a survey of car colours taken by noting the colour of cars going past a certain point.

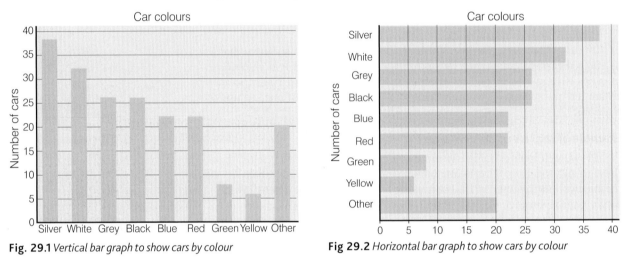

Fig. 29.1 *Vertical bar graph to show cars by colour*   **Fig 29.2** *Horizontal bar graph to show cars by colour*

One advantage that the horizontal bar graph has over the vertical one is that there is more room for long category labels. There are variations on bar charts, such as stacked bars (where the count is divided into two or more categories) and the showing of two different counts side by side on the same axis, but the principles are the same.

Note that bar graphs are best used when the categories do not necessarily fall into any particular order. If, instead, we were showing ice cream sales for each month of the year, a line chart may be preferable as the months can be ordered. However, both types are regularly used for this sort of data.

Line graphs

Line graphs are used to show how one variable changes with another. The horizontal axis usually represents time but could be, for example, the ages of the subjects of an investigation. The values are represented by dots or other symbols and it is conventional to join these up with lines. The use of lines between the points is not always appropriate as it implies a linear variation, but it is used as a method of drawing the eye to trends. **Fig. 29.3** shows the number of train passengers leaving a station at various times of the day.

Line graphs may also show more than one variable. It is important to use the correct scaling of the vertical axis. Sometimes, if all the data is well removed from zero, it is necessary to start the axis at a point other than zero. This should be clearly shown; it is a tactic often used in newspapers and by pressure groups to show a lot of variation or a trend where there is very little.

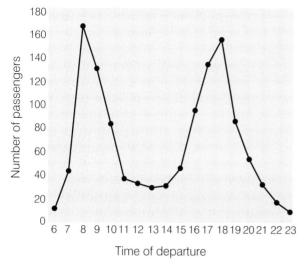

Fig. 29.3 *Line graph to show: passenger numbers by time of day*

Pie chart

A pie chart is used to show how component parts make up a whole. In general, the entire area of the chart will represent 100% and the area of each segment represents how much of the whole is made up by that category. The data may be counted (for example we could use the car-counting data opposite) or continuous (the percentage of the price of petrol which comes from oil cost, taxes, profit, etc.). The breakdown of petrol costs in South Africa is shown in **Fig. 29.4**.

Again, the appearance can be varied a lot. The chart can be given a three-dimensional appearance, or the sectors separated (exploded) but the method of construction is the same.

Scattergraphs

Scattergraphs are used to compare the variation of two related factors and can show correlation. Lines are not used to connect the points, but sometimes a best-fit line may be included to show a trend. Broadly speaking, they can show three kinds of trend: a positive correlation, a negative correlation or no significant correlation at all.

Fig. 29.5, 29.6 and **29.7** show possible results of students in two different examinations. Each dot represents one student's mark in the two subjects.

Fig. 29.5 shows *no correlation* between results in the two subjects. **Fig. 29.6** shows a *positive correlation*: generally, those who do well in one subject do well in the other. **Fig. 29.7** shows a *negative correlation*: generally those who do well in one subject do badly in the other. It must always be remembered that the existence of a correlation does not imply cause and effect.

Averages

An 'average' is a representative value of a set of data. Mathematically, there are three types of average:

- The *mean* is obtained by adding up all the values and dividing the total by the number of values.
- The *median* is obtained by writing the values in order and finding the middle one (or the number halfway between the middle two numbers).

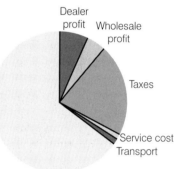

Fig. 29.4 *Pie chart to show fuel cost breakdown in South Africa*

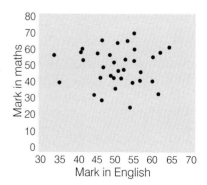

Fig. 29.5 *Comparison of exam marks in English and maths*

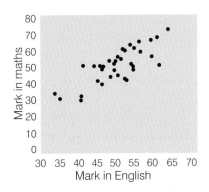

Fig. **29.6** *Comparison of exam marks in English and maths*

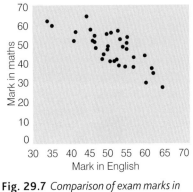

Fig. **29.7** *Comparison of exam marks in English and maths*

■ The *mode* is obtained by finding the most frequently occurring value (some sets of data have more than one mode).

For the following set of data:

    1 2 2 3 5 6 6 7 7 7 8 9

The *mean* is the sum (63) divided by the number of values (12): 63/12 = 5.25.

The *median* is the middle value; in this case the middle lies between the 6th and 7th value in numerical order. These are both 6, so the median is 6.

The *mode* is the most frequent value; there are three 7s, so the mode is 7.

Sometimes (for example in the computer program Excel) the word 'average' is used instead of 'mean'.

The three averages have different uses, advantages and disadvantages. Fig. 29.8 shows the distribution of incomes of US scientists in the US in 2003. The mean, median and mode are shown on the graph.

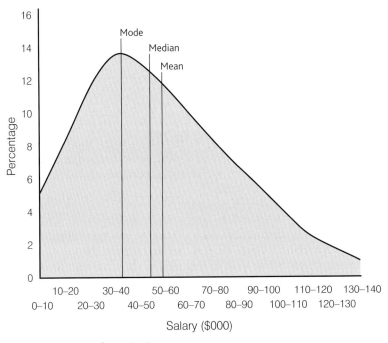

Fig. **29.8** *Incomes of US scientists*

The mean is most often used when we make a series of measurements which are subject to error. In order to obtain the best estimate of what we are measuring, we repeat the measurement a number of times and take the mean value. The mean uses all our measurements but can be greatly affected by a small number of extreme values. It is also of limited use if the distribution of results is not symmetrical. In Fig. 29.8 the small number of very high salaries pull the mean above the other two averages.

The median is often used as the most representative value when the results are not symmetrical. It does not take into account all the values, especially those a long way from the middle. In the salary graph, the median divides the *area under the graph* (shaded area) exactly in half; half the area lies to the left and half to the right.

The mode can be used, for example, when a shop needs to decide what sizes of clothes to stock. The most sales will be of the most common size, or the mode. In the salary graph, it represents the most common salary.

Probability

One of the most familiar ideas of probability comes from the throwing of dice. Since there is an equal chance of any side ending on top (assuming fair dice), the chance of any given number being shown on a single throw is 1 in 6. Probabilities may be expressed in different ways, so this 1 in 6 may also be 1/6 or 16.7%.

What happens when we throw two dice or the same die twice? In order to calculate the probabilities here, we need to introduce the concept of *independence*. A die does not know what number came up last time, neither does one die know what another die will show. The two cases are identical, so we will only consider the throwing of two dice. In this case the chances of the two numbers are not influenced by the earlier throw or the other die. When two probabilities are independent, we can multiply them together. We use the fractional form to do this, so the chance of two 6s is $1/6 \times 1/6$ or 1/36.

We can now ask a different question. What is the probability of the numbers shown on the two dice adding to 9? There are various ways to approach this. There are clearly a few ways this could happen. The first die could show 6 and the other 3. The first die could show 5 and the other 4. These are the only two combinations of numbers which will give a 9. However, we must include the first die showing 3 and the second 6, and the first die showing 4 and the second 5. This is quite different from the other way round (this is more obvious when you consider one die being thrown twice). So we now have four ways of doing it. We can work out the probability of each one of these combinations and, as for the two 6s, it is 1/36. As the probabilities of all possible combinations of two numbers must add up to 1, we can add these four probabilities, so the chance of obtaining 9 with two dice is 4/36 or 1/9.

These two simple ways of combining probabilities can be used in a wide range of situations.

Earlier, we mentioned the concept of independence. Suppose, instead of dice, we had six balls in a bag numbered 1 to 6. Is this now any different from throwing dice? If we just withdraw one ball, the chance of it being a given number is 1/6, as for throwing one die. If we do not replace this ball and withdraw another, one number has already gone, so the chances of drawing any of the other numbers is now 1/5. The methods we used before, assuming independence, no longer apply as the result will depend on what we have already done.

If you withdraw two balls from this bag, see if you can work out the chances of them adding to 9.

Each combination we had before (6 and 3, 5 and 4, etc.) has probability $1/6 \times 1/5 = 1/30$. So the chances are now 4/30 or 2/15. Can you see why the probability is higher than before? It may help to write down all the possible combinations (and sums) of two throws or two withdrawals.

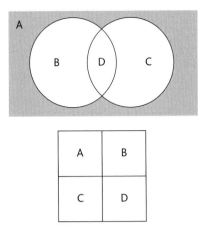

Fig. 29.9 *Venn and Carroll diagrams*

■ Venn and Carroll diagrams

Venn and Carroll diagrams are simple ways of illustrating how things can be divided into categories. They are best described using an example. **Fig. 29.9** shows how we can categorise which sports pupils take part in at school.

The two diagrams in **Fig. 29.9** are exactly equivalent. Each has four areas which represent:

■ those who do neither football nor hockey (in the Venn diagram this is the area outside both circles)
■ those who do football but not hockey
■ those who do hockey but not football
■ those who do both football and hockey.

We could write, in each area on the diagram, either the numbers of those in each subgroup or their names. The rectangle surrounding the entire area in both diagrams is known as the *universal set* and it includes all things we are considering (in this case all the pupils at the school). In the Carroll diagram, the columns and rows are usually labelled with their category. Various areas of the diagram can mean different subsets; for example, B and D taken together represents those who do football (with or without hockey).

These diagrams can be taken further, to include more categories. Beyond three categories they become quite complicated. **Fig. 29.10** shows Venn and Carroll diagrams for sorting cars by three factors: red or not red; hatchback or not hatchback, and under or over 1,400 cc engine capacity. Before looking at the list of categories, see if you can label the areas yourself. The top left circle and right-hand column represent red cars, the top right circle and bottom row represent hatchbacks and the lower circle and inner rectangle represents cars over 1,400 cc.

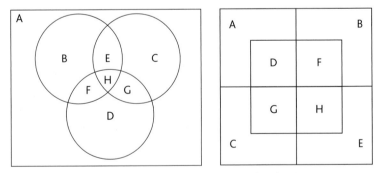

Fig. 29.10 *Venn and Carroll diagrams illustrating car classification*

The categories are as follows:

■ A: not red, not hatchback, under 1,400 cc
■ B: red, not hatchback, under 1,400 cc
■ C: not red, hatchback, under 1,400 cc
■ D: not red, not hatchback, over 1,400 cc
■ E: red, hatchback, under 1,400 cc
■ F: red, not hatchback, over 1,400 cc
■ G: not red, hatchback, over 1,400 cc
■ H: red, hatchback, over 1,400 cc.

30 Introduction

At the end of the Unit 1 and Unit 2 exam papers, you will be asked to write a longer argument in which you put forward your own point of view on an issue raised in source materials. The examiner will be judging both the quality of your reasoning and how well you communicate it. Many marks are available, and this section will give you tips about how to answer these questions effectively.

The section, comprising Chapters 30 to 35, looks at:

- organisation and coherence: the importance of planning
- arguing and asserting: supporting key claims
- moving your argument forwards: making full use of your materials; reaching for principles; strengthening support for non-factual claims
- strengthening further: identifying unwarranted assumptions and adding support; detecting your own reasoning errors
- reading through and checking.

In the exam, you will have been prepared to some extent for writing about the question at the end of the paper by answering critical questions on the source documents supplied. Here we will be diving straight into writing an argument, which makes things a little harder. Nevertheless, we can still have our critical thinking caps on. For example, you may notice that the question asked by the web blog (**document A**) perhaps presents a *false dichotomy*. (If you noticed this, you can feel quite pleased with your progress at flaw-spotting.) Even if you haven't been asked a critical question on something, spotting a potential reasoning problem or issue with the reasoning or material in any of the documents could present you with some materials for your essay.

Make sure you read the materials *critically*, thinking about the kinds of claims, the support given to them, and how effective it is. You may wish to highlight, underline or make a note of any claims or pieces of evidence that you think might be useful to include in your argument. When you've done that, start thinking about how to go about composing a longer argument in answer to the question.

We will be using the following exam-style question as a basis for our discussion of the relevant skills.

AQA Examination-style question

Decide whether or not you agree with Jerry's view that humans are naturally more evil than they are good, and write a reasoned argument to support your view. (You may decide that humans are naturally more good than they are evil, or that neither view is true.) Refer and respond to information and arguments in the source documents provided overleaf.

Document A

A web blog has asked its readers to comment on the following question: are human beings naturally good or evil at heart? Here are a selection of the replies the question obtained:

It's a sad truth but one we might as well face up to. Humans just are NOT nice creatures. Take one good look at the world around you and I'm sure you'll agree.

Jerry

This is a very simplistic attitude. Children are not born good or bad – they are brought up well or badly! Good parenting equals good children.

Isha

You criticise Jerry's post for being simplistic, but your argument is no better. As if it were that simple. I suppose all the people who worked in the concentration camps were the product of poor parenting – that Hitler would not have got into power if German parents had got their acts together …?

Dixon

I'm just saying that good needs to be nurtured. And bad impulses need to be kept in check.

Isha

Jerry – There are good actions; and there are bad actions. You'll find evidence of either if you go looking. Have more faith in the world and it will appear nicer!

Melanie

Yes, but when you weigh it all up, I think you'll agree that there is more evidence of bad acts going on than good ones. Therefore humans are naturally more evil than they are good. It's as simple as that.

Jerry

Source: author's own

Document B

The Stanford Prison Experiment

In 1971 psychology professor Philip Zimbardo created the Stanford Prison Experiment in which 24 college students were randomly assigned the roles of prison guards and prisoners at a makeshift jail on campus. The experiment was scheduled to run for two weeks. By Day Two, the guards were going far beyond just keeping the prisoners behind bars. Several guards became increasingly cruel as the experiment continued. Experimenters said that approximately one-third of the guards exhibited genuine sadistic tendencies. Prisoners were stripped naked, bags put on their heads and sexually humiliated. The two-week experiment had to be cancelled after just six days.

Participants were recruited using an advertisement in the local newspapers and offered $15 a day, or $80 in current 2008 dollars. They were told they would participate in a two-week "prison simulation." Of the 70 respondents, Zimbardo and his team selected the 24 males whom they deemed to be the most psychologically stable and healthy.

*Source: Adapted from **http://en.wikipedia.org**/wiki/Stanford_prison_experiment*

31 Organisation and coherence: the importance of planning

Learning objectives:

- to understand what is meant by good communication, and how and why marks are awarded for this in the critical thinking exams

- to understand the difference between organised and coherent writing, and writing that is disorganised and incoherent

- to appreciate the role of thinking and planning before (and as) you write

- to consider, and to practise, different forms of planning and structuring writing

- to write better planned, structured, and more coherent arguments.

AQA Examiner's tip

A good way to check if your overall argument is clear is to ask yourself if it could easily be summarised neatly into a standard form (see page 9). If this is not easy then it's likely that your argument has not come across clearly to the reader.

What is good communication?

In the exam, you will be judged on the quality of your reasoning and your communication, but what do we mean by 'communication' and how are the two things linked?

Take a look at these two paragraphs. Which do you think is better communicated?

a

> No one has to do an evel act. It mite be in you're nature to do something, but you can always chose not to, unless you are actualy forsed to by others. even if you are bad tempered you can learn to controle it to some extent. For example people can go on anger manidgement. And also when people do things out of anger its not so much evel as if they had chosen to do it. For example murder and manslorter is treeted differrant.

b

> It is indisputable that there is an inherently bad side to people. Animals have no need for morality: they just obey the natural law, the law of the jungle. Many countries have examples of notorious serial killers, each one convicted of horrible evil crimes. The Stanford prison experiment illustrates how people who were not evil were made to do evil things when placed in a certain situation.

Because we are talking about communicating an *argument*, a critical thinking examiner (and hopefully you, as a critical thinker) will say that paragraph **a** is better communicated than **b**. This is because, although the writing in **b** is much smoother and more accurate in spelling, punctuation and grammar – and shows off a wide range of vocabulary – it is difficult to make a lot of sense of it. It is almost as if the writer has paid more attention to the sound of the writing than the meaning. Although the individual sentences make sense, they make no sense together. Trying to interpret them as an argument, perhaps to support the first claim, is impossible. None of the claims support any of the others. There is no logic or coherence.

In contrast, the argument in **a** is clear. You could take the argument away, think about it, put it in different words, respond to it. Although it is not accurately written, it is *coherent*. It is clear how and why the different sentences relate to each other.

The experience of reading an incoherent piece of writing is never a particularly pleasant one. Points are picked up, put down, leaving you baffled and frustrated as to what the overall significance of each of them is, or where the piece of writing is going. Rather like being in a car with a driver who doesn't know how to control the vehicle, when the writing is disorganised or incoherent it doesn't help to put the reader at ease.

Ideally your argument should be both accurately written and well organised, since this will communicate itself best to the reader. However, an argument which is inaccurately written but clearly organised and coherent will in most cases score *better* for communication than one which is accurately written but poorly organised, unless the accuracy is so bad that what you are saying is unclear.

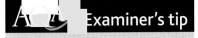

Make sure you control your argument. Don't let it control you!

Think about the relevance of what you are saying to the particular reason you are developing, and the relevance of the reason to the overall argument.

Avoid staying away from your main line of argument.

Your conclusion

Make sure your conclusion is one that answers the question and that you have stated it clearly at least once throughout the argument. It is a good idea to put the conclusion at the top of your plan as a heading (or in the middle if you are doing some kind of flow chart or mind map) and then write reasons underneath (or coming off it).

Planning: the key to clear and coherent communication

To avoid paragraphs like **A**, the answer is simple: planning! The reason the first paragraph makes more sense to the reader than the second is that the writer has thought more about what they are saying. Throughout it they are aware of what their main point is, and they are sticking to it. The paragraph has a purpose beyond that of the individual sentences.

Before you begin writing any of the paragraphs, though, you need to think about what your overall angle is; in other words, what your answer is to the question. It's very important that you read the question really carefully, as it's surprisingly easy to write an argument that doesn't *quite* answer the question. For example, if you weren't careful, you might start writing an argument in which you argued for the view that 'not all humans are naturally evil'. Even if your argument was excellent, you would lose credit for the fact that it was not what the question was asking.

The first thing to think about, then, is precisely what the question is asking, and precisely what kind of conclusions (i.e. answers) address the question. If you do not have a clear opinion on the matter, spend a short time thinking what the strongest reasons are on either side, and decide which you think gives a stronger argument. Once you have decided, spend some more time getting the reasons really clear.

Don't just scribble down what sound like reasons to you; think about each reason. With a little critical reflection, what initially seem like reasons often turn out not to be. Remember, the examiner will be reflecting critically on your thinking, so you should too! Spend a little time thinking about what your *strongest* reasons are going to be. These are those you want to develop. Think about what you would need to develop them. (You may want to have a look at the section entitled 'Before you start' (page 81) and **Table 13.1**, which considers some suggestions for how to develop points; there is more about this in Chapter 33.)

Then think about how they are going to fit together.

- Do any of the reasons have anything in common?
- Could they both be used to support an intermediate conclusion that in turn will help support your main one?

If so, then it might make sense to make them together, or one after the other, before moving onto a different line of argument altogether. For example, you might have more than one reason for thinking that good and bad are things that are learnt from other people or society, in which case it makes sense to group these points together. All this makes for a more coherent, smoother and more pleasurable reading experience – writing which is better communicated.

Planning techniques

In some ways, *how* you plan doesn't really matter. If you're a more visual person, you may prefer to do things in a visual way so that you can see the connections, like a mind map. Alternatively, a rough list of numbered points or a table can work well, but leave some space between each main point in case you think of more, and to develop the points you've thought of (which we will be looking at below). **Fig. 31.1** shows points jotted down as soon as they were thought of and then numbered to show the order in which they will be developed; and an alternative approach.

Table-style plan (numbers show order points will go in)   *Flow-style plan (shows structure)*

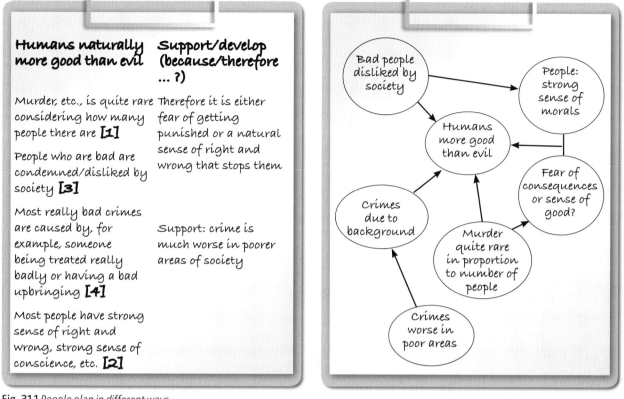

Fig. 31.1 *People plan in different ways*

As a general rule, the more thinking you do initially about the organisation and coherence of your writing, the better the result will be. Looking round a classroom or an examination room and seeing students crazily scribbling away is not always a sign that the quality will be good. Often, the students you see reading back what they've written – frowning, pausing, *thinking* – are the ones who produce the best results.

Obviously you can't spend forever on your plan, which, like your writing, doesn't need to be beautiful. The important thing is that you have *thought* about it, so that your writing has a logic, a coherence and a structure. And remember that planning is not all about 'the plan'; it's really about *thinking* – thinking ahead, thinking about what you've said, what you're going to say, how it all hangs together.

Thinking ahead

Chapter 33 discusses extending your points, drawing further inferences and moving your argument forwards, but you can begin doing this now, if you like, by performing a very simple task. Look at the points you've pulled out as possible reasons or supporting evidence, either for your argument or the counter-argument, and ask of each one: *So what? How does this take me closer towards my conclusion?* If you can see something that might follow from your points, some further significance which is useful for your argument, add it to your plan (as in the example above).

Obviously you might not think of all the significance before you write – and later we will be looking at how to extend your arguments as you write – but the more you know where your argument is going in advance, the more controlled it sounds and consequently the more convincing.

Over to you

- We have suggested an idea for how one of the reasons could be developed and how another could be better supported. Try to think of other points that could go in the develop/support column of the table-style plan. Then try mapping out the argument as a flow chart or diagram such as the flow-style plan, with arrows indicating inferences.

- Complete a plan for an argument in response to the question on page 135. (Hold on to it; we will return to it later.)

32 Arguing and asserting

Learning objectives:

- to understand the difference between a claim which is argued from one which is merely asserted

- to appreciate the need to support certain claims

- to avoid relying too heavily on assertion (including assertions made through rhetorical questions)

- to understand and recognise the difference between genuine and apparent support

- to produce more effectively reasoned written arguments.

In this chapter we turn to the (more significant) aspect of *reasoning*. Start by considering a paragraph from a possible answer to the question you've been asked to write about. (You may wish to remind yourself quickly of the source documents on page 136, and paragraphs **a** and **b** on page 137.)

c

> It's difficult to argue that people are naturally good. If anything, people are naturally the opposite. Jerry is completely justified in claiming, as he does, that 'humans are naturally more evil than they are good'. Unless people are taught things like what is right or wrong then how will they know which path to choose?

Over to you

How well-reasoned do you think paragraph **c** is, and why?

Answer: it is not very well reasoned. While the points it makes are relevant, and there is no obvious problem with coherence, there is no real support for the points it makes.

The main view being presented is that Jerry is correct in his judgement about human nature, yet we are not given any reason for why we should accept this view, other than a series of claims which say the same kind of thing in different ways. None of the claims is supported, yet they are all very debatable; they have merely been stated as if they were true. Their truth has been assumed. A good way to think of it is that the claims are merely being asserted, not argued.

The final claim is made as a rhetorical question. Yet this, too, is unsupported. Although rhetorical questions can be persuasive, they are only a different way of claiming something. They work because they make it sound as if the answer is obvious, which makes you more likely to agree with it. The trouble is, rhetorical questions are often used when the answer *isn't* obvious. In this case the claim being implied is that humans need to be told what is right or wrong, that they have no instinctive sense of morality. This is not only not obvious, but it begs the very question that the argument has been asked to answer. Again, the author of the argument is merely asserting their view, rather than arguing for it.

If the claim that is implied by a rhetorical question is one that needs support, and no support is given, then the rhetorical question adds nothing more than the impression that reasoning is taking place when in fact it isn't.

Genuine – not *apparent* – support

Imagine the following sentence had been inserted in order to strengthen the claim that the author is right to make the claim about there being no evidence that people are naturally good when left on their own:

> As the philosopher Thomas Hobbes argued, people are all essentially selfish by nature.

AQA Examiner's tip

- Whenever you express an important claim that is not obviously factually true or generally agreed by everyone as being true – *argue, don't just assert!*

- When using someone's view from the source materials, make sure you don't just present it uncritically as a 'fact'. Make sure you show whether or not you agree with it (but of course make sure you also explain why).

  For example:

  As Jerry says, ... This is a plausible view/I agree with this view *because* ...

  Or:

  Although Dixon says ..., I do not agree with this *because* ...

This sounds impressive, and indeed it is on the level of general knowledge, but it does not constitute good reasoning. You should have spotted an *appeal to authority* here. Hobbes as a philosopher is famous for his views and arguments about human nature, so it is easy to see him as an authority on the matter. However, merely stating his opinion does not give a reason for why the opinion is true. Unless you give his argument, or give an argument of your own as to why he is right, you have not actually added any real support, just the appearance of support. If it is a matter of judgement, then the same applies to Hobbes as to you: we do not care what he thought but why he thought it.

Summary

1 If you are:

- commenting critically on the usefulness, credibility or plausibility of a claim, a view or other information from the source materials, or

- making a claim that is not obviously, commonly accepted as true

   make sure the claim is not merely asserted, but argued.

2 Do not rely too heavily on rhetorical questions; these can be effective but, more often than not, students overuse them. Make sure that if the answer to the rhetorical question is not obvious, then you provide support.

3 Make sure the support is real support, not just apparent support. Watch out for appeals to authority, expertise or popularity. When using these appeals to back up your argument, make sure that they are relevant and, where necessary, fully explained.

Over to you

Using the plan you made in the previous section, take one of the main points and try to write a solid, coherent and well-reasoned paragraph in which all key claims that need support are supported. (Once again, keep it as we will return to it later.)

33

Moving your argument forward: making good use of your materials

In the exam, the question will ask you to make use of the source documents, and it is important that you do so. There is nothing wrong with using your own knowledge from outside the texts to help support your argument, and this could be very effective, but bear in mind that:

▢ You do not *need* to do this (you can easily get full marks just by making good use of the materials that are there).

▢ You *must* make at least some use of the materials which are there in order to get all the marks.

In the last chapter we saw an attempt to engage with a part of the source materials (paragraph **C**, page 140). While the author would get some credit for this, they would not get very much, since they did not actually provide any reasoning for their disagreement.

This chapter looks at how to make sure you are engaging well with the materials that you are presenting, whether they are from the source materials or from your own life experience or knowledge base.

Developing your argument

At the end of Chapter 1, we asked you to try to extend your points where possible by asking 'so what?' of each of them. The idea was for you to bring out the full significance of your points and so develop your argument further.

Over to you

Look at the following paragraph and decide how well you think the points have been developed. Which ones have been developed well, and which not so well?

> Much of human behaviour is learnt. Why should our morals or values be any different? People who are treated badly when they are young can end up being traumatised. If you are treated badly, you are more likely to treat someone else badly. Also, if you hang around with people who act in a certain way, you may feel peer pressure to copy them. The evidence of the Stanford experiment showed that totally normal people – 'psychologically stable and healthy' – could be made to do horrible things once they were put in a certain situation. Approximately one-third of the guards 'exhibited genuine sadistic tendencies', according to reports from the experiment. This shows that human behaviour is definitely learnt, not innate.

We are looking at how to develop your writing here. This level of response would score fairly well in an AS critical thinking exam, because it shows that reasoning is going on. Important claims are not just asserted, but some attempt is made to justify them. The writing is clear and mostly coherent. However, as we shall see, there is still room for improvement.

■ Using evidence

In the paragraph shown, has the author selected useful evidence, and has it been used well?

The author first considers what happens to people who are 'treated badly' when they are young, and the consequences of this for their behaviour later in life. But the relevance, and thus significance, of this is not made clear. Perhaps it is not really relevant. Perhaps it could be made relevant or significant by inserting a sentence beginning 'This shows that'.

What *does* it show? Perhaps that people's personality can be significantly affected by their upbringing – to the extent that it can make you 'more likely to treat someone else badly'. (This is not quite the same as the final sentence, so a separate sentence saying this is required.)

But so what? Is *this* relevant? What significance does *this* have for the question? Still it's not really clear. Presumably it goes *against* the view that humans are naturally good or evil, as it shows that people's personality depends on how they are brought up and the experiences they've had. But this further inference is essential. Without going this step further, the significance of the evidence is left unclear.

So remember the golden rule: tell us what the evidence shows.

As for the rest of the evidence, the author does draw a clear inference, explaining its significance, but as we shall see, it is not necessarily the right inference to draw. The result is that, despite a good effort to do so, the author has certainly not made the best use of the evidence.

■ Drawing the right inference

So what inference should they have drawn? A better – safer and more relevant – inference to draw from the evidence about peer pressure and the results of the Stanford prison experiment is, instead of the claim that:

> **This shows that human behaviour is definitely learnt, not innate.**

perhaps something like:

> **What a person considers as normal or acceptable behaviour is not fixed – it can change according to circumstances.**

Not only is this second claim better supported by the evidence, but it has greater significance for the question. The first is too general and does not apply directly to issues of morality, of good and evil; the second is more focused and more useful in progressing the argument.

(The question is about whether or not we're good or bad at heart, not where our behaviour comes from.)

■ Going further

We've already seen one example of where evidence needed to be taken further in order to make it relevant (and advance the argument towards the conclusion).

There was also a golden opportunity to take the better conclusion we've just identified and go one stage further.

They were on the right lines at the start, where they seemed to be implying that our 'morals or values' could also be 'learnt'. This would certainly have been a very good place to have got to. But the argument

AQA Examiner's tip

■ Think about the material you're selecting. Make sure the relevance and significance for your argument is clear. (Always try to ask 'so what?' of any evidence you use, either at the planning stage, or as you think about and write the actual paragraph in which you are using it.)

■ A good phrase to use is 'This shows that ...' or, if it's a little more ambiguous or uncertain say 'This suggests that ...' or 'This indicates that ...'. As a general rule, it's best to avoid saying 'This proves that ...' even if you feel it sounds more persuasive. To a trained critical thinker, it usually doesn't! Proof is a very strong word, and most evidence is less than conclusive.

doesn't really take us there. There is a missing step between the evidence and this implied claim. We have to do the thinking, and therefore construct the argument ourselves. It's frustrating because it's almost a very good argument. If they'd drawn a better inference – that was not only safer but also more relevant – then it would have been an easy step to the final conclusion.

Here is the paragraph rewritten. The material and evidence is unchanged. The first sentence shows the significance of the evidence which follows it; a further conclusion is drawn at the end of the paragraph:

> What a person considers as normal or acceptable behaviour is not fixed – it can change according to circumstances. People can often be led by peer pressure to do things they would previously have thought wrong or unacceptable. If you had asked a bully when they were younger if they thought it was okay to pick on someone till they cried, they would probably have said no. The evidence of the Stanford experiment showed that totally normal people – 'psychologically stable and healthy' – could be made to do horrible things once they were put in a certain situation. Approximately one-third of the guards 'exhibited genuine sadistic tendencies', according to reports from the experiment. This shows that not only does our behaviour change, but what we actually think of as right or wrong – in other words our morals or values.

Is this as far as we can go? Is there any further conclusion we can draw from this that moves us closer to where we want to go?

Have a think. There is a possible way of moving from this conclusion directly to a final conclusion which fully answers the question.

But be *careful*! You may want to read the next section before trying.

■ Going too far

While the author did not go far enough with some of their points, you probably noticed that with one of them they went too far. The last sentence of the original version is a conclusion that the author believes follows from the information they have selected about the Stanford prison experiment. The problem is that it doesn't, and for this reason, as well as the fact that it doesn't relate directly to the argument, they would lose credit for the quality of their reasoning, in just the same way as they would for failing to draw useful inferences that would have moved their argument forwards.

(We'll be thinking some more about detecting and ironing out errors in the reasoning in the next chapters.)

Judging how far you can take a point and what conclusions can and cannot safely be drawn is of course a key critical thinking skill and applies as much when you are writing your own arguments as when criticising and evaluating others'.

There are times, of course, when you might not think of writing something because you feel the point has been successfully implied by the reasoning. Sometimes that may be the case, but it's probably safer in an exam to spell out important, useful steps that progress your argument than to leave them unstated. We will be looking at the contrast of what is implied and what is stated explicitly in the next chapter.

■ General rule

As a general rule, then, for developing your arguments, take your points as far as you can but not too far.

■ Over to you

How would you move from the rewritten paragraph above to a final conclusion in answer to the question? Think carefully about any further inferences you could draw that would be able to take you there smoothly (i.e. without jumping too far).

Structuring tip

When you have decided what point you *can* safely conclude from a paragraph, you might find you can then build another argument from that, using the conclusion of one as a starting point, or premise in another.

For example, the conclusion we identified earlier as being a much better one to draw from the evidence could have been used to begin a following paragraph, where the next step in the reasoning (as identified earlier) could be made and developed:

> If it is the case then that people's sense of morals and values can change according to their upbringing or situation, this means that people do not have a fixed sense of right or wrong. This makes it difficult to make strong claims about whether or not people are good or evil at heart. In fact, it becomes very difficult to talk about good or evil in any general sense, as what is meant by good and evil tends to change with people's context and situation.

We could then end with a final paragraph in which the final, main conclusion is drawn:

> For these reasons, the claims that people are naturally more good than evil, or more evil than good, cannot be supported, and so neither view can be considered true.

Developing an argument in this way can be very effective, as it leads to a very strongly reasoned piece of writing that also reads very well. It's possible to have a whole argument where one paragraph provides support for the next, leading to a chain of reasoning, with a series of intermediate conclusions, leading finally to a main conclusion. Just be careful not to take any of the reasons too far. If the point you are making runs out of steam, start a new one. For example, a new paragraph could begin:

> **As well as the fact that what seems to be normal or acceptable behaviour can be influenced by external factors …**

Or:

> **Another reason for thinking that humans are not naturally good or evil, is …**

Thinking ahead

As well as extending your argument forwards, you can also extend it backwards. What we mean by this is strengthening the support you give your argument. If you have used a claim that is factual in kind but not necessarily one everyone would agree with, ask yourself if you can think of any evidence, either in the documents or from your own general knowledge, that might help convince people that the claim is true. If you are using a claim which entails some kind of personal judgement or opinion, see if you can find a more general principle that underlies the opinion. (We'll be practising this more in the next chapter.)

Over to you

1 Take the paragraph(s) you wrote before and see if there is anywhere you can extend the points a little further in a way that is interesting and progresses your argument in the direction you want it to go.

2 Separate out the material from the documents that is factual in kind from that which is based more on a judgement. For the former, ask what you think follows from it and what its significance is. For the latter, ask which are general principles, and whether for some there are wider, more general principles that apply. Try fleshing out what you have into an extended argument which is coherent, in which important claims are supported, and where the full significance for the question of the points and evidence raised is made clear by drawing appropriate inferences to develop and extend your argument in the direction you want it to go. Once again, keep it aside; we will return to it in the next chapter.

34 Strengthening further and supporting opinions

AQA Examiner's tip

When you are asked to argue for or justify a view or opinion on something, try where possible to think of some deeper or wider principle which might give it some support. (You may be specifically asked in the question to choose which principle(s) you think are important. Look for the deepest or widest one you can, that applies in this situation.)

Principles and opinions

Any claim which expresses an opinion needs supporting. Sometimes the only way to support it is with another opinion or, rather, a statement of principle.

In a way, principles are also kinds of opinions. But it always sounds better if your opinion is based on some kind of deeper, wider principle for the following reasons:

- It shows that you have thought about it enough to realise *what* the principles are that are involved.

- It enables you to give some justification other than simply 'I think it's good' or 'I think its bad'. You can say, 'I think it's good *because* I think (principle X) is an important principle.'

- It creates the impression that your views are not just based on individual whims, but might actually form some sort of coherent, systematic, consistent framework.

Criteria

A similar thing applies if you are asked what criterion or criteria you think are important to use in helping you reach your decision. When you select a criterion to help decide on a view or reach a value judgement, by definition there are a range of others you could choose. If you can, give support to the one you think best. It often only needs a sentence or so to explain why you think a certain criterion is important. Think about the implications of using (or not using) different criteria, but try to avoid rushing off down slippery slopes.

Remember that you don't need to use the *word* 'criterion' (or 'criteria'). It will be clear in your answer what kind of things you are using to support your judgement. For example, in the examples we have been using, it has been fairly clear that the criteria being used are:

- people's behaviour
- people's sense of morals and values
- how learnt or innate these things are.

Each of these could be explained very briefly. For example, you could justify using people's behaviour as a criterion as follows:

> Since it is impossible to see inside someone's heart or mind, the only way to judge whether or not someone is 'good' or 'evil' is to consider their actions. That's why I am taking people's behaviour as a way of judging how good or evil they are.

You don't actually need the second sentence, as it is clear what you are doing from the first. But there's something to be said in an exam, where possible, for spelling it out, just to be on the safe side.

Spelling it out: make the important inferences explicit

In the last chapter we claimed that sometimes it's acceptable for a claim to be implied. Here is an example:

> If you tried to argue that our sense of morals is innate, you would have to admit that there is no need to teach children what is right or wrong. However, this is clearly absurd, as children obviously need to be told this.

Here the final conclusion has been left implicit, which is fine here as it is 100% clear what that is. Although not actually stated, the claim – that our sense of morals cannot be innate – has been argued, not just asserted, and the examiner will credit it accordingly.

But as a general rule, it is probably safer in the exam to spell out any important inferences that progress the argument. This is especially so if the inference is not completely obvious, as the above one, but one which has been carefully drawn, such as the one showing the true significance of the evidence in the rewritten version of the paragraph on page 144.

Spelling it out: make the important assumptions explicit

A similar question arises about the support for your argument. Almost any inference makes a number of implicit assumptions. Should you spell all of them out?

The danger is you'd be there forever. Implicit assumptions are not a problem with an argument unless they are highly debatable ones which themselves need supporting. These are the ones you need to watch out for.

AQA Examiner's tip

Sometimes the significance of what you're saying might be clear or obvious to you, but not to the reader. Make sure you spell it out by making any important inferences explicit in your writing.

AQA Examiner's tip

Your argument will not be penalised if you make implicit assumptions, unless the assumptions are major ones, and particularly so if they are unwarranted.

Over to you

Here is the rewritten paragraph once again from the previous section. Can you see any important assumptions it is making? Do any strike you as being especially unwarranted?

> What a person considers as normal or acceptable behaviour is not fixed – it can change according to circumstances. People can often be led by peer pressure to do things they would previously have thought wrong or unacceptable. If you had asked a bully when they were younger if they thought it was okay to pick on someone till they cried, they would probably have said no. The evidence of the Stanford experiment showed that totally normal people – 'psychologically stable and healthy' – could be made to do horrible things once they were put in a certain situation. Approximately one-third of the guards 'exhibited genuine sadistic tendencies', according to reports from the experiment. This shows that not only does our behaviour change, but what we actually think of as right or wrong; in other words, our morals or values.

The argument has made two implicit assumptions:

- that people in the experiment would previously have thought the things they did were wrong
- that people's behaviour reflects their morals, or that people wouldn't do something they thought was morally bad.

Both of these assumptions are required for the argument to work. Yet which is a more major (i.e. less warranted) assumption?

Probably the second one. The second one is more questionable, and therefore less warranted. We can say this is a more major assumption, as it requires more to be taken for granted than the other, and therefore is more of a danger to the quality of the reasoning, which is otherwise good.

(Remember that we are looking at taking your writing to the highest level here. An argument which was this well reasoned and communicated throughout in an exam would be looking at getting a very high mark as it stands.)

Amending and filling in key assumptions

Now, if you were to spot this assumption as you were writing (or as you were reading back), you could do certain things:

- You might decide the assumption is such a dangerous one that you want to abort your whole line of argument. This might be the right thing to do in an essay you are doing, e.g. at home, when you have unlimited time to develop your arguments as strongly as possible.

- You might decide to leave it there as an assumption; the argument is still good and the occasional unwarranted assumption won't do your mark too much damage.

- If you are really after writing the best argument you can in the time available and have identified a slightly questionable assumption, you might bring it out and either support it as best you can and/or admit the impact or limitations it has for your argument, i.e. give a *qualification*:

> **Of course, there is a possible objection to this – that people do not ... However, it is harder to do something against your conscience.**

Remember, don't just assert a claim like this, support it:

> **Many people would feel a strong sense of guilt at doing something that they think is wrong – this is after all often what stops people doing bad things when there is no danger of being caught, e.g. ...**

Remember that there is no such thing as a perfect argument, especially when the question is complex and there are good arguments on both sides (as there will be with the questions you are asked to reach a judgement on in the exam). Do not be paranoid about making assumptions. You *have* to make assumptions to argue anything. (An argument has to *get* somewhere; if you are always going back to support things, you will never get where you are going.) As with much of critical thinking, it's all a matter of judgement and good reasoning; in this case, judging and reasoning when and where the assumptions you are making need supporting.

Essentially the question is, is your argument making a lot of *questionable* or *unwarranted* assumptions? The more you are answering yes to this (and the more the *examiner* is answering yes), the less convincing your argument is.

Note that by 'questionable' we mean from an objective point of view. The examiner will judge a claim not according to whether or not he or she agrees with it, but whether or not there are good objective reasons to agree with it. Even if it is a belief they hold, if it is not commonly accepted and therefore needs support, but support has not been given, it will be seen as a weakness in the reasoning. After all, the examiner will not be judging whether or not he or she agrees with you, but whether or not you have provided good reasons, where necessary, for what you say.

AQA Examiner's tip

It's possible that your choice of criterion or general principle, should you be asked to provide one, entails a number of assumptions in terms of what you are valuing that may be important. Think about what assumptions you are making by choosing one criterion or principle over another.

Over to you

Return to the argument you wrote at the end of the last chapter. Can you find any unwarranted assumptions that it is making? (It's often easier to spot implicit assumptions in someone else's reasoning than in your own. If you have the opportunity, try swapping with someone else. Since assumptions are like blind spots in your thinking, it sometimes helps to have someone else point them out to you.) Your argument is now finished; it just needs a final (critical) check through, so keep it stored somewhere so we can return to it in the last chapter.

Learning objectives:

- to know what to look through when you self-assess your own writing
- to consider some key aspects of style and expressions.

Examiner's tip

Check *as* you write, not just *after*.

As you have seen throughout the book, a lot of critical thinking is just about being careful – not jumping to conclusions, but considering the true meaning or significance of some information. The same is true of your own writing. Many errors can be detected simply by taking the time to check – not just after you write, but as you write. Read sentences and paragraphs back to yourself as you are going, so that what you are saying makes sense. As we mentioned earlier, the best pieces of writing are usually the ones where students have spent less time actually physically writing and more time reading and thinking about what they are writing.

When you read through, check for both communication and reasoning. Imagine you are looking at what you have written from the point of view of a reader who only has the words on the page and not a privileged position inside your own human mind with all the assumptions it is endlessly making.

Communication

Coherence

- Is it possible to follow the sense of what you're saying easily – to follow your *argument*?
- Do the sentences hang together in a meaningful and logical way, so that one sentence follows smoothly and there are no surprising jumps in topic or direction?

Clarity

- Is it clear what the main point is of each paragraph and how you got there?
- Is it clear what your conclusion is? Has it been clearly stated at least once in the argument?
- Watch out for words like 'this' or 'it'. It might be clear to you, but is it clear to your audience (e.g. the examiner)? It's better to repeat a word or phrase rather than leaving the meaning ambiguous (it's about writing clearly, not beautifully, remember).

Reasoning

- Is your line of argument consistent? If you think a principle or criterion is the most important, have you stuck with it throughout or said something that suggests otherwise? Have you contradicted yourself at all?
- Are key claims well supported? Have you argued for them or just asserted them?
- Have you relied too heavily on rhetorical questions (where the 'answers' are not as obvious as you've made out)?
- Could you have taken any of your points further or have you taken any *too* far?
- Is the overall conclusion well supported, or do you need to amend it slightly? Does it seem to follow well from what you've written – is it the natural conclusion to draw from the rest of the writing, or does it seem like a surprising twist?

Over to you

It's time for a final check of the argument you have been writing. Look for any problems with clarity, coherence or the reasoning and amend them. (Again, you may like to swap with someone else if this is feasible.)

■ Are there any assertions or assumptions that need further support? Do you recognise any flaws, such as irrelevant appeals to authority, *tu quoque*s, straw men or slippery slopes?

■ Some last tips on style and expression

In terms of your style, remember that it's not a beauty contest. Clear, coherent and mostly accurate expression is enough to warrant you full marks for communication. There is no need for flights of rhetorical fancy or showy displays of vocabulary (although these *can* be effective if done well).

Another thing to remember is that it's not an *essay* in the usual sense. It's an argument. Although good essays will contain arguments, their purpose is usually to discuss things, and to reach a conclusion after considering all the different points of view, not primarily to persuade people of a particular point of view.

What this means is that your answer doesn't need to follow the conventions of an essay with an introduction and a concluding paragraph. All it needs is to have the conclusion stated clearly somewhere (at least once), and otherwise be organised into paragraphs for clarity.

Otherwise style is relatively unimportant. It often helps to clarify the meaning if you make the reasoning very explicit, and show the functions of claims and how they relate with introductory and linking words and phrases such as:

> **A reason for thinking this is ... This can be shown by ... Another reason is ... Furthermore ... Moreover ... This helps to support the view that ... This shows that ... This is why ...**

This kind of signposting usually makes the argument read more fluently and helps you seem in control of what you are saying. (In fact, it often helps you to think about the coherence and therefore makes it more coherent.) However, if the reasoning is good and the argument is clear, the structure should be clear and, in principle, you could score a very high mark for both reasoning and communication with a minimum of such words and phrases.

Should you consider both sides?

This is entirely up to you. If you have enough materials to put together a strong argument which only gives one side, this is absolutely fine and can be very effective if it is well reasoned. Normally when writing an argument, people tend to take at least one point from the other side that they are able to counter successfully with a good argument or effective piece of counter-evidence. This also is very successful when done well.

There is also nothing wrong with admitting the *strength* of a particular point, piece of evidence or argument on the other side, admitting that perhaps the other side is stronger on that particular point, as long as you feel your reasons still make a stronger case when taken together. There can be something very convincing about appearing open-minded enough to have considered honestly the strength of the other side, and also some of the weaknesses of your own, and yet still deciding your view is correct. But it must be correct because it is better supported, not just because you want to believe it.

Glossary

Appeal to emotion: when someone uses an emotive tone, language or imagery in order to make their case sound stronger or more persuasive; when they aim to persuade by appealing to the heart rather than the head.

Argue from analogy: analogies are comparisons. They are often used in arguments to make the point that if something applies in one situation then it applies, or should apply, in a comparable one. This strategy is called 'arguing from analogy'. The adjective 'analogous' means comparable in some relevant way; the noun 'analogue' refers to something that is said to be analogous to the object being discussed.

B

Biased: a person or a person's viewpoint is termed 'biased' if he/she/it favours one side rather than another.

C

Claim: statement that is supposedly true. Claims can be factual or non-factual, and can be supported or unsupported. In an argument, the claims which are supported by other claims are conclusions; those giving the support are the reasons.

Clarifying: giving words which have open meanings more focused, closed ones that fit the author's meaning as closely as possible as indicated by their line of argument.

Conflation: when a point about one thing has slipped into being a point about something else, or when two separate things have been muddled together so that a point about one leads to a conclusion about the other.

Consistent: two or more statements are consistent with each other if it is possible for them to be true together, i.e. the truth of one does not conflict with/contradict the truth of another.

Corroboration: where two or more sources provide pieces of information which agree or which support each other. As in a court trial, evidence from one witness that bears out another's can strengthen the *probability* of its being true.

Counter-argument: an argument which takes the oposing view.

Counter-example: an example chosen to show why a general statement, viewpoint or explanation is not necessarily true.

Credibility: the credibility of a person, a source or a claim is a measure of how likely it is to be true.

Critical: suspending judgement until sufficient evidence is presented either way.

D

Dichotomy: a pair of opposing ideas which cannot both be true or both be false. It is similar to a dilemma, which means a choice between two (usually unattractive) alternatives. Restricting the options is sometimes called a false dilemma.

E

Embedded argument: where reasons for a new conclusion are presented somewhere within a text but the author has not given the argument directly, for example because they have reported or quoted from someone else's argument.

F

Factual in kind: a claim is factual in kind if its real true value is not just a matter of opinion (even if no-one knows for sure or there is disagreement about what that truth is. 'There is life on other planets' is factual in kind.

False dichotomy: a flawed way of reasoning that assumes there are only two options when there may in fact be others. (By doing this, the arguer can persuade the audience that if one of the options is false or undesirable, they *have* to choose the other.) Note that it is also sometimes known as restricting the options, as it does not need to be limited to two. The arguer may assume three options and then dismiss two of them in order to prove that one is right, but the assumption of three may have been wrong/inadequate to start with.

G

Genre: a kind of text. It has partly to do with the subject matter, but also to do with a style of writing.

H

Hypothetical: something imagined to be true in order to consider what effects it might have, for example on a statement, viewpoint or explanation, if it were true.

I

Imply: to mean something without actually saying it, e.g. 'You didn't invite me but you implied I was welcome.' To say one thing from which another follows logically or naturally, e.g. 'Telling me to pack warm clothes implied that it would be cold where we're going.'

Inconsistent: two or more statements are inconsistent if it is not possible for them to be true together.

Infer: to take one claim or assertion as grounds for a second, and to draw the second (as a conclusion) from the first.

L

Leading language: language which carries with it an implicit judgement, and which encourages the audience to share that judgement simply through the way something has been described, rather than through reasoned argument. Note that 'leading' when used in this sense is not a technical term specific to critical thinking, but identifying where language has been used to persuade or manipulate someone's response to a question or topic is an important critical skill.

N

Necessary condition: that which needs to take place for something else to happen; without it, the other thing cannot occur.

Neutrality: a person or person's viewpoint is deemed 'neutral' if he/she/it considers both sides fairly and equally and judges them on their own merits.

P

Phenomenon (*plural* phenomena): a fact or occurrence which is directly observable to the senses. (The word is also used, conversationally, to mean something extraordinary or amazing. That is not the sense here.)

Premise: this is another word for a reason. 'Premise' is the more technical term and is sometimes more precise. It is the word normally used in logic. 'Reason' is a plainer word for the kind of support people offer for their conclusions when they are arguing naturally. In this book and in the AQA specification both words are used, and you should use whichever you find more appropriate. It is mostly a matter of preference.

R

Refutation: the successful defeat of an argument, either by identifying something wrong with it or by making a better counter-argument. The word is often used loosely to mean opposing or denying something: 'I completely refute that.' In critical thinking it should be used only in the stricter (some would say correct) sense.

Rhetorical question: a sentence with the grammatical form of a question but used to make a statement. It can be a more forceful or effective way of making a statement. 'Have I got news for you?' is an example of a rhetorical question. It means 'I have' but it also conveys the message that it is very important or very interesting news for the person I am speaking to.

S

Sceptical: assuming or suspecting something is likely to be false until proven otherwise.

Slippery slope: the assumption that a small or moderate change or concession will necessarily lead to extremes, either directly or in stages. For example, if you give the workers the small pay rise they are demanding this year, next year it will be twice as much and they won't be satisfied until they have bankrupted the company. There is no necessity that this will follow from a moderate pay rise this year.

Statement of principle: a claim expressing a basic truth, rule or guideline. The mark of a principle is that it is more *general* than other claims. Statements of principle are therefore powerful claims, for the purposes of

argument, because if we accept a general principle, then we must accept all the particular claims covered by it.

Sufficient condition: that which, if it does take place, is enough to make sure something else happens; with it, the other thing must occur.

T

Tu quoque: term used for an argument which tries to justify a wrong action on the grounds that a similar wrong action is being done by someone else.

U

Unwarranted assumption: an assumption which is at best questionable and at worst false.

V

Vague: a statement that makes grammatical sense but whose meaning is unclear or too imprecise. This makes it hard to judge its relevance or significance in a given context.

Value judgement: a judgement is an opinion rather than a matter of fact. A value judgement is an opinion about the value or worth of something, including whether it is good or bad, right or wrong, harmful or beneficial, deserving or undeserving, etc. 'Claudia paid £2000 for a hairdo' is either a fact or it's false. 'It is wrong for anyone to pay £2000 for a hairdo' is a value judgement.

Vested interest: when someone has something to lose or gain in a particular debate or conflict (either materially or in terms of their reputation).

References

Dawkins, Richard, *The God Delusion*, Black Swan, London 2007

Golding, William, *Lord of the Flies*, Faber and Faber, London 2004. First published 1954

Warburton, Nigel, *Thinking from A to Z*, Routledge, London 2007

Other references are as noted in source lines within the text.

Index